Environment
and
Psychopathology

Dr. Abdu'l-Missagh A. Ghadirian completed his postdoctoral training with a degree of M.Sc. in psychiatry in the United States. Formerly Director of Medical Education of the Montreal-World Health Organization Collaborating Centre for Research and Training in Mental Health, he is currently a senior psychiatrist at the Royal Victoria Hospital and Douglas Hospital in Montreal. He is also a Professor of Psychiatry at McGill University and is the author of numerous research publications, with special interest in the psychosocial and biological aspects of mood disorders, stress, and substance abuse. He published a book on substance-abuse prevention and currently is studying the effect of environmental light on seasonal depression.

Dr. Heinz E. Lehmann received his medical education in Germany and came to Canada before World War II. He worked for many years with psychiatric patients and published the first results of a major study in North America of the new antipsychotic drugs.

A former chairperson of the Department of Psychiatry at McGill University in Montreal, he is now Emeritus Professor there. He has published extensively on schizophrenia, depression, and psychopharmacology and is now doing research on clinical and nosological issues in psychiatry.

Environment and Psychopathology

Abdu'l-Missagh A. Ghadirian
Heinz E. Lehmann
Editors

 SPRINGER PUBLISHING COMPANY • NEW YORK

Cover design by Holly Block

Springer Publishing Company, Inc.
536 Broadway
New York, NY 10012–3955

93 94 95 96 97 / 5 4 3 2 1

Library of Congress Cataloging-in-Publication Data

Environment and psychopathology / A-M. Ghadirian and H.E. Lehman, editors.
    p. cm.
    Includes bibliographical references and index.
    ISBN 0-8261-7460-4
    1. Mental illness—Environmental aspects. 2. Mental illness—Etiology—Social aspects. 3. Social Environment. I. Ghadirian, A-M. (Abdul-Missagh) II. Lehmann, Heinz E. (Heinz Edgar), 1911–
    [DNLM: 1. Environment. 2. Mental Disorders. 3. Psychopathology. WM 31 E602]
    RC455.4.E58E53   1993
    615.89'h071—dc20
    DNLM/DLC
    for Library of Congress   92-49539
                                                                    CIP

Printed in the United States of America

Contents

Contributors

F. A. Allodi, M.D., Associate Professor, Director, Cross-Cultural Psychiatry Programme, Department of Psychiatry, University of Toronto, Toronto

P. A. Bell, Ph.D., Professor, Department of Psychology, Colorado State University, Colorado

R. Bolin, Ph.D., Professor and Head of Department of Sociology and Anthropology, New Mexico State University, New Mexico

A-M. Ghadirian, M.D., Professor, Department of Psychiatry, McGill University, Montreal

G. L. Klerman, M.D. (deceased), Professor and Associate Chair for Research, Department of Psychiatry, Cornell University, New York

H. E. Lehmann, M.D., Professor Emeritus, Department of Psychiatry, McGill University, Montreal

D. A. Oren, M. D., Senior Clinical Investigator, Clinical Psychobiology Branch, National Institute of Mental Health, Bethesda, MD

R. H. Prince, M.D., Professor and Former Director of Division of Social and Transcultural Psychiatry, Department of Psychiatry, McGill University, Montreal

N. E. Rosenthal, M.D., Chief, Section on Environmental Psychiatry, Clinical Psychobiology Branch, National Institute of Mental Health, Bethesda, MD

J. J. Sigal, Ph.D., Professor, Department of Psychiatry, McGill University, Montreal

E. L. Struening, Ph.D., Associate Professor, Columbia University, School of Public Health, Director, Epidemiology of Mental Disorders Research Department, New York State Psychiatric Institute, New York

E. Susser, M.D., M.P.H., Assistant Professor of Clinical Psychiatry, Columbia University, New York

R. Wallace, Ph.D., Research Scientist, Epidemiology of Mental Disorders Research Department, New York State Psychiatric Institute, New York

S. N. Young, Ph.D., Professor, Department of Psychiatry, McGill University, Montreal

Foreword

The stunning success of molecular biology toward understanding some medical illnesses has detracted from the fact that the major improvement in health has often been the result of changes in environmental risks. For example, the reduction of air pollution, the improvement in sanitation, the removal of lead from buildings, have had major impact on improving the health of large numbers of people. Understanding environmental risk at this time in history is even more pertinent in psychiatry where molecular biological approaches are still a promise, although considerable research is under way. Ghadirian and Lehmann have attempted to re-equilibrate the balance between environment and psychiatry in this book. Most importantly, they have expanded beyond the usual environmental variables studied in psychopathology, namely stress, social supports, or coping, and have invited authors to contribute chapters in new areas of risk, such as geography, nutrition, noise, air pollution, diet, catastrophes, drug abuse, and terrorism. They have examined which syndromes may be exclusively culture-bound. Within an epidemiologic framework they have documented recent increases in the rates of depression and suicide. The presence of a birth-cohort effect suggests the effect of environmental risks. This book can be seen as an effort to re-equilibrate or re-focus our thinking from an exclusively genetic one to the study of factors in the environment. Coexistence and cross-fertilization between environmental and genetic studies may be the optimal modus operandi (Baron, 1991). However, Ghadirian and Lehmann are to be congratulated for taking a bold step in identifying new areas for consideration.

MYRNA M. WEISSMAN, PH.D.
Professor of Epidemiology in Psychiatry
Columbia University, Chief, Division
of Clinical and Genetic Epidemiology,
New York State Psychiatric Institute, New York, New York

REFERENCE

Baron, M. (1991). Editorial: Genes, environment and psychopathology. *Biological Psychiatry*, 1055–1057.

Introduction

Mental health is one of the foremost concerns of the industrialized world and a significant component of public health worldwide. However, the concept of health, physical or mental, although well-understood, is not easy to define. There is general agreement that health is more than the mere absence of disease, yet health is most often discussed specifically in terms of its negative component, pathology, because it is easier to define pathology operationally.

We know much about the manifold adverse effects of certain environmental factors on physical health—from the earliest observations of the destructive effects of excess heat and cold and the damage caused by poisons and alleged "miasms" to the spectacular scientific discoveries of pathogenic microorganisms and the recent hotly debated findings on the pathogenic potentials of diet and radiation. In contrast, we have little firm knowledge about the influence of environmental variables on emotional, mental and behavioral health. This book has been conceived with the intention of bringing together more of the existing information in this field.

The book is not simply a collection of papers presented at a conference on environment and psychopathology. There have not been many major conferences with this central theme. Rather, each contributor has been chosen and asked to write a chapter concerning an issue about which he or she has special interest and expertise.

We all live in an individual environment. And although we may be able to change it, we can never liberate ourselves entirely from its influence on our physical condition and our behavior. Environment, in the context of this discussion, will be defined as the total of all external factors that may impinge on the physical, social, or psychological state of individuals, groups, and populations. Genetic and psychodynamic factors are, by definition, not included because they are not external and affect only very small and highly interdependent groups.

Social and cultural parameters are typical environmental factors that may affect an individual's mental status and for which there already exists a considerable literature. This book focuses also on less-studied variables such as food, illumination, noise, pollution, time-period effects, disaster, torture, and imprisonment.

Psychopathology has been defined in this book as any persistently abnormal or deviant experience or behavior that is perceived by the subject, or by others, as interfering with normal adaptive function in one's daily life. The most typical psychopathological phenomena related to environmental factors are panic and anxiety, depression, aggression, and, occasionally, psychosis or cognitive disorder.

In the interaction between environment and people, some of the psychopathological manifestations have been known for centuries in different forms: for instance, mass hysteria was known as "dancing mania" at the time of the great plague in the Middle Ages. Others, like seasonal affective disorder, were not recognized until a few years ago. Correspondingly, many environmental conditions, such as natural disasters and imprisonment, have existed throughout history, whereas others made their appearance only in modern times; for example, nuclear accidents, urban homelessness, and expectations of the baby-boom generation.

Seasonal affective disorder (SAD) is a new psychiatric diagnosis that has been created during the last decade. Its etiology is related to the season and to the geographical site of the affected individual. D. A. Oren and N. E. Rosenthal describe the manifestations and treatment of this disorder which, according to one survey, may affect 4% to 10% of the population, the majority of whom are women in their twenties. Exposure to high-intensity light can alter the circadian amplitude and has antidepressant effects.

Noise and pollution are discussed by P. A. Bell, who points out that a weak but positive association has been found between noisy areas (for example, London's Heathrow Airport) and admission to mental hospitals. Such association has also been observed for high levels of air pollution. Laboratory studies have shown that noise enhances aggressive tendencies and impairs social behavior. Moreover, research has identified an air pollution syndrome characterized by headache, fatigue, insomnia, irritability, impaired judgment, and gastrointestinal problems.

S. N. Young debunks some myths about therapeutic effects of the

Feingold diet (without food additives or salicylates) for hyperactive children and shows that in a double-blind controlled study of food allergies, oligoantigenic diets had much less dramatic effects than suggested by many practitioners in the field who take folklore for truth. On the other hand, he points out that anorexia secondary to depression may lead to unsuspected folate deficiency associated with a lowering of serotonin, and thus may produce a vicious cycle. Certain nutritional deficiencies may lead to psychiatric disorders as outlined in this chapter.

R. H. Prince defines culture as the nongenetic blueprint for living that is passed from one generation to the next. Although recent sources refer to some 140 examples of culture-bound syndromes, Prince's analysis reduces their number to four. Devoting his chapter to a methodological discussion of social phobias in the Japanese as compared to Western culture and diagnosis, he reports that a spectrum of social phobias in Japan affects up to 35% of psychiatric patient populations and may even manifest itself in the form of transient easily treated delusions.

In an unusual reversal of roles, G. L. Klerman starts with an epidemiological phenomenon as the independent factor and then seeks the environmental etiology. Recent epidemiological discoveries have revealed unexpected and significant increases of depression and suicide in the adolescent and young adult U.S. postwar population. This phenomenon occurs in a generation that otherwise has enjoyed very good physical health and that grew up in unprecedented economic prosperity in the Western world. Klerman discusses this cohort-period effect, which appears to be a paradox.

What are the causal relationships between the recent environmental blight of urban homelessness and psychopathological symptoms? The complex feedback loops involved in these processes are discussed by R. Wallace, E. Struening, and E. Susser, who stress the importance of social networks for the development of coping strategies of individuals threatened by the loss of their regular domiciles, a loss that is viewed by the authors as a "slow disaster."

Psychoactive drug abuse, another post-war effect, is discussed by A-M. Ghadirian, who points out that 30% to 50% of substance abusers suffer from concurrent nondrug psychopathology. Cultural value systems may determine the choice of the abused substance. For alcoholism, one study reports rates of preexisting depression varying from 8.6% to 66%, depending on the measurement instruments used. There is a high prevalence of affective disorders among cocaine abusers. Cognitive impairment, depression, and personality change are the main psychopathological features that persist after cessation of substance abuse. However, whether psychopathology is predisposing to, resulting from, or simply concurrent with substance abuse is often difficult to ascertain.

R. Bolin reminds us that regardless of class, many people live in areas prone to disaster. In victims of natural disasters there often arises a post-event solidarity, whereas technological disasters are more likely to create divisiveness. Uncertainty about delayed health impacts of technological disasters frequently produces general anxiety, depression, despair, and anger in the potential victims. Pre-existing psychiatric conditions render individuals more vulnerable to disaster-related psychological trauma. Posttraumatic stress syndrome may not manifest itself until two months after the traumatic event and may persist for years.

Terrorism and torture, their psychopathological consequences, psychodynamics, and therapeutic interventions, are discussed by F. Allodi, who points out that terrorism and torture are closely related phenomena. However, these two atrocities also differ in some respects. All countries officially repudiate torture, but not every agent of terrorism may be considered a criminal, depending on motivation and on the perspective of the observer. A follow-up study of 500 victims of hostage-takings 9 years later revealed that about half of the victims and 29% of their families suffered from symptoms of posttraumatic stress disorder. Interestingly, a lower proportion of victims reported some positive value from their experiences.

This is not the case with torture victims, who often also fit the diagnostic criteria of posttraumatic stress disorder given in DSM–III. The needs of torture victims are multiple and differ in their home country and in exile. Although 85% to 90% of recent torture victims can be supported in centers for victims of torture, 10% to 15% require referral to the medical network.

Many studies have been conducted to document the psychological damage that followed the horrors of Hitler's concentration camps and Japanese prisoner-of-war camps after World War II. J. J. Sigal has reviewed these reports from Scandinavia, the United States, Israel, and Canada. These studies show that the survivors have higher rates of mortality by violent means (suicide, accidents) and greater prevalence of anxiety, depression, persistent dysphoria, irrational fear, sleep disturbances, reduced memory, and concentration. In contrast to most other stressful experiences, the overwhelming trauma of the camps seems to have erased all pre-existing individual differences and vulnerability and resistance.

These sociocultural and environmental factors are in constant interaction with the human mind and emotions. As a result of these interactions, vulnerable individuals are exposed to the pathogenic influences of environmental forces. It is therefore essential to study the nature and consequences of the dynamic relationship between human beings and their environment. Today's environment is growing more complex and challenging at a rate that often exceeds normal human ability to cope with the ensuing changes and problems that may result in stress and chronic psychopathology. We have to learn more about the intervening processes if we want to prevent such outcomes.

PART *I*

Physical Factors and Psychopathology

Chapter 1

Environmental Light and Mood

Dan A. Oren and Norman E. Rosenthal

> When the winter sets in . . . there is first a
> disappearance of the sun for only a few
> minutes, the next day it is double that
> time, and the next day it is double that
> time. . . . It takes two months before it en-
> tirely disappears. Then the gloom of the
> Arctic night sets in, and although Eskimos
> . . . tried hard to amuse us, I could notice a
> depression among ourselves . . . that
> reached its climax about Christmas. . . . Al-
> though we had a very good Christmas din-
> ner and everything we could wish for in the
> way of food, we were all very blue.
> —*Cook, 1894a*

The idea that light could affect our moods must date back to hu-
mankind's first awareness of emotions. In a world in which the sun
was once the central deity and today remains a powerful regulator
of human behavior, only recently has a scientific appreciation of the
impact of environmental light on mood emerged. Recognizing the
still-dawning history of the impact of light on psychopathology, we
will illuminate the beginnings and status of this fertile field of
inquiry.

Although seasonally distributed influences on affective illness
have been recorded by physicians as ancient as Hippocrates (1931),
Cook's observations are the earliest we know of that specifically
link seasonal loss of sunlight to a mood disorder. Accompanying
Robert E. Peary on one of his early Arctic expeditions, Cook noted
the profound influences of light on the voyagers and the Eskimos.
Such symptoms as loss of sexual desire, fatigue, loss of energy, and

profoundly depressed mood were noted by Cook not just in the observed Eskimos but in the observers as well. Cook believed that lack of light, not the winter cold, caused the syndrome as the Eskimos kept their igloos well heated. As for the explorers, Cook noted that he "never suffered from the cold and none of our party did" (1894a, p. 164; 1894b).

Remarkably, in a century whose earliest decades saw humanity making great strides toward understanding the influence of environmental nutrients and pathogens on health, significant interest in light and mood disorders lay dormant until the late 1970s. One patient in particular was a catalyst for the resurgent interest in light. Herbert E. Kern had carefully recorded his long history of fall–winter depressive episodes, which he attributed to changing periods of environmental light, a theory that piqued the interest of researchers at the National Institute of Mental Health (Lewy, Kern, Rosenthal, & Wehr, 1982; Rosenthal, Lewy, Wehr, Kern, & Goodwin, 1983). Speculating that two periods of bright light that extended normal daylight hours would be beneficial to Mr. Kern, they found a dramatic improvement in the patient's affect (Lewy et al., 1982). The next winter Rosenthal and colleagues (1984) delineated the winter-depression syndrome of "seasonal affective disorder" (SAD) and treated 11 of these patients with light therapy. Confirmatory studies involving hundreds of patients treated by other independent groups continue to support the basic findings of the original reports (Rosenthal, Sack, Skwerer, Jacobsen, & Wehr, 1988b). In recognition of the solid nature of the syndrome, the most recent psychiatric diagnostic guidebook, the DSM–III–R, calls for noting the presence of seasonality in cases of recurrent mood disorders (American Psychiatric Association, 1987).

PHENOMENOLOGY

We currently define "winter SAD" as occurring in patients with a history of at least one incident of major affective disorder, depressed (Spitzer, Endicott, & Robins, 1978) and recurrent fall–winter depressions that remit during spring or summer, with at least two consecutive prior winter-depressive episodes. Initial criteria required that the winter pattern be unaccounted for by psychosocial variables.

Characteristic symptoms of winter depression noted in winter SAD patients are dysphoria and decreased activity with concomitant irritability, anxiety, decreased libido, and social withdrawal usually seen. Unlike classically depressed patients, most SAD patients suffer "atypical" depressed symptoms of increased appetite and weight, despite their increased quantities of sleep (Rosenthal et al., 1984). Some SAD patients are more disturbed by these vegetative symptoms than by the mood changes themselves. Because physical manifestations of the disorder frequently precede the psychological changes (Young, Watel, Lahmeyer, & Eastman, 1990), SAD patients often consult their family physicians rather than seek psychiatric assistance. The depressions are usually mild to moderate, but occasional patients have histories of hospitalization and 2% have had prior electroconvulsive treatments (Oren & Rosenthal, 1992).

Nearly 80% of the 366 winter SAD patients seen in our clinic have been women. Given potential selection biases, this figure may overstate the true relative prevalence of the disorder among women (Terman et al., 1989a). Epidemiological studies, however, tend to corroborate that women are more vulnerable to being troubled by seasonal changes in mood (Kasper, Wehr, Bartko, Gaist & Rosenthal, 1989b; Rosen et al., 1990). The average onset of the disorder is at age 25 (Oren & Rosenthal, 1992). For patients residing near the 38.9° N latitude of Washington, DC, depressive episodes typically begin in November when total hours of daylight drop below 10 (Rosenthal et al., 1984). Untreated depressive episodes generally resolve by springtime, although some individuals do not fully recover before the early summer. Travel to latitudes nearer the equator often results in diminution of symptoms. Many of our patients have reported a history of briefly depressed moods, even in spring and midsummer, if the weather is cloudy or they spend time in a dimly lit area (Rosenthal et al., 1984). Mild hypomania with elation, increased libido, social activity, increased energy, diminished sleep requirements, reduced appetite, and loss of winter weight often appear during the summers (Jacobsen & Rosenthal, 1988).

EPIDEMIOLOGY

Most winter SAD patients have unipolar depression, with a substantial minority of patients having bipolar II disorder, and very few having bipolar I disorder (Sack et al., 1990; Terman et al., 1989a). Familial factors may be involved in the disorder, given that approximately half the patients have reported a history of major affective disorder in at least one first-degree relative (Oren & Rosenthal, 1992). SAD has also been seen in children, who present with fatigue, irritability, difficulty getting out of bed in the morning, and school problems (Rosenthal et al., 1986a).

Clinical studies document the presence of the syndrome in five continents (Boyce & Parker, 1988; Hanada et al., 1991; Terman et al., 1989a; Thompson, 1986; Wirz-Justice et al., 1989). Subclinical *forme fruste* versions of the syndrome (S-SAD) appear as well (Kasper et al., 1989a). One canvass in Maryland found approximately 4% of the population to have SAD and greater than 10% to have subsyndromal SAD (Kasper et al., 1989b). Many more people among the general population may have mild seasonal changes in mood, energy, or weight as well (Kasper et al., 1989b; Terman, 1988).

BIOLOGY

Certain biological parameters have been found to be abnormal in patients with seasonal winter depressions. Hormonal profiles, biochemical challenges, immune responses, and visually evoked phenomena all provide some understanding of the pathophysiology of SAD and the way in which this is affected by light treatment.

Sleep studies reveal significant differences between those with winter depressions and normals. In consonance with patients' own reports, winter sleep in SAD patients is increased in length, though slow wave (delta) sleep is decreased. Light therapy partially counters this distortion in sleep architecture (Skwerer et al., 1988). Though others have found thyroid abnormalities to be present in some forms of major depression, we have been unable to document any particular thyroid abnormality in winter SAD (Joseph-Vanderpool et al., 1990b; Rosenthal et al., 1984).

Joseph-Vanderpool and colleagues (1991) have shown that depressed winter SAD patients have normal basal plasma cortisol and adrenocorticotropic hormone (ACTH) levels, but blunted ACTH responses to infusions of corticotropin-releasing hormone (CRH), an abnormality that can largely be corrected with phototherapy. This blunted response is also seen in hypercortisolemic patients, such as melancholic depressives. In the case of SAD patients, however, we believe it reflects an underactive hypothalamo-pituitary-adrenal axis, which would be consistent with the lethargy, hypersomnia, and hyperphagia typical of SAD as opposed to the agitation, insomnia, and anorexia seen in melancholic depression. The dexamethasone suppression test has been found to be consistently normal in patients with winter SAD (James et al., 1986).

In contrast to those depressed patients who manifest decreased response of peripheral blood lymphocytes to mitogen stimulation (Kronfol et al., 1983; Schleifer, Keller, Bond, Cohen, & Stein, 1989), depressed SAD patients have been found to have an abnormally increased response to the mitogens phytohemaglutinin and Concanavalin A. Whereas eye exposure to bright white light enhanced lymphocyte blastogenesis in normals, in SAD patients the over-responsiveness was normalized (Skwerer et al., 1988).

The hypothesis that the eye plays a special role in SAD is supported by a phototherapy study suggesting that the antidepressant effects of light are mediated through the eyes (Wehr et al., 1987). There is only limited evidence, however, to support the idea that ophthalmic function itself is abnormal in SAD. Dr. Norio Ozaki of our group has replicated the statistical finding that electrooculograms are abnormal in SAD (Lam et al., 1990).

MECHANISM

Two clues offer promise for revealing the mechanism of the disorder. One is the association between SAD and the time of year when people are exposed to low levels of sunlight. The second is that alteration of ambient light in winter can effectively treat the depressive symptoms. From these clues, however, the possible lines of reasoning diverge.

One possible explanation for the disorder is that the short days of winter deprive susceptible patients of sufficient quanta of light for maintenance of a euthymic state. This "photon-deficient" depression is treated by replacing the relatively deficient winter light. The initial report on SAD by Rosenthal and colleagues (1984) documenting that bright light acted as an antidepressant whereas dim light did not, forms the cornerstone of this hypothesis. The failure of ordinary light to prevent depression in this population suggested that a critical number of photons might be necessary for the antidepressant response.

The potential importance of melatonin in SAD was also suggested by the superior antidepressant effect of bright versus dim light, given that bright light suppresses melatonin secretion in humans (Lewy et al., 1980, 1982). One theory maintained that bright light's suppression of melatonin induced an antidepressant effect. Arguments against this proposition were encountered when the administration of melatonin to successfully treated SAD patients failed to blunt the antidepressant effect of light therapy (Rosenthal et al., 1986b). When other SAD patients were treated with atenolol—a beta-adrenergic blocker that can reduce night-time melatonin levels—and failed to improve, it became clear that there were limits to the "melatonin hypothesis." If pharmacological suppression of melatonin failed to have an antidepressant effect, it seemed unlikely that the suppression of melatonin was specifically responsible for the antidepressant effect (Rosenthal et al., 1988a).

The eyes, not the skin, appear to mediate the effects of light treatment (Wehr et al., 1987). Visual P300s (dynamic brain event-related potentials measuring the amount of brain attention or processing committed to a stimulus) in winter SAD are enhanced by light in direct proportion to its antidepressant effects—a phenomenon not seen with auditory P300s (Duncan, Deldin, Skwerer, Jacobsen, & Rosenthal, 1987, personal communication; Duncan-Johnson & Donchin, 1982). Combined results from two trials of treatment with light of different wavelengths suggest that green light is a more effective antidepressant than either red or blue (Brainard et al., 1990; Oren et al., 1991). These findings are consistent with our knowledge of the rod-and-cone photoreceptors that absorb maximally at about 510 nm and 550 nm, respectively (Fein & Szuts, 1982). Retinal illumination may act in SAD by increasing dopamine production and suppressing melatonin in the retina (Oren, 1991) or increasing photoreceptor metabolic activity (Terman, Remé, Rafferty, Gallin, & Terman, 1990).

A "phase-shift" hypothesis of phototherapy was built on the capacity of bright light in the morning to advance the nocturnal rise of melatonin to an earlier hour (Lewy, 1984, 1985a; Lewy, 1987; Lewy & Sack, 1986). Two groups have suggested that SAD patients have abnormally delayed melatonin rhythms which are advanced by bright light therapy in the morning (Lewy, Sack, Miller, & Hoban, 1987a; Sack et al., 1990; Terman et al., 1988). There is considerable controversy as to whether light works by shifting circadian rhythms or not (Isaacs, Stainer, Sensky, Moor, & Thompson, 1988; Thompson, Franey, Arendt, & Checkley, 1988; Wehr et al., 1986).

Depending on the timing of light exposure, endogenous circadian amplitudes of variables such as temperature, melatonin, and heart rate can be markedly enhanced or attenuated depending on when the light is administered (Czeisler, Kronauer, Mooney, Anderson, &

Allan, 1987; Kronauer, 1987). Based on this model, Kronauer and Czeisler proposed that an increased circadian amplitude induced by phototherapy may result in light's antidepressant effect (Czeisler et al., 1987; Kronauer, 1987; Kronauer & Frangioni, 1987). Although we have found no difference in 24-hour core temperature measurements of SAD patients and normals either in winter (Rosenthal et al., 1990) or in summer (Levendosky, et al., 1991), light treatment significantly enhanced the amplitude of the patients' circadian rhythms in winter.

Several lines of research suggest that serotonin plays an important role in winter depressions (Coppen, 1967). Winter reductions in serotonin concentrations have been observed in the human postmortem hypothalamus (Carlsson, Svennerholm, & Winblad, 1980). Wurtman and colleagues (1981) have postulated that carbohydrate craving, which is prominent in winter depressives (Jacobsen, Murphy, & Rosenthal, 1989; Rosenthal et al., 1984), may reflect a functional serotonin deficiency. Rosenthal and colleagues (1989) found that carbohydrate-rich meals activate SAD patients and sedate normal controls, which may also be consistent with a serotonergic abnormality in SAD. Two studies have shown abnormal behavioral and hormonal responses to infusions of the postsynaptic serotonin agonist m-CPP (Jacobsen et al., 1989; Joseph-Vanderpool et al., 1990a). Recent reports that light exposure may alter serotonin receptor sensitivity in rat neurons (Cox, Mason, Meal, & Parker, 1986; Mason, 1984) and in platelets of patients with winter SAD (Szádóczky et al., 1989) are compatible with a serotonergic explanation of light therapy. Further support of this hypothesis comes from a study demonstrating the serotonergic agonist d-Fenfluramine to be highly effective in reversing symptoms of the syndrome (O'Rourke, Wurtman, Chebli, & Gleason, 1989).

Depue and colleagues (1989b) have proposed that dopamine might play a key role in SAD by modulating a "Behavioral Facilitation System." Several studies of physiological, behavioral, and hormonal systems thought to be regulated by dopamine have supported this hypothesis (Arbisi, Depue, Spoont, Leon, & Ainsworth, 1989; Depue, Iacono, Muir, & Arbisi, 1988; Depue et al., 1989a, 1990; Levendosky et al., 1990b). These studies have been explained with models of excess dopamine activity inducing dopamine receptor down-regulation or with models of reduced dopaminergic activity in various brain systems. Despite the indefinite nature of these models, so many abnormalities in dopamine systems have been documented in SAD that it seems likely that these systems play some role in the pathophysiology of the condition.

TREATMENT

Alteration of environmental light is but one viable treatment approach for winter SAD. Although we know of no clinical trials of commercially available antidepressant medications in SAD patients, our clinical experience suggests that patients with SAD can be successfully treated with cyclic antidepressants, monoamine oxidase inhibitors, or lithium. Use of fluoxetine has also appeared helpful in several cases. Many SAD patients turn to phototherapy, however, to avoid the well-known side effects of the standard pharmaceutical agents.

Illuminance, measured in terms of quanta of light sensed over time by a certain surface area, was the first phototherapy variable studied systematically (Rosenthal et al., 1988b). Integral to this measurement is the distance of the subject from the light source. Initially, researchers used a set of bulbs situated 90 centimeters from the subject to achieve an illuminance of 2,500 lux (Rosenthal et al., 1984). In recent years fixtures delivering 10,000 lux have been found to be effective with less than an hour of treatment per day (Terman et al. 1990). It is essential that patients sit facing the lights, though it may not be necessary for them to stare directly at the fixture.

We cannot say with certainty what hour of the day is best for daily light treatment. The "phase-shift" theory of light treatment was derived from the observation that morning light, by advancing circadian rhythms, appeared to have superior antidepressant effects (Lewy et al., 1984). Several studies seem to confirm this hypothesis (Avery, D. H., Khan, A., & Dunner, D. L., personal communication 1988; Lewy, Sack, & Singer, 1985b; Lewy, Sack, Singer, & White, 1987b; Terman, Quitkin, Terman, Stewart, & McGrath, 1987). Other carefully conducted studies, however, have shown that light treatment at other times of day induces significant antidepressant effects (James, Wehr, Sack, Parry, & Rosenthal, 1985; Wehr et al., 1986).

Duration may interact inversely with intensity in the delivery of a total quantity of light for successful treatment (Terman et al., 1990). High levels of bright light, though, may be harmful to the retina (Sykes, Robison, Waxler, & Kuwabara, 1981). In our view, a reasonable treatment approach begins with 30 minutes of light each morning. If this regimen fails to trigger an antidepressant response within 5 days, then using the lights for the first hours of the day, or dividing the hour between morning and evening, may be considered.

Our own longitudinal experience suggests that the two-thirds of SAD patients who respond to phototherapy should be maintained on the treatment until they gain sufficient daily light exposure from other sources, typically in the spring. Premature withdrawal from phototherapy usually results in a return of the depressive syndrome. Following the summer, it is often appropriate to resume phototherapy prophylactically near the calendar date when the patient's depressive episodes historically have begun.

Early investigators employed fluorescent lighting that closely followed the special distribution of natural outdoor light. The results of more recent studies differed in assessing the therapeutic effect of ultraviolet-bearing light (Frank et al., 1989; Lam, Buchanan, Clark, & Remick, 1989; Oren et al., 1991). This point is of concern because of the theoretical possibility that ultraviolet light exposure might adversely affect the eyes or the skin (Oren, Rosenthal, Rosenthal, Waxler, & Wehr, 1990d). There is some evidence that incandescent light sources also may be effective in the treatment of winter SAD (Moul et al., 1990; Yerevanian, Anderson, Grota, & Bray, 1986). Because there is no convincing evidence that ultraviolet light is critical to the antidepressant effect of light, we usually recommend that patients begin treatment with an ultraviolet-free light source.

Use of bright light treatment has been a benign experience for most patients. Side effects are few, though some patients complain about eyestrain, headaches, irritability, overactivity, or insomnia (Oren et al., 1991; Rosenthal et al., 1984). Eyestrain and headaches often diminish after a few days of treatment, and they may be minimized by decreasing the duration of therapy or increasing distance from the light. Light administered too late in the evening may sometimes result in difficulty falling asleep.

IS LIGHT THERAPY MERELY A PLACEBO?

A controversy that challenges researchers who study the effects of light on mood is the suggestion that phototherapy succeeds only as a placebo (Eastman, 1990). Although it is difficult to rule out any involvement of the placebo effect, several arguments suggest that placebo effects alone do not account for the efficacy of phototherapy. These arguments include the demonstration of light's efficacy by several groups, the repeated responses within some individual patients over the course of years, the characteristic time course of response to treatment and relapse following treatment withdrawal, the existence of a dose-response curve for light intensity, and the suggestion of a circadian rhythm of treatment sensitivity (Rosenthal et al., 1988b).

NONSEASONAL DEPRESSION

Kripke and coworkers have pioneered the research in treatment of nonseasonal depression by increasing environmental light. Two initial studies were unsuccessful in inducing antidepressant response (Kripke, 1985; Kripke, Mullaney, Gillin, Risch, & Janowsky, 1985). Use of inadequate illuminance for inadequate intervals may have contributed to these failures (Kripke, Risch, & Janowsky, 1983a; 1983b). Although others have found incandescent light unhelpful in nonseasonally depressed patients (Yerevanian et al., 1986), Kripke and colleagues (Kripke, Gillin, Mullaney, Risch, & Janowsky, 1987; Kripke, Mullaney, Savides, & Gillin, 1989) have reported modest but significant antidepressant responses using 3 hours of evening bright light. These findings offer hope that certain light treatment paradigms might prove beneficial in some nonseasonally depressed patients.

BRIGHT LIGHT AND NORMALS

Bright light benefits subjects with mild winter depression, as in subsyndromal SAD (Kasper et al., 1989a; Rosenthal et al., 1985; Terman et al., 1989c). Common experience suggests that many of us will choose to be in a brightly-lit room rather than a dim one. But there are limits to the beneficial effects of bright lights. A recent study indicated that seniors living in residential housing complexes had little tolerance of the bright lights commonly used for phototherapy (Genhart, Kelly, Coursey, & Rosenthal, 1988). Two formal studies of light exposure to normals have demonstrated no mood-altering effects (Kasper, Rogers, Madden, Joseph-Vanderpool, & Rosenthal, 1990; Rosenthal, Rotter, Jacobsen, & Skwerer, 1987). To ease them into the dark world of sleep, those who read in bed at night may prefer an adequate bedside lamp to a bright ceiling fixture. Light, therefore, is not a universal euphoriant.

CONCLUSION

From a public health perspective, research on light and mood does not yet offer specific guidelines. It seems that environmental light plays a critical role in maintaining a euthymic state for many people. Most people, however, have evolved so that their moods are tolerably stable within the environment in which they live. Given cost and some people's lack of reaction or adverse reaction to high-intensity lamps, installation of bright lights at every desk or work station does not seem wise. Nevertheless, accommodating the needs of those who are sensitive to dim light by permitting brightly-lit "micro-environments" may improve the mood and productivity of many adults and children (Jacobsen, Wehr, Sack, James, & Rosenthal, 1987; Kasper et al., 1990; London, 1987). If forthcoming methods of light delivery such as portable "light visors" or bedside "dawn simulators" prove helpful (Moul et al., 1990; Terman, Schlager, Fairhurst, & Perlman, 1989b), light treatment may be even more attractive than it is presently. Meanwhile architects and urban planners may wish to consider the idea of preserving environmental light as a factor in their design of homes, schools, and work places.

If we return to the Arctic night where this chapter began, we may note a small irony of history. Frederick A. Cook, perhaps the first author specifically to link seasonal sunlight changes to mood, was a man obsessed by his quest for fame. In the early years of this century he deceptively contended that he had beaten Peary (1987) in the race to the North Pole. His latter years were spent in jail for fraud. Had he appreciated that his connection of environmental light to mood would blossom in the ways we have outlined here, he might have pursued his early findings and avoided prison. Whether SAD would subsequently have been named "Cook's Disease" we cannot say, but observations linking light to mood will keep many psychiatrists and scientists busy for years to come and, we hope, many patients satisfied through what would have been the winters of their discontent.

REFERENCES

American Psychiatric Association. (1987). *Diagnostic and statistical manual of mental disorders 3rd revised edition.* Washington, DC: Author.

Arbisi, P. A., Depue, R. A., Spoont, M. R., Leon, A., & Ainsworth, B. (1989). Thermoregulatory response to thermal challenge in seasonal affective disorder: A preliminary report. *Psychiatry Research, 28,* 323–334.

Boyce, P., & Parker, G. (1988). Seasonal affective disorder in the southern hemisphere. *American Journal of Psychiatry, 145,* 96–99.

Brainard, G. C., Rosenthal, N. E., Sherry, D., Kelly, D., Skwerer, R. G., Schulz, P. M., Waxler, M., & Wehr, T. A. (1990). Personal communication.

Carlsson, A., Svennerholm, L., & Winblad, B. (1980). Seasonal and circadian monoamine variations in human brains examined post mortem. *Acta Psychiatrica Scandinavica, 61*(Suppl 280), 75–85.

Cook. F. A. (1894a). Gynecology and obstetrics among the Eskimos. *Brooklyn Medical Journal, 8,* 154–169.

Cook, F. A. , (1894b). Medical observations among the Esquimaux. *NY Journal of Gynecology and Obstetrics, 4,* 282–286.

Coppen, A. (1967). The biochemistry of affective disorders. *British Journal of Psychiatry, 113,* 1237–1264.

Cox, C. M., Mason, R., Meal, A., & Parker, T. L. (1986). Altered 5-HT sensitivity and synaptic morphology in rat CNS induced by long-term exposure to continuous light. *British Journal of Pharmacology, 89,* 528P.

Czeisler, C. A., Kronauer, R. E., Mooney, J. J., Anderson, J. L., & Allan, J. S. (1987). Biologic rhythm disorders, depression, and phototherapy: A new hypothesis. *Psychiatric Clinics of North America, 10,* 687–709.

Depue, R. A., Arbisi, P., Krauss, S., Iacono, W. G., Leon, A., Muir, R., & Allen, J. (1990). Seasonal independence of low prolactin concentration and high spontaneous eye blink rates in unipolar and bipolar II seasonal affective disorder. *Archives of General Psychiatry, 47,* 356–364.

Depue, R. A., Arbisi, P., Spoont, M. R., Krauss, S., Leon, A., & Ainsworth, B. (1989a). Seasonal and mood independence of low basal prolactin secretion in premenopausal women with seasonal affective disorder. *American Journal of Psychiatry, 146,* 989–995.

Depue, R. A., Arbisi, P., Spoont, M. R., Leon, A., & Ainsworth, B. (1989b). Dopamine functioning in the behavioral facilitation system and seasonal variation in behavior: Normal population and clinical studies. In Rosenthal, N. E., and Blehar, M. C. *Seasonal Affective Disorders and Phototherapy* pp. 230–259. New York: Guilford Press.

Depue, R. A., Iacono, W. G., Muir, R., & Arbisi, P. (1988). Effects of phototherapy on spontaneous eye-blink rate in seasonal affective disorder. *American Journal of Psychiatry, 145,* 1457–1459.

Duncan-Johnson, C. C., & Donchin, E. (1982). "The P300 component of the event-related potential as an Index of Information processing." *Biological Psychiatry, 14,* 1–52.

Eastman, C. I. (1990). What the placebo literature can tell us about phototherapy for SAD. *Psychopharmacology Bulletin, 26,* 495–504.

Fein, A., & Szuts, E. Z. (1982). *Photoreceptors: Their role in vision.* IUPAB Biophysics Series. Cambridge: Cambridge Univ. Press.

Frank, A., Docherty, J., Welch, B., Souci, M., Fierman, E., Merkl, K., Frankel, F., & Rosenthal, N. E. (1989). Personal communication.

Genhart, M., Kelly, K. A., Coursey, R. D., & Rosenthal, N. E. (1988). Personal communication.

Hanada, K., Takahashi, S., & Takahashi, K., (1991). Clinical features of seasonal affective disorder in Japan. *Biological Psychiatry, 29*: 342S.

Hippocrates. (1931). Aphorisms. *Hippocrates* pp. 128–129. Cambridge: Harvard Univ. Press.

Isaacs, G., Stainer, D. S., Sensky, T. E., Moor, S., & Thompson, C. (1988). "Phototherapy and its mechanisms of action in seasonal affective disorder." *Journal of Affective Disorders, 14*, 13–19.

Jacobsen, F. M., Joseph-Vanderpool, J. R., & Rosenthal, N. E. (1988). Personal communication.

Jacobsen, F. M., Murphy, D. L., & Rosenthal, N. E. (1989). The role of serotonin in seasonal affective disorder and the antidepressant response to phototherapy. In Rosenthal, N. E., and Blehar, M. C. *Seasonal Affective Disorders and Phototherapy* pp. 333–341. New York: Guilford Press.

Jacobsen, F. M., & Rosenthal, N. E. (1988). Seasonal affective disorder. In Georgotas, A., and Cancro, R. *Depression and Mania: A Comprehensive Textbook* pp. 104–116. New York: Elsevier Science.

Jacobsen, F. M., Wehr, T. A., Sack, D. A., James, S. P., & Rosenthal, N. E. (1987). Seasonal affective disorder: A review of the syndrome and its public health implications. *American Journal of Public Health, 77*, 57–60.

James, S. P., Wehr, T. A., Sack, D. A., Parry, B. L., Rogers, S., & Rosenthal, N. E. (1986). The dexamethasone suppression test in seasonal affective disorder. *Comprehensive Psychiatry, 27*, 224–226.

James, S. P., Wehr, T. A., Sack, D. A., Parry, B. L. & Rosenthal, N. E. (1985). Treatment of seasonal affective disorder with light in the evening. *British Journal of Psychiatry, 147*, 424–428.

Joseph-Vanderpool, J. R., Jacobsen, F. M., Murphy, D. L., Sorek, E., Hill, J. L., & Rosenthal, N. E. (1990a). Personal communication.

Joseph-Vanderpool, J. R., Oren, D. A., Sorek, E., Madden, P., Brown, C., & Rosenthal, N. E. (1990b). Personal communication.

Joseph-Vanderpool, J. R., Rosenthal, N. E., Chrousos, G. P., Wehr, T. A., Skwerer, R., Kasper, S., & Gold, P. W. (1991). Abnormal pituitary-adrenal responses to corticotropin-releasing hormone (CRH) in patients with seasonal affective disorder: Clinical and pathophysiological implications. *Journal of Clinical Endocrinology and Metabolism, 72*, 1382–1387.

Kasper, S., Rogers, S. L. B., Madden, P. A., Joseph-Vanderpool, J. R., & Rosenthal, N. E. (1990). The effects of phototherapy in the general population. *Journal of Affective Disorders, 18*, 211–219.

Kasper, S., Rogers, S. L. B., Yancey, A., Schulz, P. M., Skwerer, R. G., & Rosenthal, N. E. (1989a). Phototherapy in individuals with and without subsyndromal seasonal affective disorder. *Archives of General Psychiatry, 46*, 837–844.

Kasper, S., Wehr, T. A., Bartko, J. J., Gaist, P. A., & Rosenthal, N. E.

(1989b). Epidemiological findings of seasonal changes in mood and behavior. *Archives of General Psychiatry, 46,* 823–833.

Kripke, D. F. (1985). Therapeutic effects of bright light in depressed patients. *Annals of the New York Academy of Sciences, 453,* 270–281.

Kripke, D. F., Gillin, J. C., Mullaney, D. J., Risch, S. C., & Janowsky, D. S. (1987). Treatment of major depressive disorders by bright white light for 5 days. In Halaris, A., *Chronobiology and Psychiatric Disorders* pp. 207–239. New York: Elsevier.

Kripke, D. F., Mullaney, D. J., Gillin, J. C., Risch, S. C., & Janowsky, D. S. (1985). Phototherapy of non-seasonal depression. In Shagass, C., Josiassen, R. C., Bridger, W. H., Weiss, K. J., Stoff, D., & Simpson, G. M. *Biological Psychiatry* pp. 993–995. New York: Elsevier Science.

Kripke, D. F., Mullaney, D. J., Savides, T. J., & Gillin, J. C. (1989). Phototherapy for nonseasonal major depressive disorders. In Rosenthal, N. E., & Blehar, M. *Seasonal Affective Disorders and Phototherapy* pp. 342–356. New York: Guilford Press.

Kripke, D. F., Risch, S. C., & Janowsky, D. (1983a). "Bright white light alleviates depression." *Psychiatry Research, 10,* 105–112.

Kripke, D. F., Risch, S. C., & Janowsky, D. (1983b). Lighting up depression. *Psychopharmacology Bulletin, 19,* 526–530.

Kronauer, R. E. (1987). A model for the effect of light on the human "deep" circadian pacemaker. *Sleep Research, 16,* 621.

Kronauer, R. E., & Frangioni, J. V. (1987). Modeling laboratory bright light protocols. *Sleep Research, 16,* 622.

Kronfol, Z., Silva, J., Greden, J., Demginski, S., Gardner, R., & Carroll, B. J. (1983). Impaired lymphocyte function in depressive illness. *Life Sciences, 33,* 241.

Lam, R. W., Beattie, C., Buchanan, A., Remick, R. A., & Zis, A. P. (1990). Light treatment & biological rhythms. New York: 34.

Lam, R. W., Buchanan, A., Clark, C., & Remick, R. A. (1989). First annual meeting of the society for light treatment and biological rhythms. Bethesda, MD: 12.

Levendosky, A. A., Joseph-Vanderpool, J. R., Hardin, T., Sorek, E., & Rosenthal, N. E. (1990a). Personal communication.

Levendosky, A. A., Joseph-Vanderpool, J. R., Hardin, T., Sorek, E., Rosenthal, N. E. (1991). Core body temperature in patients with seasonal affective disorder and normal controls in summer and winter. *Biological Psychiatry, 29,* 524–534.

Levendosky, A. A., Joseph-Vanderpool, J. R., Kasper, S., Duncan, C. C., Skwerer, R. A., Jacobsen, F. M., Hardin, T. A., & Rosenthal, N. E. (1990b). Personal communication.

Lewy, A. H., Kern, H. A., Rosenthal, N. E., & Wehr, T. A. (1982). Bright artificial light treatment of a manic-depressive patient with a seasonal mood cycle. *American Journal of Psychiatry, 139,* 1496–1498.

Lewy, A. J. (1987). Treating chronobiologic sleep and mood disorders with bright light. *Psychiatric Annals, 17,* 664–669.

Lewy, A. J., & Sack, R. L. (1986). Light therapy and psychiatry. *Proceedings of the Society of Experimental Biology and Medicine, 183,* 11–18.

Lewy, A. J., Sack, R. L., Miller, L. S., & Hoban, T. M. (1987a). Antidepressant and circadian phase-shifting effects of light. *Science, 235*, 352–353.

Lewy, A. J., Sack, R. L., & Singer, C. M. (1984). Assessment and treatment of chronobiologic disorders using plasma melatonin levels and bright light exposure: The clock–gate model and the phase response curve. *Psychopharmacology Bulletin, 20*, 561–565.

Lewy, A. J., Sack, R. L., & Singer, C. M. (1985a). Immediate and delayed effects of bright light on human melatonin production: Shifting "dawn" and "dusk" shifts the dim light melatonin onset (DLMO). *Annals of the New York Academy of Sciences, 453*, 253–259.

Lewy, A. J., Sack, R. L., & Singer, C. M. (1985b). Treating phase typed chronobiologic sleep and mood disorders using appropriately timed bright artificial light. *Psychopharmacology Bulletin, 21*, 368–372.

Lewy, A. J., Sack, R. L., Singer, C. M., & White, D. M. (1987b). The phase shift hypothesis for bright light's therapeutic mechanism of action: Theoretical considerations and experimental evidence." *Psychopharmacology Bulletin, 23*, 349–353.

Lewy, A. J., Wehr, T. A., Goodwin, F. K., Newsome, D. A., & Markey, S. P. (1980). Light suppresses melatonin secretion in humans. *Science, 210*: 1267–1269.

London, W. P. (1987). Full-spectrum classroom light and sickness in pupils. *Lancet, 2*, 1205–1206.

Mason, R. (1984). Effects of chronic constant illumination on the responsiveness of rat suprachiasmatic, lateral geniculate and hippocampal neurons to ionophoresed 5-HT. *Journal of Physiology, 357*, 13P.

Moul, D. E., Hellekson, C. J., Oren, D. A., Frank, A., Brainard, G. C., Murray, M. G., Wehr, T. A., & Rosenthal, N. E. (1990). Second annual conference on light treatment and biological rhythms. New York: 15.

Oren, D. A. (1991). Retinal melatonin and dopamine in seasonal affective disorder. *Journal of Neural Transmission*, (in sect), 83; 85–91.

Oren, D. A., & Rosenthal, N. E. (1992). Seasonal affective disorders. In Paykel, E. S. *Handbook of Affective Disorders. 2nd Edition* (pp. 551–567). London: Churchill Livingstone.

Oren, D. A., Brainard, G. C., Johnston, S. H., Joseph-Vanderpool, J. R., Sorek, E., & Rosenthal, N. E. (1991). Treatment of seasonal affective disorder with green light and red light. *American Journal of Psychiatry, 148*, 509–511.

Oren, D. A., Rosenthal, F. S., Rosenthal, N. E., Waxler, M., & Wehr, T. A. (1990d). Exposure to ultraviolet B radiation during phototherapy. *American Journal of Psychiatry, 147*, 675–676.

Oren, D. A., Shannon, N. J., Carpenter, C. J., & Rosenthal, N. E. (1991). Usage patterns of phototherapy in seasonal affective disorders. *Comprehensive Psychiatry, 32*, 147–152.

O'Rourke, D., Wurtman, J. J., Wurtman, R. J., Chebli, R., & Gleason, R. (1989). Treatment of seasonal depression with d-fenfluramine. *Journal of Clinical Psychiatry, 50*, 343–347.

"Peary, Robert E." (1987). *Encyclopedia Americana, 21*, 584–585.

Rosen, L. N., Targum, S. D., Terman, M., Bryant, M. J., Hoffman, H., Kasper, S. F., Hamovit, J. R., Docherty, J. P., Welch, B., & Rosenthal, N. E.

(1990). Prevalence of seasonal affective disorder at four latitudes. *Psychiatry Research, 31*, 131–144.

Rosenthal, N. E., Carpenter, C. J., James, S. P., Parry, B. L., Rogers, S. L. B., & Wehr, T. A. (1986a). Seasonal affective disorder in children and adolescents. *American Journal of Psychiatry, 143*, 356–358.

Rosenthal, N. E., Genhart, M. J., Caballero, B., Jacobsen, F. M., Skwerer, R. G., Coursey, R. D., Rogers, S., & Spring, B. J. (1989). Psychobiological effects of carbohydrate- and protein-rich meals in patients with seasonal affective disorder and normal controls. *Biological Psychiatry, 25*, 1029–1040.

Rosenthal, N. E., Jacobsen, F. M., Sack, D. A., Arendt, J., James, S. P., Parry, B. L., & Wehr, T. A. (1988a). Atenolol in seasonal affective disorder: A test of the melatonin hypothesis. *American Journal of Psychiatry, 145*, 52–56.

Rosenthal, N. E., Levendosky, A. A., Skwerer, R. G., Joseph-Vanderpool, J. R., Kelly, K. A., Hardin, T., Kasper, S., DellaBella, P., & Wehr, T. A. (1990). Effects of light treatment on core body temperature in seasonal affective disorder. *Biological Psychiatry, 27*, 39–50.

Rosenthal, N. E., Lewy, A. J., Wehr, T., A., Kern, H. E., & Goodwin, F. K. (1983). Seasonal cycling in a bipolar patient. *Psychiatry Research, 8*, 25–31.

Rosenthal, N. E., Rotter, A., Jacobsen, F. M., & Skwerer, R. G. (1987). No mood-altering effects found after treatment of normal subjects with bright light in the morning. *Psychiatry Research, 22*, 1–9.

Rosenthal, N. E., Sack, D. A., Carpenter, C. J., Parry, B. L., Mendelson, W. B., & Wehr, T. A. (1985). Antidepressant effects of light in seasonal affective disorder. *American Journal of Psychiatry, 142*, 163–170.

Rosenthal, N. E., Sack, D. A., Gillin, J. C., Lewy, A. J., Goodwin, F. K., Davenport, Y., Mueller, P. S., Newsome, D. A., & Wehr, T. A. (1984). Seasonal affective disorder: A description of the syndrome and preliminary findings with light therapy. *Archives of General Psychiatry, 41*, 72–80.

Rosenthal, N. E., Sack, D. A., Jacobsen, F. M., James, S. P., Parry, B. L., Arendt, J., Tamarkin, L., & Wehr, T. A. (1986b). Melatonin in seasonal affective disorder and phototherapy. *Journal of Neural Transmission, [Suppl 21]*, 257–267.

Rosenthal, N. E., Sack, D. A., Skwerer, R. G., Jacobsen, F. M., & Wehr, T. A. (1988b). Phototherapy for seasonal affective disorder. *Journal of Biological Rhythms, 3*, 101–120.

Sack, R. L., Lewy, A. J., White, D. M., Singer, C. M., Fireman, M. J. & Vandiver, R. (1990). Morning vs evening light treatment for winter depression. *Archives of General Psychiatry, 47*, 343–351.

Schleifer, S. J., Keller, S. E., Bond, R. N., Cohen, J., & Stein, M. (1989). Major depressive disorder and immunity. *Archives of General Psychiatry, 46*, 81–87.

Skwerer, R. G., Jacobsen, F. M., Duncan, C. C., Kelly, K. A., Sack, D. A., Tamarkin, L., Gaist, P. A., & Rosenthal, N. E. (1988). Neurobiology of seasonal affective disorder and phototherapy. *Journal of Biological Rhythms, 3*, 135–154.

Spitzer, R. L., Endicott, J., & Robins, E. (1978). Research diagnostic criteria: Rationale and reliability. *Archives of General Psychiatry, 35*, 773–782.

Sykes, S. M., Robison, Jr., W. G., Waxler, M., & Kuwabara, T. (1981). Damage to the monkey retina by broad-spectrum fluorescent light. *Investigative Opthalmology and Visual Sciences, 20*, 425–434.

Szádóczky, E., Falus, A., Arató, M., Németh, A., Teszéri, G., & Moussong-Kovács, E. (1989). Phototherapy increases platelet ^{3}H-imipramine binding in patients with winter depression. *Journal of Affective Disorders, 16*, 121–125.

Terman, J. S., Terman, M., Schlager, D., Rafferty, B., Rosofsky, M., Link, M. J., & Quitkin, F. M. (1990). Efficacy of brief, intense light exposure for treatment of winter depression. *Psychopharmacology Bulletin, 26*, 3–11.

Terman, M. (1988). On the question of mechanism in phototherapy for seasonal affective disorder: Considerations of clinical efficacy. *Journal of Biological Rhythms, 3*, 155–172.

Terman, M., Botticelli, S. R., Link, B. G., Link, M. J., Quitkin, F. M., Hardin, T. E., & Rosenthal, N. E. (1989a). Seasonal symptom patterns in New York: Patients and population. In Thompson, C., & Silverstone, T. *Seasonal affective disorder* (pp. 77–95). London: CNS (Clinical Neuroscience) Publishers.

Terman, M., Quitkin, F. M., Terman, J. S., Stewart, J. W., & McGrath, P. J. (1987). The timing of phototherapy: Effects on clinical response and the melatonin cycle. *Psychopharmacology Bulletin, 23*, 354–357.

Terman, M., Remé, C. E., Rafferty, B., Gallin, P. F., & Terman, J. S. (1990). Bright light therapy for winter depression: Potential ocular effects and theoretical implications. *Photochemistry and Photobiology 51*, 781–792.

Terman, M., Schlager, D., Fairhurst, S., & Perlman, B. (1989b). Dawn and dusk simulation as a therapeutic intervention. *Biological Psychiatry, 25*, 966–970.

Terman, M., Terman, J. S., Quitkin, F. M., Cooper, T. B., Lo, E. S., Gorman, J. M., Stewart, J. W., & McGrath, P. J. (1988). Response of the melatonin cycle to phototherapy for seasonal affective disorder. *Journal of Neural Transmission, 72*, 147–165.

Terman, M., Terman, J. S., Quitkin, F. M., Stewart, J. W., McGrath, P. J., Nunes, E. V., Wager, S. G., & Tricamo, E. (1989c). Dosing dimensions of light therapy: Duration and time of day. In Thompson, C., & Silverstone, T. *Seasonal affective disorder* (pp. 187–204). London: CNS (Clinical Neuroscience) Publishers.

Thompson, C. (1986). Seasonal affective disorder and phototherapy: Experience in Britain. *Clinical Neuropsychology, 9, (Suppl 4)*, 190–192.

Thompson, C., Franey, C., Arendt, J., & Checkley, S. A. (1988). A comparison of melatonin secretion in depressed patients and normal subjects. *British Journal of Psychiatry, 152*, 260–265.

Wehr, T. A., Jacobsen, F. M., Sack, D. A., Arendt, J., Tamarkin, L., & Rosenthal, N. E. (1986). Phototherapy of seasonal affective disorder: Time of day and suppression of melatonin are not critical for antidepressant effects. *Archives of General Psychiatry, 43*, 870–875.

Wehr, T. A., Skwerer, R. G., Jacobsen, F. M., Sack, D. A., & Rosenthal, N. E. (1987). Eye versus skin phototherapy of seasonal affective disorder. *American Journal of Psychiatry, 144*, 753–757.

Wirz-Justice, A., Graw, P., Bucheli, C., Schmid, A. C., Gisin, A., Jochum, A., & Pöldinger, W. (1989). Seasonal affective disorder in Switzerland: A clinical perspective. In Thompson, C., & Silverstone, T. *Seasonal Affective Disorder* (pp. 69–76). London: CNS (Clinical Neuroscience).

Wurtman, J. J., Wurtman, R. J., Growdon, J. H., Henry, P., Lipscomb, A., & Zeisel, S. H. (1981). Carbohydrate craving in obese people: Suppression by treatments affecting serotonergic transmission. *International Journal of Eating Disorders, 1*, 2–15.

Yerevanian, B. I., Anderson, J. L., Grota, L. J., & Bray, M. (1986). Effects of bright incandescent light on seasonal and nonseasonal major depressive disorder. *Psychiatry Research, 18*, 355–364.

Young, M. A., Watel, L. G., Lahmeyer, H. W., & Eastman, C. I. (1990). Second annual conference on light treatment and biological rhythms. New York: 42.

Chapter 2

Noise, Pollution, and Psychopathology

Paul A. Bell

Over the centuries there has been much suspicion that the physical environment has played some role in the development of manifest psychopathology, or at least of symptoms of pathological behavior. For example, exposure of a pregnant woman to the wrong "vapors" or to traumatic events in the physical environment were once thought to result in physical and emotional abnormalities in the infant. In technologically advanced societies over the past two centuries or so, however, the battleground of the etiology of psychopathology has been dominated by biological and psychosocial forces. Hypotheses involving genetic, biopathogenic, biochemical, psychodynamic, and social/developmental influences have gained various degrees of support and favor in the etiological literature.

Although outside of the psychopathology literature there has been considerable recognition of the role of the physical environment within the domain of each of these etiological pathways, it is only in the past few decades that serious consideration has been given to the possibility that the physical environment could have more direct influences on the appearance of pathological behavior (cf. Maurissen, 1981). For example, there has been mounting evidence that some varieties of toxic waste can influence genetic mutation, that biopathogens and industrial wastes can be neurotoxic, and that noise can increase stress and exacerbate antisocial behavior. The increased awareness of these influences is no doubt heavily tied to cultural awareness of human contributions to the destruction of the natural environment. The realization that such pollutants are tied to psychopathology has paralleled environmental awareness, and the evidence is mounting sufficiently that mental

21

health professionals are giving more and more credence to the etiological significance of noise and toxic pollution.

This chapter will provide a brief review of some of the major evidence for the influence of noise and toxic pollution on psychopathology and antisocial behavior. As will be seen, it is difficult to link most of these factors to a specific psychopathology (except for neuropathy in the case of toxins), but the contribution of noise and pollutants to symptoms that are psychopathological is readily substantiated.

As with other behavioral research, a note of methodological caution is warranted. Most of the relevant research with humans is correlational in nature. Rarely do high noise or toxic conditions occur in the absence of other contributory factors. For example, loud noise usually occurs in the presence of other known pathogens, such as poverty, deterioration in family infrastructure, low educational opportunity, high levels of air pollution, or even battlefield conditions. Similarly, toxicity such as lead poisoning is most often studied in lower socioeconomic areas (e.g., in association with lead paint in public housing) where similarly significant covariates exist. However, as evidence for the etiological significance of these factors mounts, more and more research is statistically controlling for these known potential confounds. Often, quasi-experimental designs have been employed, and the use of more than one meaningful control group has increased the confidence in the internal and external validity of the studies.

NOISE AND PSYCHOPATHOLOGY

Noise consists of a physical component—sound—and a psychological component—the interpretation of the sound as something undesirable. As a result, although there are nomothetic parameters predicting which sounds will be interpreted as noise, there is a very subjective element in determining whether a given sound will be annoying or aversive. The following section reviews the major determinants of annoyance and some of the impact of aversive noise. The next section will consider research linking noise to stress effects. Following this discussion, a review of research on airport noise shows how the implications of noise effects can be studied in the context of a specific real-world source of aversive noise. Finally, a brief review is given of the research on noise as a factor in antisocial behavior.

Annoyance and Its Determinants

The most comprehensive experimental work on noise and human stress is probably the research of Glass and Singer (1972). These scientists and their associates systematically explored the impact of different types of noise on a number of measures of human performance and psychological stress. In general, noise that is loud, unpredictable (intermittent in onset and duration), and uncontrollable is the most aversive or annoying. Noise that does not meet all three of these criteria (e.g., loud, controllable noise or noise that is constant) is less aversive and may have minimal or short-lived impact. Borsky (1969) has also observed that annoyance increases if the perceiver believes the noise to be unnecessary or generated by others unconcerned with the welfare of the perceiver; the perceiver believes the noise to be hazardous to health; the perceiver associates the noise with fear; or the perceiver is dissatisfied with other aspects of the environment. Thus, there are likely to be considerable individual differences in any impact of noise on psychopathology. For example, support for this possibility comes from Auble and Britton's (1958) finding that only individuals high in anxiety are adversely affected by noise on some tasks.

A major finding of the Glass and Singer (1972) research was that aftereffects of noise are as important (or more important) in some respects than the effects of the noise during actual exposure. In addition to impeding concentration and vigilance, the experience impaired frustration tolerance once the noise terminated. Such tolerance is typically measured by persistence of working on unsolvable puzzles. Interestingly, the more perceived control one has over noise, the greater the frustration tolerance after the noise has ceased (Sherrod et al., 1977).

Noise and Stress

By definition, noise is "unwanted sound" and, as such, there are a number of mechanisms by which it may promote psychopathological symptoms. An obvious mediator is stress. For example, Ward and Suedfeld (1973) recorded traffic noise and played it in a laboratory setting. Relative to a control group, subjects experiencing the traffic noise reported greater tension and uncertainty and talked faster. The stress connection has also been studied in research linking noise to physical ailments thought to be aggravated by stress, including ulcers and other gastrointestinal problems (Doring, Hauf,

& Seiberling, 1980; National Academy of Sciences, 1981), infant mortality (Ando & Hattori, 1973), sleep loss and increased consumption of hypnotics (Grandjean, Graf, Lauber, Meier, & Muller, 1973), and general reports of acute and chronic illness (Cameron, Robertson, & Zaks, 1972; see also, Jansen, 1973). Mass psychogenic illness has also been linked to noise exposure (Colligan & Murphy, 1982).

Some studies, however, show little or no relationship between industrial noise and health effects (e.g., Finckle & Poppen, 1948; Glorig, 1971), and Cohen, Glass, and Phillips (1977) concluded in their review of the material that the correlation between noise and stress-related illness is weak. On the other hand, numerous studies have shown that peripheral blood vessel constriction, systolic and diastolic blood pressure, electrodermal activity, and catecholamine secretion all increase with exposure to aversive noise (e.g., Cohen et al., 1980; Eggertson, Svensson, Magnusson, & Andren, 1987; Frankenhaeuser & Lundberg, 1977; Glass & Singer, 1972; Knipschild, 1980). In addition, workers who wear hearing protectors show lower blood pressure and lower epinephrine in their urine, and even without hearing protection physiological changes such as heart rate or skin conductance can moderate after repeated exposure (Borg, 1981; Glass & Singer, 1972), although vasoconstriction may not (Jansen, 1973). Interestingly, Cherek (1985) reported that cigarette smoking increased with increasing aversiveness to noise, and Woodson, Buzzi, Nil, & Battig (1986) reported that smokers not allowed to smoke during noise exposure reported increased subjective distress, but those allowed to smoke showed no such increase.

Partly because of the relatively strong connection with physiological changes and relatively weak association with stress-related disorders, some researchers prefer "arousal" rather than "stress" as a mediator of noise effects. Another important mediator is probably perceived control itself, loss of which can lead to learned helplessness and depression. Although direct linkage of noise exposure to depression has not been demonstrated, exposure to loud, uncontrollable noise can bias retrieval of memories such that memories associated with negative moods are more readily recalled (Willner & Neiva, 1986).

Noise in the Workplace

Surveys of workers in industry have shown that noise exposure is associated with a variety of psychosomatic complaints and emotional symptoms. Such correlational associations with high levels of noise include headaches, nausea, instability, argumentativeness, anxiety, sexual impotence, and mood changes (e.g., Cohen, Glass, & Phillips, 1977; Miller, 1974; Strakhov, 1966). These relationships are typically quite small statistically, and the research rarely controls for other relevant variables, such as other sources of stress and other aspects of the job that covary with noise.

Airport Noise

The nature of the methodological problem with such survey research is illustrated by the controversy over whether or not mental hospital admissions are associated with airport noise. About two-thirds of people living near airports where noise is a problem report annoyance and unhappiness with the noise (Burrows & Zamarin, 1972; McLean & Tarnopolsky, 1977). Abey-Wickrama, A'Brook, Gattoni, & Herridge (1969) compared hospital admission rates for high- and low-noise neighborhoods around London's Heathrow Airport. As might be expected, the noisy areas had higher admission rates. However the character of neighborhoods differs along numerous dimensions associated with admission rates (e.g., Chowns, 1970). Methods controlling for these factors more carefully have still shown a positive, though rather weak, association with admission rates (e.g., Herridge, 1974; Herridge & Low-Beer, 1973).

Probably the most comprehensive study of the human impact of airport noise is contained in a series of reports on children in schools around the Los Angeles International Airport (Cohen et al., 1980, 1981, 1986). Noisy schools were associated with elevated blood pressure, lower performance on cognitive tasks, reduced frustration tolerance, and increased distractibility. School achievement itself was not affected by aircraft noise, but it was associated with noise in the home. Other studies of transportation noise have shown that it can impair reading ability of children (Bronzaft & McCarthy, 1975; Cohen, Glass, & Singer, 1973).

Antisocial Behavior

Psychopathology sometimes involves antisocial behavior, though certainly most psychopathologies do not involve antisocial tendencies. To the extent noise is encountered by anyone, it may promote antisocial actions. Several laboratory studies in social psychology suggest that noise enhances aggressive tendencies and impairs prosocial behavior. For example, Green and O'Neal (1969) showed that noise can increase the willingness of subjects to administer ostensible electric shock to a confederate. Donnerstein and Wilson (1976) found that this antisocial tendency occurred primarily in subjects who had been provoked, and that the effect dissipated when subjects were given perceived control over the noise. Others (Mathews & Canon, 1975; Page, 1977) demonstrated that noise can decrease the tendency of subjects to offer assistance to someone in need, and Sherrod and Downs (1974) showed that this tendency can also be mitigated through increased perceived control over the noise. Indeed, many noise effects on behavior in the laboratory may be influenced by informed consent procedures which convey an unintended sense of perceived control over the aversive conditions (Bell & Doyle, 1983; Dill, Gilden, Hill, & Hanselka, 1982; Gardner, 1978).

To the extent noise interferes with prosocial behavior, it appears to do so by distracting attention away from relevant social cues (Cohen & Lezak, 1977; Yinon & Bizman, 1980). Since many pathological conditions also involve failure to process social cues appropriately, it is conceivable that noise would further promote antisocial behavior in some populations with psychopathologies. If so, one might expect dementias to exaggerate this tendency. However, preliminary data from a National Institute of Mental Health project by the author suggest that noise is not a particular contributory factor to assaults by patients— many of whom have a dementia—on a state hospital geriatric unit.

Summary

It appears that there is no evidence of a link between the etiology of any specific diagnosable psychopathology and exposure to noise. However, noise may contribute to other factors in a neighborhood which would promote mental illness, although the evidence for such an effect on a neighborhood level is weak and subject to numerous caveats associated with correlational data. Stronger evidence exists for noise increasing stress, arousal, distraction, and antisocial behavior, and decreasing frustration tolerance, all of which may, in the presence of other symptoms, be indicative of psychopathology.

POLLUTION AND PSYCHOPATHOLOGY

There are numerous studies on the effects of pollution on people. For convenience, discussion of potential links to psychopathology can be divided into correlational studies on air pollution, studies on exposure as a result of technological catastrophe, and studies on neurotoxicity of specific agents.

Air Pollution

Correlational studies have shown an increase in psychiatric hospital admissions associated with high levels of air pollution (Briere, Downes, & Spensley, 1983; Strahilevitz, Strahilevitz, & Miller, 1979). Higher numbers of emergency calls for psychiatric symptoms have also been associated with increased air pollution levels (Rotton & Frey, 1982). Evans, Jacobs, Dooley, & Catalano (1987) reported a higher probability of distress following major life stresses if pollution was high. As with similar noise studies, such research is subject to the control problems of correlational methods. However, a combination of pollutants has been medically identified as causing an Air Pollution Syndrome, characterized by headache, fatigue, insomnia, irritability, depression, burning of the eyes, back pain, impaired judgment, and gastrointestinal problems (Hart, 1970; LaVerne, 1970). Also, as with noise, malodorous air pollution in the lab has been found to make affect more negative and under some circumstances it can promote antisocial behavior (Rotton, 1983; Rotton, Barry, Frey, & Soler, 1978; Rotton, Frey, Barry, Milligan, & Fitzpatrick, 1979).

Toxic Exposure During Technological Catastrophe

Several recent studies have examined the psychological impact of toxic disaster such as the Three Mile Island nuclear accident and the Love Canal toxic dump tragedy. With such data it can be difficult to separate neurotoxic impact from consequences associated with fear, uncertainty, and despair. For example, immediately after the accident at the TMI nuclear power plant, nearby residents reported more psychological and emotional distress than those away from the vicinity of the plant (Bromet, 1980; Dohrenwend, Dohrenwend, Kasl, & Warheit, 1979; Flynn, 1979; Houts, Miller, Tokuhata, & Ham, 1980). Similar feelings of distress, sleeping difficulty, and elevated urinary epinephrine levels were evident 1 to 5 years later in nearby residents (Baum, Fleming, & Davidson, 1983; Davidson & Baum, 1986; Davidson, Fleming, & Baum, 1987; Gatchel, Schaeffer, & Baum, 1985). The increased levels of stress were relatively mild but chronic. Moreover, social support (Fleming, Baum,

Gisriel, & Gatchel, 1982), palliative coping strategies (Collins, Baum, & Singer, 1983), and perceived control (Davidson, Baum, & Collins, 1982) were associated with reduced stress symptoms.

Similar studies have reported increased stress and psychological distress among residents affected by the Love Canal toxic dump (Gibbs, 1982; Levine, 1982; Levine & Stone, 1986), as well as another toxic waste site (Fleming, 1985), and by residents using water from a contaminated landfill (Gibbs, 1986). Pesticide exposure and exposure to toxic smoke from an explosion have produced similar results (Markowitz & Gutterman, 1986).

Electromagnetic Fields

Over the past decade there has been some scientific research and much media publicity about the possibility that exposure to electromagnetic fields (EMFs) may be associated with a variety of biological effects, especially cancer. This research is inconsistent yet tantalizing enough that considerable scientific interest has been generated (see Beal, 1974; Persinger, Ludwig, & Ossenkopf, 1973; Nair, Morgan, & Florig, 1989; Pool, 1990a, 1990b for reviews), and issues of risk and liability have been raised (Pool, 1990c). Electric power lines, generators, and even small appliances create EMFs, so everyone in industrialized countries is almost constantly exposed to them on at least a minimal level. The consequences of EMF exposure, to the extent they appear in the literature, are quite varied. Except for nervous system tumors, the research on EMFs rarely examines mental impact. Russian scientists (reported in Pool, 1990b) in the 1960s reported headaches, fatigue, and reduced libido in workers employed in a high-voltage power switchyard. Graham (also reported in Pool, 1990b) found that humans exposed to high-voltage EMFs experienced changes in heart rate, brain activity, and reaction time.

A number of biological mechanisms mediating the effects of EMFs have been proposed, including reduction in melatonin levels. Interestingly, reduction in melatonin has been proposed as a mechanism by which phototherapy (exposure to bright light) counteracts depression in seasonal affective disorder (e.g., Rosenthal et al., 1984; Wehr et al., 1986). The evidence on melatonin as a mediator in SAD is inconsistent; and within EMF research, the hypothesized reduction in melatonin from exposure to EMFS should theoretically counter depression if it is to be consistent with the SAD hypothesis, yet no such observations have been reported. Just as fear of nuclear exposure seems to be associated with some stress effects, if fear of EMF exposure should become prominent from the same type of media coverage that is dominant about nuclear exposure, we might expect to see similar stress effects as those described above. As of this writing, no such effects have been found. At this point, it must be said that the jury is still out on EMF connections to any disease, especially mental illness, but that research in the next 10 years should be fairly definitive about the presence or absence of such effects.

Some have wondered about the risk of EMFs or other radiation for those working with video display terminals (e.g., Kirkpatrick, 1988). Although some workers complain of eyestrain and headaches after working on computer terminals, the research evidence is inconclusive since there are so many potential confounds (e.g., gender, office design, pay) in field research on the topic (cf. Starr, Thompson, & Shute, 1982). Clearly, glare on screens can cause eyestrain which can lead to headaches and perhaps irritability. Here again, the jury is still out, but any direct connections to psychopathology seem unlikely.

Neurotoxins

A recent report by the Office of Technology Assessment (1990) details the concerns about the neurotoxins in the environment. Although the U.S. Environmental Protection Agency has inventoried 65,000 chemicals for toxicity, little is known about the neurotoxic potential of any of them. Moreover, although linkage to specific psychopathology is often, if not usually, hypothetical, linkage of numerous toxins to neurological deficits is quite firm in many cases, especially for lead and other heavy metals such as mercury. Weiss (1983) notes that metals such as vanadium and manganese, which are essential for life, can be toxic enough to cause Parkinsonism, manic-depression, and other disorders. Since lead has probably received the most attention in terms of its widespread and chronic effects, a more detailed review of the research on it is presented below.

Lead

The neurotoxicity of lead is well established, although the precise mechanism is still unknown. For example, lead is thought to interfere with the way neurons process calcium, and it also may interfere with the blood–brain barrier (Taylor, 1990). In adults, lead and other heavy metal poisoning is one cause of dementia and other neuropsychological deficits, and it has been associated with anxiety (Browder, Joselow, & Louria, 1973; Grandjean, Arnvig, & Beckmann, 1978; Spivey et al., 1979) and interpersonal difficulties (Bromet, Ryan, & Parkinson, 1986; Spivey et al., 1979). It can be treated in part with chelating agents. In children the effects of lead poisoning may be long-lasting (see Rabin, 1989, for a review). Needleman, Schell, Bellinger, Leviton, & Alldred (1990) have recently reported an 11-year follow-up study of the Needleman et al. (1979) research which revealed numerous cognitive and attention-related deficits. For example, higher lead levels were associated with lower IQ (4 points on average), and higher distractibility in the classroom. Evaluations from teachers showed that as lead levels increased, so did hyperactivity, impulsivity, frustration, daydreaming, distractibility, and dependence; increases in lead were associated with decreases in persistence, organization, and inability to follow directions. Variables controlled included race, class, and parental intelligence.

After 11 years, the high-lead group scored lower than the low-lead group on neuropsychological measures (vocabulary, fine motor skills, reaction time) and were seven times less likely to complete high school, six times more likely to have reading difficulties, and had over 50% more classroom absences. It should be cautioned that the developmental impact of lead is disputed. Fisher (1990), for example, reviews the opinions of numerous experts who question the Needleman and other findings; this includes the findings of a 1983 Environmental Protection Agency panel, which concluded that the extant research neither substantiated nor refuted a causal link between childhood exposure to low levels of lead and subsequent neuropsychological deficits. Whether or not such a link exists, none of the above findings is causally tied to specific psychopathology. However, many of the symptoms associated with lead poisoning (and other toxic exposure) are found in disturbed children, adolescents, and adults, and the potential contribution of lead poisoning to symptoms in specific psychopathologies should not be overlooked.

Other Neurotoxins

Weiss (1983) reviews a number of other neurotoxic substances including mercury, pesticides, and solvents, exposure to which can result in a variety of neuropathies (especially Parkinsonism), as well as depression, anxiety, hallucinations, and difficulty in concentrating. Recent developments have been astounding with respect to previously unknown neurotoxicity and common neurological disorders. One of the most studied linkages is between the substance called MPTP and Parkinson's disease (Langston, Ballard, Tetrud, & Irwin, 1983). Originally discovered through rapid-onset cases of Parkinson's in individuals taking "designer" street drugs contaminated with the compound, laboratory evidence has substantiated that MPTP has a specific toxicity for the neurons of the substantia nigra. Another compound, BMAA, has been shown to have toxicity linked to Guam ALS-Parkinsonism-Dementia complex (Spencer et al., 1987). Numerous studies have linked aluminum to Alzheimer's disease, although other research has seriously questioned such an etiological relationships (see McLachlan, 1986, for a review). Whether these and other components are linked to psychopathologies is unknown, but the fact that a specific toxin leads to a specific neuropathy strongly supports the need for more research into the topic.

SUMMARY

Pollution can contribute to a variety of psychopathological symptoms. In addition to neurotoxic effects from specific pollutants, there is evidence that air pollution in general is associated with increased psychiatric hospital admissions and with symptoms such as fatigue, depression, irritability, and insomnia. Catastrophic exposure to toxic substances is often associated with symptoms of stress and self-reported psychological distress, which may be chronic. That social support and adaptive coping strategies can relieve some of the distress points out a particular concern for mental health professionals. In general pollution is not selective in terms of who gets exposed to it, and its impact applies to the population as a whole. However, the above evidence suggests that mental health professionals should consider whether or not pollution (and noise, for that matter) aggravates a preexisting mental disorder, and whether clients with impaired coping skills may be especially susceptible to the psychological impact of pollution.

ACKNOWLEDGMENT

The author expresses appreciation to Andrew Baum for assembling some of this material in a related coauthored work.

REFERENCES

Abey-Wickrama, I., A'Brook, M. F., Gattoni, F. E. G., & Herridge, C. F. (1969). Mental hospital admissions and aircraft noise. *Lancet, 2*, 1275–1277.

Ando, Y., & Hattori, H. (1973). Statistical studies in the effects of intense noise during human fetal life. *Journal of Sound and Vibration, 27*, 101–110.

Auble, D., & Britton, N. (1958). Anxiety as a factor influencing routine performance under auditory stimuli. *Journal of General Psychology, 58*, 111–114.

Baum, A., Fleming, R., & Davidson, L. M. (1983). Natural disaster and technological catastrophe. *Environment and Behavior, 15*, 333–354.

Beal, J. B. (1974). Electrostatic fields, electromagnetic fields and ions—Mind/body/environment interrelationships. In J. G. Llaurado, A. Sances, & J. H. Battocletti (Eds.), *Biologic and clinical effects of low-frequency magnetic and electric fields*, (pp. 5–20). Springfield, IL: Thomas.

Bell, P. A., & Doyle, D. P. (1983). Effects of heat and noise on helping behavior. *Psychological Reports, 53*, 955–959.

Borg, E. (1981). Noise, hearing, and hypertension (editorial). *Scandinavian Audiology, 10*(2), 125–126.

Borsky, P. N. (1969). Effects of noise on community behavior. In W. D. Ward & J. E. Fricke (Eds.), *Noise as a public health hazard*. Washington, DC: The American Speech and Hearing Association.

Briere, J., Downes, A., & Spensley, J. (1983). Summer in the city: Urban weather conditions and psychiatric emergency room visits. *Journal of Abnormal Psychology, 92*, 77–80.

Bromet, E. (1980). *Preliminary report on the mental health of Three Mile Island residents*. Pittsburgh, PA: Western Psychiatric Institute, University of Pittsburgh.

Bromet, E., Ryan, C., & Parkinson, D. (1986). Psychosocial correlates of occupational lead exposure. In A. H. Lebovits, A. Baum, & J. Singer (Eds.), *Advances in Environmental Psychology* (Vol. 6, pp. 19–31). Hillsdale, NJ: Erlbaum.

Bronzaft, A. L., & McCarthy, D. P. (1975). The effects of elevated train noise on reading ability. *Environment and Behavior, 7*, 517–527.

Browder, A. A., Joselow, M. M., & Louria, D. B. (1973). The problem of lead poisoning. *Medicine, 52*, 121–139.

Burrows, A. A., & Zamarin, D. M. (1972). Aircraft noise and the community: Some recent survey findings. *Aerospace Medicine, 43*, 27–33.

Cameron, P., Robertson, D., & Zaks, J. (1972). Sound pollution, noise pollution, and health: Community parameters. *Journal of Applied Psychology, 56*, 67–74.

Cherek, D. R. (1985). Effect of acute exposure to increased levels of background industrial noise and cigarette smoking behavior. *International Archives of Occupational and Environmental Health, 56*, 23–30.

Chowns, R. H. (1970). Mental hospital admissions and aircraft noise. *Lancet, 1*(7644), 467.

Cohen, S., Evans, G. W., Krantz, D. S., & Stokols, D. (1980). Physiological, motivational, and cognitive effects of aircraft noise on children: Moving from the laboratory to the field. *American Psychologist, 35,* 231–243.

Cohen, S., Evans, G. W., Krantz, D. S., Stokols, D., & Kelly, S. (1981). Aircraft noise and children: Longitudinal and cross-sectional evidence on adaptation to noise and the effectiveness of noise abatement. *Journal of Personality and Social Psychology, 40,* 331–345.

Cohen, S., Evans, G. W., Stokols, D., & Krantz, D. S. (1986). *Behavior, health and environmental stress.* New York: Plenum.

Cohen, S., Glass, D. C., & Phillips, S. (1977). Environment and health. In H. E. Freeman, S. Levine, & L. G. Reeder (Eds.), *Handbook of medical sociology.* Englewood Cliffs, NJ: Prentice-Hall.

Cohen, S., Glass, D. C., & Singer, J. E. (1973). Apartment noise, auditory discrimination, and reading ability in children. *Journal of Experimental Social Psychology, 9,* 407–422.

Cohen, S., & Lezak, A. (1977). Noise and inattentiveness to social cues. *Environment and Behavior, 9,* 559–572.

Colligan, M. J., & Murphy, L. R. (1982). A review of mass psychogenic illness in work settings. In M. J. Colligan, J. W. Pennebaker, & L. R Murphy (Eds.), *Mass psychogenic illness.* Hillsdale, NJ: Erlbaum.

Collins, D. L., Baum, A., & Singer, J. (1983). Coping with chronic stress at Three Mile Island: Psychological and biochemical evidence. *Health Psychology, 2,* 149–166.

Davidson, L. M., & Baum, A. (1986). Chronic stress and post traumatic stress disorders. *Journal of Consulting & Clinical Psychology, 54,* 303–308.

Davidson, L. M., Baum, A., & Collins, D. L. (1982). Stress and control-related problems at Three Mile Island. *Journal of Applied Social Psychology, 12,* 349–359.

Davidson, L. M., Fleming, I., & Baum, A. (1987). Chronic stress, catecholamines, and sleep disturbance at Three Mile Island. *Journal of Human Stress, 13,* 75–83.

Dill, C. A., Gilden, E. R., Hill, P. C., & Hanselka, L. L. (1982). Federal human subjects regulations: A methodological artifact? *Personality and Social Psychology Bulletin, 8,* 417–425.

Dohrenwend, B. P., Dohrenwend, B. S., Kasl, S. V., & Warheit, G. J. (1979). *Report of the Task Group on Behavioral Effects to the President's Commission on the Accident at Three Mile Island.* Washington, DC: U.S. Government Printing Office.

Donnerstein, E., & Wilson, D. W. (1976). Effects of noise and perceived control on ongoing and subsequent aggressive behavior. *Journal of Personality and Social Psychology, 34,* 774–781.

Doring, H. J., Hauf, G., & Seiberling, M. (1980). Effects of high intensity sound on the contractile function of the isolated ileum of guinea pigs and rabbits. In *Noise as a public health problem: Proceedings of the Third International Congress* (ASHA Report No. 10). Rockville, MD: American Speech and Hearing Association.

Eggertsen, R., Svensson, A., Magnusson, M., & Andren, L. (1987). Hemodynamic effects of loud noise before and after central sympathetic nervous stimulation. *Acta Medica Scandinavica, 221*(2), 159–164.

Evans, G. W., Jacobs, S. V., Dooley, D., & Catalano, R. (1987). The interaction of stressful life events and chronic strains on community mental health. *American Journal of Community Psychology, 15,* 23–34.

Finckle, A. L., & Poppen, J. R. (1948). Clinical effects of noise and mechanical vibrations of a turbo-jet engine on man. *Journal of Applied Physiology, 1,* 183–204.

Fisher, K. (1990). Research on lead yields bad news, controversy, *APA Monitor, 21*(7), 12–13.

Fleming, I. C. (1985). *The stress reducing functions of specific types of social support for victims of a technological catastrophe.* Unpublished doctoral dissertation, University of Maryland, College Park, MD.

Fleming, R., Baum, A., Gisriel, M. M., & Gatchel, R. J. (1982). Mediation of stress at Three Mile Island by social support. *Journal of Human Stress, 8,* 14–22

Flynn, C. B. (1979). *Three Mile Island telephone survey.* U.S. Nuclear Regulatory Commission (NUREG/CR–1093).

Frankenhaeuser, M., & Lundberg, U. (1977). The influence of cognitive set on performance and arousal under different noise loads. *Motivation and Emotion, 1,* 139–149.

Gardner, G. T. (1978). Effects of federal human subjects regulations on data obtained in environmental stress research. *Journal of Personality and Social Psychology, 36,* 628–634.

Gatchel, R. J., Schaeffer, M. A., & Baum, A. (1985). A psychological field study of stress at Three Mile Island. *Psychophysiology, 22,* 175–181.

Geen, R. G., & O'Neal, E. C. (1969). Activation of cue-elicited aggression by general arousal. *Journal of Personality and Social Psychology, 11,* 289–292.

Gibbs, L. (1982). *Love Canal: My story.* Albany, NY: SUNY Press.

Gibbs, M. S. (1986). Psychopathological consequences of exposure to toxins in the water supply. In A. H. Lebovits, A. Baum, & J. Singer (Eds.), *Advances in environmental psychology* (pp. 47–70). Hillsdale, NJ: Erlbaum.

Glass, D. C., & Singer, J. E. (1972). *Urban stress.* New York: Academic Press.

Glorig, A. (1971). Nonauditory effects of noise exposure. *Journal of Sound and Vibration, 5,* 28–29.

Grandjean, E., Graf, P., Lauber, A., Meier, H. P., & Muller, R. (1973). A survey on aircraft noise in Switzerland. In W. D. Ward (Ed.), *Proceedings of the International Congress on Noise as a Public Health Problem.* Washington, DC: U.S. Government Printing Office.

Grandjean, P., Arnvig, E., & Beckmann, J. (1978). Psychological dysfunctions in lead-exposed workers. *Scandinavian Journal of Work, Environment and Health, 4,* 295–303.

Hart, R. H. (1970). The concept of APS: Air Pollution Syndrome(s). *Journal of the South Carolina Medical Association, 66,* 71–73.

Herridge, C. F. (1974). Aircraft noise and mental health. *Journal of Psychosomatic Research, 18,* 239–243.

Herridge, C. F., & Low-Beer, L. (1973). Observations of the effects of aircraft noise near Heathrow Airport on mental health. In W. D. Ward (Ed.), *Proceedings of the International Congress as a Public Health Problem.* Washington, DC: U.S. Government Printing Office.

Houts, P. S., Miller, R. W., Tokuhata, G. K., & Ham, K. S. (1980, April 8). *Health-related behavioral impact of the Three Mile Island nuclear incident.* Report submitted to the TMI Advisory Panel on Health Research Studies of the Pennsylvania Department of Health, Part I.

Jansen, G. (1973). Non-auditory effects of noise—Physiological and psychological reactions in man. *Proceedings of the International Congress on Noise as a Public Health Problem.* Dubrovnik, Yugoslavia, May 13–18. Washington, DC: U.S. Environmental Protection Agency.

Kirkpatrick, D. (1988). How safe are video terminals? *Fortune,* 66–68.

Knipschild, P. G. (1980). Aircraft noise and hypertension. In J. V. Tobias, G. Jansen, & W. D. Ward (Eds.), *Noise as a public health problem: Proceedings of the Third International Congress* (ASHA Report No. 10). Rockville, MD: American Speech and Hearing Association.

Langston, J. W., Ballard, P., Tetrud, J. W., & Irwin, I. (1983). Chronic Parkinsonism in humans due to a product of meperidine-analogue synthesis. *Science, 219,* 979–980.

LaVerne, A. A. (1970). Nonspecific Air Pollution Syndrome (NAPS): Preliminary report. *Behavioral Neuropsychiatry, 2,* 19–21.

Levine, A. G. (1982). *Love Canal: Science, politics and people.* Lexington, MA: Lexington Books, D.C. Heath.

Levine, A., & Stone, R. (1986). Threats to people and what they value. Residents' perceptions of the hazards of Love Canal. In A. H. Lebovits, A. Baum, & J. Singer (Eds.), *Advances in environmental psychology* (Vol. 6, pp. 109–130). Hillsdale, NJ: Erlbaum.

Markowitz, J. S., & Gutterman, E. M. (1986). Predictors of psychological distress in the community following two toxic chemical incidents. In A. H. Lebovits, A. Baum, & J. Singer (Eds.), *Advances in environmental psychology* (Vol. 6, pp. 89–107). Hillsdale, NJ: Erlbaum.

Mathews, K. E., & Canon, L. K. (1975). Environmental noise level as a determinant of helping behavior. *Journal of Personality and Social Psychology, 32,* 571–577.

Maurissen, J. P. J. (1981). History of mercury and mercurialism. *New York State Journal of Medicine, 81,* 1902–1909.

McLachlan, D. R. C. (1986). Aluminum and Alzheimer's Disease. *Neurobiology of Aging, 7,* 525–532.

McLean, E. K., & Tarnopolsky, A. (1977). Noise, distress, and mental health. *Psychological Medicine, 7,* 19–62.

Miller, J. D. (1974). Effects of noise on people. *Journal of the Acoustical Society of America, 56,* 729–764.

Nair, I., Morgan, G., & Florig, H. K. (1989). *Biological effects of power frequency electric and magnetic fields.* Washington, DC: Office of Technology Assessment.

National Academy of Sciences (1981). *The effect on human health from long-term exposure to noise.* (Report of Working Group 81.) Washington, DC: National Academy Press.

Needleman, H. L., Gunnoe, C. G., Leviton, A., Reed, R. R., Peresie, H., Maher, C. et al. (1979). Deficits in psychologic and classroom performance of children with elevated dentine lead levels. *New England Journal of Medicine, 300,* 689–695.

Needleman, H. L., Schell, A. S., Bellinger, D., Leviton, A., & Alldred, E. N. (1990). The long-term effects of exposure to low doses of lead in childhood: An 11-year follow-up report. *New England Journal of Medicine, 322,* 83–88.

Office of Technology Assessment. (1990). *Neurotoxicity. Identifying and controlling poisons of the nervous system.* U.S. Government Printing Office.

Page, P. A. (1977). Noise and helping behavior. *Environment and Behavior, 9,* 559–572.

Persinger, M. A., Ludwig, H. W., & Ossenkopf, K. P. (1973). Psychophysiological effects of extremely low frequency electromagnetic fields: A review. *Perceptual and Motor Skills, 26,* 1131–1159.

Pool, R. (1990a). Is there an EMF-cancer connection? *Science, 249,* 1096–1098.

Pool, R. (1990b). Electromagnetic fields: The biological evidence. *Science, 249,* 1378–1381.

Pool, R. (1990c). Flying blind: The making of EMF policy. *Science, 250,* 23–25.

Rabin, R. (1989). Warnings unheeded: A history of child lead poisoning. *American Journal of Public Health, 79,* 1668–1674.

Rosenthal, N. E., Sack, D. A., Gillen, J. C., Lewy, A. J., Goodwin, F. K., Davenport, Y., Mueller, P. S., Newsome, D. A., & Wehr, T. A. (1984). Seasonal affective disorder: A description of the syndrome and preliminary findings with light therapy. *Archives of General Psychiatry, 41,* 72–80.

Rotton, J. (1983). Affective and cognitive consequences of malodorous pollution. *Basic and Applied Social Psychology, 4,* 171–191.

Rotton, J., Barry, T., Frey, J., & Soler, E. (1978). Air pollution and interpersonal attraction. *Journal of Applied Social Psychology, 8,* 57–71.

Rotton, J., & Frey, J. (1982). Air pollution, weather, and psychiatric emergencies: A constructive replication. Unpublished manuscript, Florida International University, Miami, FL.

Rotton, J., & Frey, J. (1985). Air pollution, weather, and violent crimes: Concomitant time-series analysis of archival data. *Journal of Personality and Social Psychology, 49,* 1207–1220.

Rotton, J., Frey, J., Barry, T., Milligan, M., & Fitzpatrick, M. (1979). The air pollution experience and interpersonal aggression. *Journal of Applied Social Psychology, 9,* 397–412.

Sherrod, D. R., Armstrong, D., Hewitt, J., Madonia, B., Speno, S., & Fenyd, D. (1977). Environmental attention, affect and altruism. *Journal of Applied Social Psychology, 7,* 359–371.

Sherrod, D. R., & Downs, R. (1974). Environmental determinants of altruism: The effects of stimulus overload and perceived control on helping. *Journal of Experimental Social Psychology, 10,* 468–479.

Spencer, P. S., Nunn, P. B., Hugon, J., Ludolph, A. C., Ross, S. M., Roy, D. N., & Robertson, R. C. (1987). Guam Amyotrophic Lateral Sclerosis—Parkinsonism—Dementia linked to plant excitant neurotoxin. *Science, 237,* 517–522.

Spivey, G. H., Brown, C. P., Baloh, R. W., Campion, D. S., Valentine, J. L.,

Massey, F. J., Jr., Browdy, B. L., & Culver, B. D. (1979). Subclinical effects of chronic increased lead absorption—A prospective study. I. Study design and analysis of symptoms. *Journal of Occupational Medicine, 21*, 423–429.

Starr, S. J., Thompson, C. R., & Shute, S. J. (1982). Effects of video display terminals on telephone operators. *Human Factors, 24*, 699–711.

Strahilevitz, N., Strahilevitz, A., & Miller, J. E. (1979). Air pollution and the admission rate of psychiatric patients. *American Journal of Psychiatry, 136*, 206–207.

Strakhov, A. B. (1966). *Some questions of the mechanism of the action of noise on an organism.* (Report N67–11646). Washington, DC: Joint Publication Research Service.

Taylor, R. (1990). Heavy metal, heavy toll: The lasting legacy of low-level lead in children. *Journal of NIH Research, 2*, April, 57–60.

Ward, L. M., & Suedfeld, P. (1973). Human responses to highway noise. *Environmental Research, 6*, 306–326.

Wehr, T. A., Jacobsen, F. M., Sack, D. A., Arendt, J., Tamarkin, L., & Rosenthal, N. E. (1986). Phototherapy of seasonal affective disorder. *Archives of General Psychiatry, 43*, 870–875.

Weiss, B. (1983). Behavioral toxicology and environmental health science. *American Psychologist, 38*, 1174–1187.

Willner, P., & Neiva, J. (1986). Brief exposure to uncontrollable but not to controllable noise biases the retrieval of information from memory. *British Journal of Clinical Psychology, 25*, 93–100.

Woodson, P. P., Buzzi, R., Nil, R., & Battig, K. (1986). Effects of smoking on vegetative reactivity to noise in women. *Psychophysiology, 23*, 272–282.

Yinon, Y., & Bizman, A. (1980). Noise, success, and failure as determinants of helping behavior. *Personality and Social Psychology Bulletin, 6*, 125–130.

Chapter 3

Nutrition as a Contributing Factor in Psychiatric Disorders and Their Treatment

Simon N. Young

The history connecting nutrition and psychiatry is long and varied. The treatment of pellagra with niacin was one of the first triumphs of biological psychiatry. However, more recently the topic of nutrition and psychiatry usually brings to mind the controversies surrounding a host of unconventional treatments which are often given to correct alleged adverse effects of various dietary components. The purpose of this chapter is to review several areas in which nutrition and psychiatry intersect. First there are the mental effects of nutritional deficiencies, both of total calorie intake and of vitamins and minerals. Second there is the use of purified dietary components, such as tryptophan, as drugs in the treatment of various disorders. The final section of this chapter attempts to distinguish between fact and myth in the strong folklore about how a normal diet in the developed world can produce psychopathology.

NUTRITIONAL DEFICIENCIES

A variety of different nutritional deficiencies can have adverse effects on brain function. The causes of these deficiencies vary widely, but include inadequate diet due to lack of nutritional education or social, medical, or psychiatric factors, malabsorption, and genetic factors influencing the metabolism of or requirement for nutrients. However, the most important factors worldwide are political and economic. In spite of adequate global food resources a large proportion of the population in third world countries is poorly nourished. Thus, the problems of inadequate diet are very different between developing and developed countries. While frank deficiencies tend to be confined to the third world, Carney (1990) has argued that subclinical vitamin deficiencies are not uncommon in developed countries and can play a role in the production of psychopathology.

The sections below deal with some of the more important nutritional deficiencies, in both the first and third world. The list is certainly not exhaustive. Deficiencies of any required nutrient can effect the brain either directly or indirectly. For some the mental symptoms are not well characterized or are not the most important symptoms. Other deficiencies, such as neonatal iodine deficiency which causes hypothyroidism and mental retardation, are well understood, easily treatable, and have, to a large extent, ceased to be a problem.

Prenatal Protein/Calorie Deficiencies

According to some estimates, malnutrition of pregnant women is the most common cause of mental retardation worldwide. However, as pointed out by Stein and Susser (1985) in their excellent review of this topic, malnutrition often occurs when social factors are less than optimal, and it is difficult to isolate the effects of diet from the effects of social milieu. Nonetheless, there is good evidence that malnutrition in early pregnancy can lead to mental retardation or depressed mental competence. Chronic malnutrition in later pregnancy and in the early years of a child's life can lead to cognitive deficits, particularly when combined with social deprivation. The effects of malnutrition early in pregnancy are probably not reversible to any appreciable extent because influences at critical stages in brain development can cause permanent structural changes. Malnutrition later in life has not been convincingly shown to produce untreatable deficits. Obviously the appropriate remedy for mental retardation resulting from prenatal malnutrition is to provide adequate nutrition. While this is simple on an individual level, on a political and economic level it has remained an intractable problem.

Iron Deficiency

Iron deficiency occurs most commonly in third world countries as a result of nutritional deficiencies and intestinal parasites, but it is also seen in developed countries. It can cause cognitive deficits in children and a decrease in physical work production in adults (Pollitt & Liebel, 1982; Scrimshaw, 1984). The mental effects are not necessarily a secondary result of anemia, as iron deficiency can result in various alterations in the brain, for example a decrease in dopamine receptor density (Youdim, Sills, Heydorn, Creed, & Jacobowitz, 1986). Treatment with antiparasitic agents and iron supplements will cause enhanced educational performance in anemic children (Soemantri, Pollitt, & Kim, 1985).

Niacin Deficiency

Pellagra is usually associated with diets high in corn, which has a low bioavailability of niacin and its precursor tryptophan. In the early years of this century in the southern United States, and starting early in the 19th century in southern Europe, the mental symptoms of pellagra made it one of the most prevalent major psychiatric disorders (Sebrell, 1981). Although pellagra is almost never seen in developed countries, it still occurs in developing countries. The etiology of pellagra is related not only to poor nutrition, but also to social factors. Many of the native peoples of the New World relied heavily on corn for their nutritional needs, but did not develop pellagra. In Mexico, just over the border from the southern United States, many of the same conditions which caused pellagra existed. However, in Mexico the disease was almost unknown (Carpenter, 1981).

The reason for this discrepancy did not become apparent until the early 1950s, when it was shown that the traditional methods employed by the native peoples of the American continent for cooking corn, which involved alkali treatment, increased the bioavailability of both tryptophan and niacin (Carpenter, 1981; Katz, Hediger, & Valleroy, 1974). All the cultural groups among the native Americans, who relied heavily on corn, used alkali processing, usually boiling the corn with lime or wood ashes (Katz et al., 1974). If this method of preparation had been adopted by all the peoples who have come to rely heavily on corn in their diet, pellagra would not be the problem it is today. However, there is the prospect that where the cultural transfer of information has been inadequate, technology may solve the problem. Thus, new varieties of corn have been developed which have a higher tryptophan content and lower pellagragenic effect (Xue-Cun et al., 1983).

Niacin is the precursor of the coenzyme NAD, which is involved in many chemical reactions in the brain. Thus a deficiency of niacin will affect many processes in the brain. The specific ones responsible for the mental symptoms are not known.

Thiamine

Chronic nutritional deficiency of thiamine causes beriberi. The symptoms include motor and sensory peripheral nerve lesions, together with depression and loss of appetite. In developed countries thiamine deficiency occurs most commonly in association with alcoholism. In alcoholics Wernicke's syndrome is seen, which is characterized by ataxia, ophthalmoplegia, and confusion. If prompt treatment with thiamine does not occur, it can lead to Korsakoff's syndrome, with a permanent loss of short-term memory. The primary cause of this memory loss is the degeneration of cholinergic neurons, which seem to be sensitive to thiamine deficiency (Arendt, Bigl, & Tennstedt, 1983).

Folic Acid

A high incidence of folate deficiency has been found in many studies of psychiatric patients, and in particular in depression (Young & Ghadirian, 1989; Reynolds, Carney, & Toone, 1984; Carney, 1990). As depression may result in anorexia, this result may not seem surprising. However, there is accumulating evidence that folate deficiency can contribute to depressed mood and folate supplementation may have a useful role to play in the treatment of some depressed patients. A syndrome consisting of various neuropsychological changes and lowered mood, which is associated with folate deficiency, has been defined (Botez, Botez, Léveillé, Bielmann, & Cadotte, 1979; Botez, Botez, & Maag, 1984). Patients suffering from this syndrome respond better to folic acid treatment than to placebo (Botez et al., 1979).

Recently two studies have been performed in which major affective-disorder patients, selected on the basis of low folate levels, not on the basis of the full syndrome of lowered mood and neuropsychological changes, were treated with folic acid. In the first study, affective-disorder patients who were on long-term lithium therapy were treated with folic acid or placebo under double-blind conditions. After one year, the patients with the highest folate levels showed a significant reduction in their affective morbidity (Coppen, Chaudhry, & Swade, 1986). In the second study, one-third of a group

of patients with depression or schizophrenia were found to have folate deficiency and took part in a double-blind placebo-controlled 6-
month trial of methylfolate (the form which is transported actively
across the blood-brain barrier). Methylfolate (15 mg per day) or placebo was added to standard psychotropic treatment. Among both depressed and schizophrenic patients methylfolate significantly improved clinical and social recovery (Godfrey et al., 1990).

Folate deficiency is associated with lowered CNS serotonin levels
(Botez, Young, Bachevalier, & Gauthier, 1982). The lowering of serotonin that can occur in folate deficiency may be one of the primary
factors in the etiology of depression in some patients. However, in
others the anorexia associated with depression may cause folate deficiency, and the lowering of serotonin which results may exacerbate the depression. Whether folate deficiency is the cause or result
of depression, folate supplementation should be therapeutic in fo-
late-deficient depressed patients. The studies in folate supplementation have used doses up to 75 times the normal dietary intake of folic acid. Lower doses, such as those found in over-the-counter
vitamin tablets, have not been tested. However, given that lower
doses have negligible risk and minimal cost, they could well be
given to all depressed patients.

USE OF DIETARY NEUROTRANSMITTER PRECURSORS IN PSYCHIATRY

While the majority of mental symptoms associated with nutritional
deficiencies could be avoided with adequate nutrition, the use of
neurotransmitter precursors has little to do with nutrition, although these compounds are all components of a normal diet. This
is because the doses of the precursors that are used are above the
normal dietary intake, and the effect that these compounds have on
the brain is more extreme than any acute effect of food intake. One
important advantage in the use of dietary components as drugs is
their low toxicity. Tryptophan is the most used of the dietary precursors, and in studies comparing it with placebo, side effects with
tryptophan are no more common than with placebo (Young, 1986).
Recently, serious toxic effects, termed the eosinophilia-myalgia syndrome (EMS), have been seen in subjects taking tryptophan in the
United States and various European countries. However, EMS was
caused not by tryptophan itself but by impurities in several batches
of tryptophan made by a single manufacturer (Belongia et al.,

1990). The neurotransmitter precursors themselves seem to be remarkably safe.

Dietary Neurotransmitter Precursors

The dietary precursor used most commonly is tryptophan, which the brain converts to serotonin. Serotonin itself does not cross the blood–brain barrier and cannot be used to increase brain serotonin. However, an increase in brain tryptophan will increase the rate of serotonin synthesis even in humans (Eccleston et al., 1970). Human brain serotonin can be increased up to, but no more than, two-fold by tryptophan (Young & Gauthier, 1981). This increase is adequate to have a therapeutic effect in some conditions.

Apart from tryptophan, the other neurotransmitter precursors that may be of use in psychiatry are phenylalanine and tyrosine, which are precursors of the catecholamines dopamine and noradrenaline, and choline, which is the precursor of acetylcholine.

Use of Tryptophan in Depression

Because of theories which relate low serotonin levels to the etiology of depression (Meltzer & Lowy, 1987), tryptophan has been tested as an antidepressant. Although it is probably not as effective as classical antidepressants in severe depression, it is as effective and has fewer side effects in mild or moderate depression (Thomson et al., 1982; Young, 1986). In addition, tryptophan can potentiate the antidepressant effect of monoamine oxidase inhibitors. Unfortunately, it also potentiates the side effects of monoamine oxidase inhibitors (Young, 1986), so this combination is usually confined to treatment-resistant patients. Tryptophan is available in Britain and Canada as a prescription drug for the treatment of depression.

Use of Tryptophan in Insomnia

Numerous studies have looked at the effect of tryptophan on sleep in humans, and various reviews of this topic are available (Young, 1986; Hartmann & Greenwald, 1984). In general, tryptophan decreases sleep latency in subjects with mild or moderate insomnia, but not in patients with severe insomnia. Doses above 1 g are often effective (Hartmann, Cravens, & List, 1974), while lower doses are less effective (Hartmann & Spinweber, 1979). The peak effect of tryptophan is at about 45 minutes after ingestion (Hartmann,

Spinweber, & Ware, 1976). In patients who respond to tryptophan, it is almost the ideal hypnotic, as it does not alter sleep stages (at lower doses), impair performance, elevate the threshold for arousal from sleep, or alter brain electrical activity during sleep (Spinweber, 1986). Tryptophan is available as a hypnotic in various European countries.

Other Uses of Tryptophan

Tryptophan has been tested in a variety of disorders. Several small studies suggest potential usefulness in various types of pain (Young, 1986). Two studies indicate that tryptophan may be a useful adjunct in the treatment of pathological aggression (Morand, Young, & Ervin, 1983; Volavka et al., 1990). The possible use of tryptophan in mania or in the prophylaxis of bipolar patients is still under investigation (Young, 1986). In spite of strong folklore among certain sections of the public in the United States that tryptophan is a treatment for premenstrual depression, the only study to look at this topic found no effect of tryptophan (Harrison, Endicott, Rabkin, & Nee, 1984).

Other Neurotransmitter Precursors

Tryptophan is the only dietary neurotransmitter precursor that has been approved as a prescription drug. The other precursors are still the subject of active investigation. In general, no useful effects have been demonstrated, in spite of some beliefs about the use of these compounds (Young, 1990). There is some indication that tyrosine may have a therapeutic effect in depression. However, this effect is seen only when tyrosine is given in conjunction with other agents, not when it is given by itself (Gelenberg et al., 1990; van Praag, 1990).

ADVERSE PSYCHIATRIC EFFECTS OF SPECIFIC FOOD INGESTION

With increasing concern in society about health implications of nutrition in general, it is not surprising that there are currently many theories relating psychiatric symptomatology to intake of food or dietary components. As with other theories or folklore about nutrition, there are two main types—theories that attribute curative powers to specific nutrients, and those that attribute psychiatric symptomatology to components of the diet. As attitudes to food have changed over the past few decades, so has the emphasis of the concerns. Initial interest in this field came from proponents of megavitamin therapy. Other dietary components to which therapeutic powers have been ascribed include the neurotransmitter precursors, discussed above. Although megavitamin therapy seems to have survived as a popular belief, in spite of the convincing evidence that massive doses of niacin have no therapeutic effect in schizophrenia (Skrabanek, 1990; American Psychiatric Association Task Force on Vitamin Therapy in Psychiatry, 1973), the current emphasis is on components of the diet that may have adverse psychiatric effects. This is entirely in keeping with current concerns about the purity and processing of food in general. The purpose of the next few sections is to discuss some of the theories that relate food intake to mental health, and to try to separate the facts from the myths and folklore.

Sugar and Psychopathology

Attempts have been made to link sugar to psychopathology in two ways. First there is the hypothesis that children, and in particular hyperactive children, react adversely to ingestion of simple carbohydrates. The second theory, which overlaps the first, attributes a wide variety of psychopathological behaviors to hypoglycemia, often hypoglycemia as a result of ingestion of simple carbohydrates.

The pervasive idea that sugar has adverse behavioral effects in children has been the subject of a number of studies which have been reviewed recently (Wolraich, 1988). Retrospective studies tend to support the idea that hyperactive children ingest more sugar than normal children. However, at least 13 challenge studies fail to support the idea that sugar may cause hyperactivity. This is true for studies on normal children, on children with a diagnosis of attention deficit disorder, and on children whose parents considered that they reacted adversely to sugar. While a few of these studies did find small behavioral effects of sugar, a sedative effect was seen as often as an increase in activity.

Although the diagnosis of hypoglycemia is made on the basis of postprandial symptomatology, by those who believe it is a common phenomenon, a recent study suggests that it occurs infrequently, even in a population referred for hypoglycemia (Palardy et al., 1989). Twenty-eight patients who received the diagnosis of postprandial hypoglycemia on the basis of postprandial symptomatology and a glucose tolerance test, gave blood samples when they were experiencing typical symptoms. This was done by finger prick and collection of the blood on filter paper for later assay. Only 5% of the 132 symptomatic episodes reported by the 28 patients were associated with blood glucose levels of 2.8 mmol per liter (50 mg per deciliter) or less. While blood glucose was never found to be this low in normal subjects, none of the patients showed a consistent relationship between reported symptoms and hypoglycemia. The idea that symptomatic hypoglycemia is not a common phenomenon is supported by the finding that, in a population of hospitalized patients, hypoglycemia was most often iatrogenic (Fischer, Lees, & Newman, 1986).

The data described above suggest that hypoglycemia causing mental symptoms is a rare disorder. Because the subjects under investigation for hypoglycemia were referred on the basis of glucose tolerance tests (Palardy et al., 1989), the results also suggest that glucose tolerance tests are of little use in determining whether a patient will have symptoms associated with hypoglycemia under more normal conditions of food ingestion. This applies to a study in which suicide attempts and recidivism among offenders convicted of violent crimes or arson were associated with a low blood glucose nadir during a glucose tolerance test (Virkkunen, DeJong, Bartko, Goodwin, & Linnoila, 1989a; Virkkunen, DeJong, Bartko, & Linnoila, 1989b). This finding is of interest, but does not necessarily imply that the offenses were caused by hypoglycemia. The abnormal blood glucose tolerance test may be a secondary phenomenon related to other metabolic changes, for example, the low brain serotonin found in these patients (Virkkunen et al., 1989a; Virkkunen et al., 1989b). Considerations such as these led the American Dietetic Association to publish a position paper which states that "valid evidence is lacking to support the hypothesis that reactive hypoglycemia is a common cause of violent behavior" (American Dietetic Association, 1985).

The Feingold Hypothesis

Feingold has suggested that artificial food colorings and flavors, and also salicylates, are the cause of childhood hyperactivity in a large portion of hyperactive children (Feingold, 1975). While the claims made by Feingold and his followers are dramatic, independent verification of his hypothesis gives a rather different picture. Reviews of this topic (Mattes & Gittelman, 1981; Rumsey & Rapoport, 1983) and a National Institutes of Health (U.S.) consensus conference (Office for Medical Applications of Research, 1982) concluded that there is no consistent dietary effect on symptoms of hyperactivity. Positive findings have generally resulted from uncontrolled studies. Challenge studies, in which children are placed on the type of diet recommended by Feingold and then the additives added back under double-blind conditions, have occasionally shown beneficial effects in one or two children, but no consistent therapeutic effect has been seen. The difference between the effects of challenge studies and open studies in which children are placed on additive-free diets has been attributed to placebo effects and expectation (Harley, Matthews, & Eichman, 1978). Also, it may well be that some parents who place their children on additive-free diets pay more attention to their children as a result of the requirement that they know everything the child eats, and that this has a beneficial effect. Thus, while it is undeniable that some hyperactive children respond to the Feingold diet, the therapeutic effects of this diet cannot be attributed to the absence of additives or salicylates.

Food "Allergies"

Foods can definitely cause allergies. Immediate allergic reactions are the most common and well documented. The immunologic mechanism responsible for the majority of these reactions involves the presence of an antigen to which the host has been sensitized through previous exposure, an immunoglobulin of the IgE class directed against the sensitizing antigen, and a mast cell or basophil (Atkins, 1986). What is highly controversial is the extent to which such an allergic reaction can cause adverse mental effects. In many cases in which psychological symptoms have been claimed there is no evidence of allergies, and food sensitivity would be a better term (Atkins, 1986). Effects which have been claimed include irritability, emotional lability, depression, listlessness, and even criminal behavior. Also controversial are some of the methods in use for the diagnosis of food allergies, and the American Academy of Allergy has issued a position paper stating that some of these techniques are unproven (Atkins, 1986).

One popular method for studying food allergies that has recently been subject to rigorous testing is symptom provocation (Jewett, Fein, & Greenberg, 1990). In symptom provocation food extracts are injected intradermally to see if the injection reproduces the symptoms that are suspected of being associated with food ingestion. A different dose of the offending allergen is then thought to "neutralize" the reaction and its accompanying mental effects. In the study, all 18 patients had symptoms which had been consistently provoked during previous unblinded testing. The patients were tested using the same extracts at the same dilution as those previously thought to provoke symptoms during the unblinded test. The response of the patients to the active and control injections was indistinguishable: 27% of the active injections were judged by the patients to be the active substance, as were 24% of the control injections. Neutralizing injections were given in an unblinded manner to some of the patients who reported symptoms. Despite the fact that neutralizing doses are commonly used to relieve symptoms, these doses provoked symptoms as often as the provocation doses.

One important design aspect of the study of symptom provocation is that the protocol was approved by members of the American Academy of Environmental Medicine (formerly the Society for Clinical Ecology), proponents of provocation testing.

A more valid method to determine if foods cause adverse mental effects is the use of elimination diets (Atkins, 1986). After a period of time on a diet with the suspected foods removed, the foods are reintroduced singly and the recurrence of symptoms is noted. This technique was used with 76 overactive children suspected of adverse food reactions (Egger, Carter, Graham, Gumley, & Soothill, 1985). Sixty-two improved on an oligoantigenic diet, and a normal range of behavior was achieved in 21. Of the children who improved, 28 completed a double-blind placebo-controlled crossover trial in which foods thought to provoke symptoms were reintroduced. According to the paper, the blinding was maintained by using, as the placebo, foods similar to the suspected food, for example, using goat's milk for cow's milk.

Symptoms returned or were exacerbated significantly more often when the patients were on active material than placebo. However, the authors point out that many of the patients who responded still had considerable behavior problems, and their families continued to require counseling. Also, only a part of the patient's response to the oligoantigenic diet could be attributed to adverse food reactions, as demonstrated in the double-blind reintroduction phase of the study when not all the suspected allergens produced effects. This suggests that the effects of food "allergies" are not as dramatic as suggested by many of the practitioners in this field.

While available evidence supports a limited effect of food "allergies," little change in the folklore surrounding this topic can be expected, given the human characteristic of believing in "truths" in the face of convincing rebuttals. A group of 23 patients, who believed they were suffering from food allergy, were studied at the time of their presentation to an allergy clinic (Rix, Pearson, & Bentley, 1984). The presence of organic food hypersensitivity could not be confirmed in 19 who attributed common neurotic symptoms to allergy. This group was nearly identical in terms of psychiatric symptomatology and general characteristics with a group of new psychiatric outpatient referrals. The other four patients had food-related symptoms, but there was no evidence that this included psychological symptoms.

CONCLUSIONS

Problems related to nutrition and psychopathology are very different in nature in developing and developed countries. In developing countries the main concern is the economic resources needed to provide an adequate diet. In developed countries the main problem is one of education, both as to the nature of an adequate diet in some sections of the population, and the myths and truths about adverse reactions to components of the diet. The efforts by some in developed countries to avoid safe and nutritious foods, because of irrational fears about their effects, stands in stark contrast to efforts by millions in the developing countries to acquire any food that will provide adequate nutrition.

REFERENCES

American Dietetic Association. (1985). Position paper of the American Dietetic Association on diet and criminal behavior. *Journal of the American Dietetic Association, 85*, 361–362.

American Psychiatric Association Task Force on Vitamin Therapy in Psychiatry. (1973). *Megavitamin and orthomolecular therapy in psychiatry.* Washington, DC: American Psychiatric Press, Inc.

Arendt, T., Bigl, V., & Tennstedt, A. (1983). Loss of neurones in the nucleus basalis of Meynert in Alzheimer's disease, paralysis agitans, and Korsakoff's disease. *Acta Neuropathologica, 61*, 101–108.

Atkins, F. M. (1986). Food allergy and behavior: definitions, mechanisms and a review of the evidence. *Nutrition Reviews, 44* (supplement), 104–112.

Belongia, E. A., Hedberg, C. W., Gleich, G. J., White, K. E., Mayeno, A. N., Loegering, D. A., Dunnette, S. L., Pirie, P. L., MacDonald, K. L., & Osterholm, M. T. (1990). An investigation of the cause of the eosinophilia-myalgia syndrome associated with tryptophan use. *New England Journal of Medicine, 323*, 357–365.

Botez, M. I., Botez, T., Léveillé, J., Bielmann, P., & Cadotte, M. (1979). Neuropsychological correlates of folic acid deficiency: facts and hypotheses. In Botez, M. I. and Reynolds, E. H. (Eds.) *Folic acid in neurology, psychiatry and internal medicine* (pp. 435–461). New York: Raven Press.

Botez, M. I., Botez, T. and Maag, U. (1984). The Wechsler subtests in mild organic brain damage associated with folate deficiency. *Psychological Medicine, 14*, 431–437.

Botez, M. I., Young, S. N., Bachevalier, J., & Gauthier, S. (1982). The effect of folic acid and vitamin B12 deficiencies on 5-hydroxyindoleacetic acid in human cerebrospinal fluid. *Annals of Neurology, 12*, 479–484.

Carney, M. W. P. (1990). Vitamin deficiency and mental symptoms. *British Journal of Psychiatry, 156*, 878–882.

Carpenter, K. J. (1981). Effects of different methods of processing maize on its pellagragenic activity. *Federation Proceedings, 40*, 1531–1535.

Coppen, A., Chaudhry, S., & Swade, C. (1986). Folic acid enhances lithium prophylaxis. *Journal of Affective Disorders, 10*, 9–13.

Eccleston, D., Ashcroft, G. W., Crawford, T. B. B., Stanton, J. B., Wood, D., & McTurk, P. H. (1970). Effect of tryptophan administration on 5HIAA in cerebrospinal fluid in man. *Journal of Neurology, Neurosurgery, and Psychiatry, 33*, 269–272.

Egger, J., Carter, C. M., Graham, P. J., Gumley, D., & Soothill, J. F. (1985). Controlled trial of oligoantigenic treatment in the hyperkinetic syndrome. *Lancet, i*, 540–545.

Feingold, B. F. (1975). *Why your child is hyperactive.* New York: Random House.

Fischer, K. F., Lees, J. A., & Newman, J. H. (1986). Hypoglycemia in hospitalized patients: Causes and outcomes. *New England Journal of Medicine, 315*, 1245–1250.

Gelenberg, A. J., Wojcik, J. D., Falk, W. E., Baldessarini, R. J., Zeisel, S. H., Schoenfeld, D., & Mok, G. S. (1990). Tyrosine for depression: A double-blind study. *Journal of Affective Disorders, 19*, 125–132.

Godfrey, P. S. A., Toone, B. K., Carney, M. W. P., Flynn, T. G., Bottiglieri, T., Laundy, M., Chanarin, I., & Reynolds, E. H. (1990). Enhancement of recovery from psychiatric illness by methylfolate. *Lancet, 336*, 392–395.

Harley, J. P., Matthews, C. G., & Eichman, P. (1978). Synthetic food colors and hyperactivity in children: A double-blind challenge experiment. *Pediatrics, 62*, 975–983.

Harrison, W. M., Endicott, J., Rabkin, J. G., & Nee, J. (1984). Treatment of premenstrual dysphoric changes: Clinical outcome and methodological implications. *Psychopharmacology Bulletin, 20*, 118–122.

Hartmann, E., Cravens, J., & List, S. (1974). Hypnotic effects of L-tryptophan, *Archives of General Psychiatry, 31*, 394–397.

Hartmann, E., & Greenwald, D. (1984). Tryptophan and human sleep: An analysis of 43 studies. In Schlossberger, H. G., Kochen, W., Linzen, B., & Steinhart, H. (Eds.) *Progress in tryptophan and serotonin research.* (pp. 297–304). Berlin: Walter de Gruyter.

Hartmann, E., Spinweber, C. L., & Ware, C. (1976). L-Tryptophan, L-leucine, and placebo: Effects on subjective alertness. *Sleep Research, 5,* 57.

Hartmann, E., & Spinweber, C. L. (1979). Sleep induced by L-tryptophan: Effect of dosages within the normal dietary intake. *Journal of Nervous and Mental Disorders, 167,* 497–499.

Jewett, D. L., Fein, G., & Greenberg, M. H. (1990). A double blind study of symptom provocation to determine food sensitivity. *New England Journal of Medicine, 323,* 429–433.

Katz, S. H., Hediger, M. L., & Valleroy, L. A. (1974). Traditional maize processing techniques in the new world: Traditional alkali processing enhances the nutritional quality of the maize. *Science, 184,* 765–773.

Mattes, J. A., & Gittelman, R. (1981). Effects of artificial food colorings in children with hyperactive symptoms. *Archives of General Psychiatry, 38,* 714–718.

Meltzer, H. Y., & Lowy, M. T. (1987). The serotonin hypothesis of depression. In Meltzer, H. Y. (Ed.) *Psychopharmacology: The third generation of progress.* (pp. 513–526). New York: Raven Press.

Morand, C., Young, S. N., & Ervin, F. R. (1983). Clinical response of aggressive schizophrenics to oral tryptophan. *Biological Psychiatry, 18,* 575–578.

Office for Medical Applications of Research, National Institutes of Health, Bethesda, MD. (1982). Defined diets and childhood hyperactivity. *Journal of the American Medical Association, 248,* 290–292.

Palardy, J., Havrankova, J., Lepage, R., Matte, R., Belanger, R., Damour, P., & Stemarie, L. G. (1989). Blood glucose measurements during symptomatic episodes in patients with suspected postprandial hypoglycemia. *New England Journal of Medicine, 321,* 1421–1425.

Pollitt, E., & Liebel, R. L. (1982). *Iron deficiency: brain biochemistry and behavior.* New York: Raven Press.

Reynolds, E. H., Carney, M. W. P., & Toone, B. K. (1984). Methylation and mood. *Lancet, ii,* 196–198.

Rix, K. J. B., Pearson, D. J., & Bentley, S. J. (1984). A psychiatric study of patients with supposed food allergy. *British Journal of Psychiatry, 145,* 121–126.

Rumsey, J. M., & Rapoport, J. L. (1983). Assessing behavioral and cognitive effects of diet in pediatric populations. In Wurtman, R. J., & Wurtman, J. J. (Eds.). *Nutrition and the brain, volume 6 physiological and behavioral effects of food constituents.* (pp. 101–161). New York: Raven Press.

Scrimshaw, N. S. (1984). Functional consequences of iron deficiency in human populations. *Journal of Nutritional Science and Vitaminology, 30,* 47–63.

Sebrell, W. H. (1981). History of pellagra. *Federation Proceedings, 40,* 1520–1522.

Skrabanek, P. (1990). Reductionist fallacies in the theory and treatment of mental disorders. *International Journal of Mental Health, 19,* 6–18.

Soemantri, A. G., Pollitt, E., & Kim, I. (1985). Iron deficiency and educational achievement. *American Journal of Clinical Nutrition, 42,* 1221–1228.

Spinweber, C. L. (1986). L-tryptophan administered to chronic sleep-onset insomniacs: Late-appearing reduction of sleep latency. *Psychopharmacology, 90,* 151–155.

Stein, Z., & Susser, M. (1985). Effects of early nutrition on neurological and mental competence in human beings. *Psychological Medicine, 15,* 717–726.

Thomson, J., Rankin, H., Ashcroft, G. W., Yates, C., McQueen, J. K., & Cummings, S. W. (1982). The treatment of depression in general practice: A comparison of L-tryptophan, amitriptyline, and a combination of L-tryptophan and amitriptyline with placebo. *Psychological Medicine, 12,* 741–751.

van Praag, H. M. (1990). Catecholamine precursor research in depression: the practical and scientific yield. In Richardson, M. A. (Ed.). *Amino acids in psychiatric disease.* (pp. 77–97). Washington, DC: American Psychiatric Press.

Virkkunen, M., DeJong, J., Bartko, J., Goodwin, F. K., & Linnoila, M. (1989a). Relationships of psychobiological variables to recidivism in violent offenders and impulsive fire setters: A follow-up study. *Archives of General Psychiatry, 46,* 601–603.

Virkkunen, M., DeJong, J., Bartko, J., & Linnoila, M. (1989b). Psychobiological concomitants of life-time history of suicide attempts among violent offenders and impulsive fire setters. *Archives of General Psychiatry, 46,* 604–608.

Volavka, J., Crowner, M., Brizer, D., Convit, A., van Praag, H. M., & Suckow, R. F. (1990). Tryptophan treatment of aggressive psychiatric inpatients. *Biological Psychiatry, 28,* 728–732.

Wolraich, M. L. (1988). Sugar intolerance: Is there evidence for its effects on behavior in children. *Annals of Allergy, 61,* 58–62.

Xue-Cun, C., Tai-An, Y., Xiu-Zhen, T., Yu-Fang, H., Xiao-Yue, Y., Shu-Rong, L., & Huai-Cheng, Y. (1983). Opaque-2 maize in the prevention and treatment of pellagra. *Nutrition Research, 3,* 171–180.

Youdim, M. B. H., Sills, M. A., Heydorn, W. E., Creed, G. J., & Jacobowitz, D. M. (1986). Iron deficiency alters discrete proteins in rat caudate nucleus and nucleus accumbens. *Journal of Neurochemistry, 47,* 794–799.

Young, S. N. (1986). The clinical psychopharmacology of tryptophan. In Wurtman, R. J., & Wurtman, J. J. (Eds.). *Nutrition and the brain, volume 7, food constituents affecting normal and abnormal behaviors.* (pp. 49–88). New York: Raven Press.

Young, S. N. (1990). The abuse of amino acids: Pseudoscientific distortion of legitimate psychopharmacotherapies. *International Journal of Mental Health, 19,* 45–55.

Young, S. N., & Gauthier, S. (1981). Effect of tryptophan administration on tryptophan, 5-hydroxyindoleacetic acid, and indoleacetic acid in human lumbar and cisternal cerebrospinal fluid. *Journal of Neurology, Neurosurgery, and Psychiatry, 44,* 323–327.

Young, S. N., & Ghadirian, A-M. (1989). Folic acid and psychopathology. *Progress in Neuropsychopharmacology and Biological Psychiatry, 13,* 841–863.

PART *II*

Social and Cultural Forces

Chapter 4

Culture-Bound Syndromes: The Example of Social Phobias

Raymond H. Prince

Culture is a universal feature of the human environment. Among factors considered to influence psychopathology, culture is at once the most pervasive and most neglected. Psychiatrists are often unaware of the importance of culture because of their total immersion within their own; paradoxically, it is so familiar and fundamental as to go unnoticed. We may define culture as the nongenetic blueprint for living that is passed from one generation to the next. It is the sum total of habits, beliefs, values, and attitudes and includes such components as language, styles of nonverbal communication, dietary habits, marital and sexual patterns, religious beliefs, art forms, and the acceptable spectrum of occupations. Germans, Crees, Kuwaitis, and Koreans think, feel, and act differently and culture accounts for much of the variance. The branch of psychiatry that concerns itself with cultural influences upon phenomena of psychiatric interest is variously known as comparative, transcultural, cross-cultural, or simply cultural psychiatry.

CULTURE-BOUND SYNDROMES

One of the key questions for transcultural psychiatry is whether the distinctive beliefs and values of given cultures can create psychiatric disorders that do not occur in other cultures. This question was probably first raised by European colonial psychiatrists in the late 19th century. They discovered disorders such as *latah* among the Malaysians (episodes of echolalia, echopraxia, coprolalia, and automatic obedience) and *koro* (panic due to supposed genital retraction

55

into the abdomen resulting in death) among the Celebese islanders, which they had not seen at home in Europe. In 1962, Yap, Pow-Meng, a Western-trained Chinese psychiatrist working in Hong Kong, coined the term culture-bound syndromes (CBSs) for these disorders that occurred in some cultures but not in others. In the past 20 years dozens of illnesses have been labelled CBSs. In a recent book devoted to the subject (Simons & Hughes, 1985) an appendix lists some 140 examples. This unwarranted proliferation is a result of the considerable looseness and inconsistency which has developed in the use of the CBS concept. Some illnesses seem to have been designated CBSs merely because they have been given a local name. The above-mentioned syndrome of echolalia, echopraxia, and coprolalia (*latah*) occurs in many cultures and has been labeled differently according to the local language—*miryachit* in some Siberian cultures; "jumpers" among Americans (particularly French-Canadian immigrants) in Maine; *imu* among the Ainu of the northern islands of Japan; and *mali-mali* among Filipinos, to mention only a few. The result is that the literature contains 10 or 12 different CBS labels designating the same illness pattern (Prince & Tcheng-Laroche, 1987).

Further proliferation has resulted from the argument of some authors, particularly anthropologists, that because each culture attributes a different cause or meaning to a given syndrome, each should be regarded as a separate CBS. Thus Cassidy (1982) has proposed a meaning-centered definition which holds that when considering the CBS status of a given disease, it is important that notions of etiology and treatment be included. Cassidy elaborated her views by reference to protein energy malnutrition (PEM) or *kwashiorkor* (a childhood disease characterized by peevishness, edema, skin lesions, abdominal swelling, failure to thrive, and a high mortality rate). Although she admits that the signs and symptoms of PEM are the same around the world, patients and their families hold notions of cause which often differ radically from the notions of the Western-trained physicians who treat them, with the result that treatment or prevention programs usually fail. On this basis, according to Cassidy, PEM should be designated a culture-bound syndrome.

The use of causal notions as a basis for the classification of diseases is ancient and pervasive and the reason is easily understood. To know the cause of a disease is to be at least partway to its cure, so healers have traditionally preoccupied themselves with causal formulations. Although superseded within scientific medicine by the syndrome-based approach to classification, the method of classification by etiology does have merit within a given cultural monad. As medical anthropologists like to point out, etiological notions of illness often form part of a well-integrated world view. Healing concepts intermesh with concepts of good and evil, male and female, hot and cold, and with high and low status in social hierarchies (as described for the Yoruba culture by Buckley [1985], for example). Such delineations of cultural totalities and inner homogeneities are not only intellectually satisfying but they also suggest that the source of some powers of healers in a prescientific medical system may arise from these highly homogeneous symbol systems. Shared by healers, communities, and patients, such symbol systems provide a powerful background of agreement and "social truth," which render the healers' therapeutic suggestions much more powerful than among more culturally fragmented systems. Conflicting etiological notions and modes of cure in complex urban societies no doubt weaken the contemporary physicians' suggestive powers. It goes without saying that the ultimate goal of medicine is also an etiologically based classification system, but one based on causal connections determined by scientific method.

PROBLEMS WITH ETIOLOGICAL NOTIONS AS CLASSIFICATION PRINCIPLES

The problem with disease classifications based on etiological notions for the transcultural psychiatrist is, of course, that comparisons of illnesses and their epidemiology across cultures is impossible. There are wide differences of opinion as to the cause of a particular illness, both within cultures and between cultures. Canadian physicians never attribute illness to *djinns* or other spirits the way Arab healers do; and the Yoruba healers of Nigeria (at least as of the 1960s) had never heard of Oedipal conflicts. Some historical examples will further illustrate these difficulties.

Homer's famous account of the war between the Greeks and the Trojans opens with the description of a plague that swept the Greek forces as soon as they beached on the Trojan shore. According to the *Iliad*, the plague was the result of the Greek commander Agamemnon's discourtesy to a favorite priest of the god Apollo. Apollo angrily retaliated by raining his arrows upon the Greeks: "His descent was like nightfall. He sat opposite the ships and shot an arrow, with a dreadful twang from his silver bow. He attacked the mules first and the nimble dogs; then he aimed his sharp arrows at the men, and struck again and again. Day and night innumerable fires consumed the dead" (Homer, 1950, p. 24). Although Homer's poem provides a glimpse of early Greek explanatory models of disease and his contemporary audience no doubt found these explanations meaningful, from a medical point of view we have no idea of the nature of that prehistoric epidemic. In a similar way, many other accounts of illness which focus upon notions of etiology cannot be identified in current medical terms. Examples include: the plagues inflicted upon the Egyptians in the Old Testament; early descriptions of epidemics in the Middle East and in China (McNeill, 1976, pp. 69–131); and, according to McNeill (1976), the humoral theory of the eminent Roman physician Galen interfered with his description of the Antonine plague (165 to 180 A.D.) in such a way that even his portrayal does not permit medical identification.

One of the first physicians to break through this preoccupation with etiological notions and present us with a clear description of the signs and symptoms of diseases was the pioneer luminary of Persian medicine, *Abu Bakr Muhammad ibn Zakariyya Ar-Razi* (238–320 A.H.) known in the West as Rhazes (850–932 A.D.) In his *Kitab al-Jadari Wal-hasba* (Treatise on Smallpox and Measles), he described measles and smallpox in such a refreshingly clear manner that they are easily recognizable by the modern physician. In describing the signs and symptoms of smallpox, he not only provided general observations on the febrile state, but also gave a clear description of the skin eruptions, distinguished the discrete and confluent types of pustules, and noted their important differential implications for prognosis (Sadi, 1935).

Rhazes was one of the important pioneers in the shift from folk medicine to scientific medicine (which in Europe began some 800 years later). Thomas Sydenham (1624–1698), who can be called the English Rhazes, extended the latter's insight of the importance of careful symptom description to clearly perceive that each illness or disease was characterized by its own distinctive symptom pattern and natural history. It became important to separate fever, for example, into characteristic disease patterns such as malaria, tuberculosis, and scarlet fever. It was realized that if the physician carefully distinguished which of these distinctive diseases was being dealt with in a particular patient, prediction of outcome and treatment was greatly facilitated.

But the problem of mixing etiological notions and symptom patterns within disease classifications continues into modern times, especially within psychiatry. One of the important advances in the last decade has been the DSM–III's attempt to purge psychiatric diagnoses of overt or covert etiological notions. As Spitzer and Williams (1988) note, "The DSM–III task force believed that, given our present state of ignorance about etiology, we should avoid including etiological assumptions in the definitions of the various mental disorders, so that people who have different theories about etiology can at least agree on the features of the various disorders, without having to agree on how these disorders come about" (p. 84). In a similar vein, a new definition of culture-bound syndromes has been formulated which specifically rules out etiological notions.

"A culture-bound syndrome is a collection of signs and symptoms (excluding notions of cause) which is restricted to a limited number of cultures primarily by reason of certain of their psychosocial features" (Prince, 1985, p. 201). In this way, dozens of so-called culture-bound syndromes have been purged from our list, and indeed after ruling out causal notions and local meanings and labels, we may wonder whether there are any CBSs left. I would argue that there may be a few. One likely candidate is anorexia nervosa, which seems restricted to Western or intensely Westernizing cultures (another recent advance in our understanding of CBSs is the realization that the Western world also has them [Prince, 1985; Littlewood & Lipsedge, 1986]).

This chapter, however, will be devoted to *taijin kyofu sho* (TKS), a Japanese designation for a spectrum of social phobias which has long been considered a culture-bound syndrome restricted to Japanese culture. TKS will be examined in the context of other phobias, including social phobias, as well as in relation to the recently delineated monosymptomatic hypochondriacal psychoses. It will be argued that the Japanese/Western difference may be attributed largely to a much greater prevalence of social phobias in Japan, but also to a difference in psychiatrists' conceptions and pigeonholing rather than important differences in patient's symptom patterns.

SOCIAL PHOBIAS AS CULTURE-BOUND SYNDROMES

Phobias in Western Psychiatry

The American physician Benjamin Rush (1745–1813) was one of the first to use the term phobia in a psychiatric context. His article, in a half humorous vein, "On the different species of phobias" was published in the first edition of a Philadelphia weekly magazine in 1798 (Hunter & Macalpine, 1963, pp. 669–670). He listed 18 phobias including "church phobia," which he characterized as "that disease (which) has become epidemic in the City of Philadelphia." But other definitions indicate that he had also had experience with phobias of pathological intensity such as "the water phobia . . . (which) includes not the dread of swallowing, but of *crossing* water. I have known some people who sweat with terror in crossing an ordinary ferry;" and "the thunder phobia . . . (which) is common to all ages and to both sexes: I have seen it produce the most distressing appearances and emotions upon many people." Rush did not mention a phobia of public places (DSM–III's agoraphobia) or a fear of social situations in which one's performance is likely to be criticized (DSM–III's social phobia).

But credit for first identification of agoraphobia as a distinct psychiatric syndrome is usually afforded the German psychiatrist Westphal who, in his 1871 article "*Die Agoraphobie*," described three cases in the following terms: "Patients complained of the . . . impossibility of walking through certain streets or squares, or possibility of doing so only with resulting dread of anxiety . . . no loss of consciousness . . . vertigo was excluded by all patients . . . no hallucinations or delusions to cause this strange fear . . . agony was much increased at those hours when the particular streets dreaded were deserted and the shops closed. The patients experience great comfort from the companionship of men or even an inanimate object, such as a vehicle or a cane. The use of beer or wine also allowed the patient to pass through the feared locality with comparative comfort. One man even sought, without immoral motives, the companionship of a prostitute as far as his own door . . . some localities are more difficult of access than others; the patient walking far in order not to traverse them . . . strange to say, in one instance, the open country was less feared than sparsely housed streets in town. Case 3 also had a dislike for crossing a certain bridge. He feared he would fall in the water. In this case there was also an apprehension of impending insanity." (Snaith, 1968, p. 673)

In 1895 Freud separated common phobias of things most Westerners fear to some extent (such as death, illness, and snakes) from specific phobias of things or situations that inspire no fear in the average Westerner, such as of public places. Phobias achieved a separate diagnostic label in the International Classification of Diseases of the World Health Organization only in 1947, and in the American Psychiatric Association classification (DSM–I) in 1952.

Social Phobias: Japan and Korea

The separation of the social phobias from agoraphobia and the host of simple phobias probably first occurred in the Japanese literature. In the 1920s, Shoma Morita wrote extensively about *shinkeishitsu* (neurasthenia) in which he included a subcategory *taijin kyofu-sho* (TKS) which means fear of people. TKS does not mean a wish to avoid people; TKS patients have a sincere wish to socialize, but they are unable to do so because of imagined deficiencies in themselves, which they fear will embarrass, disturb, or even damage others in some way. TKS has been extensively described in the Japanese literature, and to some extent in the English literature (Yamashita, 1977; Murphy, 1982; Kasahara & Sakamoto, 1971). TKS is most common among males and adolescents or individuals in their early twenties (Yamashita, 1977).

Offending or hurting may occur in many ways in Japan: embarrassing others by blushing; making others uncomfortable by the nature or intensity of one's gaze; through one's facial expression, which may be thought derisive or otherwise offensive; through facial or other deformities that cause uneasiness in others; by body odors, either general or emanating from the axilla or genital areas; irritation of others by shakiness of the voice or limbs; or of offending by speaking one's thoughts aloud. Of these various versions of the disorder, offense by blushing, odor, or gaze seem to be the most frequent. TKS is extremely common in Japan and affects some 10% to 35% of psychiatric patient populations (depending upon the clinical setting of the observations). The following is an abbreviated case history of a 48-year-old, unmarried Japanese woman from Honda (1983):

> Her chief complaint was of "thinking aloud unknowingly and hurting the feelings of other people around her." Her brother had begun to think aloud while bathing; this the patient disliked and she was afraid she might do the same. At age 45 she began to feel that she herself was thinking aloud, and believed she must have spoken ill of other people and hurt their feelings. She thought the whole community knew of her habit and she hesitated to go shopping or even out on the street, fearing people would avoid her, or turn their heads away from her. She wanted to die rather than live under such miserable circum-

stances. Her judgment remained intact except for her unreasonable fear of thinking aloud. She continued to work both at home and at outside jobs. (p. 193)

Kasahara (1988) has divided TKS into four stages of increasing intensity: (1) a transient type that breaks out temporarily during a particular period of life (usually adolescence); (2) "pure" social phobia that fits the definition of DSM–III; (3) social phobia that takes on the quality of a "delusion of reference" (for want of a better term); and (4) social phobia accompanied by schizophrenia "arising as a prodrome of schizophrenia or as a post-psychotic symptom during remission." As an example of stage 3, he cites the following self-report involving a "delusion of reference" regarding the eyes:

> "It is not the partner's eyes but my own eyes that worry me. In the presence of others, my looks become so peculiarly sharp that my piercing eyes must hurt the feelings of others, because I always notice that the eyes of the partner move slightly with embarrassment. He or she seems to become stiff and unnatural. It would be more appropriate if I say it is a kind of infection, because it is really infectious. The partner tries to avoid my eyes or sometimes leaves the place. Formerly it was only my eyes but recently, strangely enough, I began to feel as though there were other eyes coming out of my body, even from my back. It is not exactly eyes but some queer atmosphere emitting towards others. I cannot do anything but commit suicide to stop it." (p. 146)

The author points out that the characteristic feature of the TKS patient is his belief that he is offending or harming others because of the behavior of others toward him. The other person makes peculiar eye movements, coughs, makes remarks, or moves out of the room to avoid him. In addition, he notes that the "delusion" of harming others disappears as soon as he separates from them. Another interesting point about TKS patients is that they usually experience their fear, not among family members and not among total strangers, but almost always among those with whom they are only moderately acquainted (e.g., with their neighbors or with their work group). TKS pseudo-delusions tend to disappear after the age of 30.

Although TKS had long been regarded as a culture-bound syndrome in Japan, an interesting conference was convened in February 1987 in which Korean psychiatrists presented case material indicating that the same disorder was very common in Korea (Lee, 1988). Lee reported on 315 cases seen at the Korea General Hospital, Seoul, over a 3 1/2 year period. These social phobias comprised 4.9% of the total new cases seen at the outpatient department over the time period. Lee followed Kasahara (cited above) in distinguishing four stages of social phobia: social anxiety; social phobia, simple type (48%); social phobia, delusional type (37.8%); and social phobia, borderline type (14.2%). He felt that the first two categories could be included in the DSM–III "social phobia" category.

In distinguishing the delusional type from simple phobia, he noted that in the simple type the fear of humiliation, embarrassment or the scrutiny of others is a self-centered concern similar to Western stage fright. But in the delusional type the patient believes that his or her physical defects cause others to feel uncomfortable, or that they harm or infect others, and thus the patient experiences guilt and self-reproach. This other-centeredness is of an almost delusional intensity and it is this quasi-delusional aspect of the third stage of TKS which created difficulties for placement in DSM–III.

Lee noted that when American psychiatrists hear the word "delusion," they diagnose psychosis without hesitation; but for Japanese and Korean psychiatrists, TKS is a neurosis. Lee warned, "A proper term for this particular kind of delusion should be found, lest it confuse our Western colleagues." He also noted that true delusions are very resistant to therapy, whereas in his experience the "delusions" of TKS patients respond rapidly to cognitive reconstruction therapy (Lee, 1988, p. 148).

Social Phobias in the West

In contrast to Japanese and Korean cultures, social phobias are relatively unimportant in the Western world. They were not mentioned in DSM–I, DSM–II, or in the various versions of the International Classification of Disease (World Health Organization) at least until ICD-9. They are not listed in Hinsie and Campbell's (1970) *Psychiatric Dictionary*, nor indexed in the major Western psychiatric textbooks before the 1980s. Social phobias seem to have been first mentioned by Isaac Marks in his 1969 *Fears and Phobias*, and it was probably on the basis of this pioneering work that they entered DSM–III in 1980.

The literature on phobias was extensively reviewed (with 2000 references) in Marks' more recent volume, *Fears, Phobias, and Rituals* (1987). In this Western compendium, social phobias are defined as fears of situations in which other people may scrutinize one's performance. Unlike agoraphobics who avoid public places because of their fear of confinement or suffocation, social phobics fear being watched and criticized by others. Social phobics in the Western world agree to such statements as, "I am afraid I may look ridiculous or make a fool of myself or make a foolish mistake, or seem unintelligent or ignorant;" "I hate walking past a crowd;" "I am uncomfortable with people I don't know or when I am the center of attention (for instance, when crossing a dance floor)" (Marks, 1987, p. 363).

According to Amies, Gelder, & Shaw, (1983), who compared 57 Western cases of agoraphobia with 87 of social phobia, there is a marked excess of females among agoraphobics (86% female to 14% male), but an excess of males among social phobics (60% male to 40% female). They also found a later age of onset among agoraphobics (age 24 versus age 19 among social phobics). Alcohol was used excessively by more social phobics (20% among social phobics versus 7% among agoraphobics). They felt that the distinction between social phobias and agoraphobias was justified, noting that social phobias tended to begin in the second half of the teenage years when social embarrassment and lack of social confidence were greatest. Amies and his colleagues found that social phobias were most common among the offspring of upwardly mobile families (i.e., family situations in which the child was of higher social class than the parents), a feature which was not present among agoraphobics' families. Most of these same distinctions have been confirmed in other studies (Marks, 1987).

It seems probable that social phobias have been present in the Western world for many years but because of their relatively low intensity and similarity to the symptomatology of agoraphobias, they have not received distinct recognition until the last 20 years. It is important to note that within the Western literature there has been no mention of the "delusions of reference" which figure so prominently in that of Japan and Korea.

Social Phobias in the Arab World

It is interesting that there is some indication that social phobias may be relatively common in the Arab world. Chaleby (1987) diagnosed social phobias in some 13% of the total neurotic population at a Saudi Arabian psychiatric clinic. He suggested that this was a much higher rate than reported among comparable Western populations. Chaleby found the disorder to be most prevalent among young unmarried males of relatively high educational and occupational

status. Patients usually complained of shyness and fear accompanied by excessive avoidance of situations in which they felt under
scrutiny (speaking, eating, or performing in public). Al-Radi and Al-
Mahdy (1989), in an article on Islamic group therapy in Saudi Ara-
bia, mentioned in passing that 47% of the 68 patients they studied
were diagnosed as social phobics. They pointed out that "social phobias have been resistant to individual supportive psychotherapy
and classical behavior therapy, but that the present Islamic form of
group therapy has been highly effective in producing symptom re-
lief among those suffering such phobias" (p. 276).

Once again it should be noted that with Arab, as with Western
patients, "delusions of reference" are not mentioned. It is clear that
social phobias in the Arab world will repay further study. In particular, a comparative analysis of the cultural contexts of social phobias in Japan and Korea on the one hand, and Arab cultures on the
other, would be of considerable interest.

Social Phobias and Paranoia

We have already noted the reluctance of Japanese/Korean psychiatrists to equate the "quasi-delusional ideas of reference" found in a
considerable proportion of social phobic patients in their cultures to
the true delusions of psychotic patients. TKS is a neurosis, not a
psychosis, according to Japanese psychiatrists. TKS quasi-delusions
are relatively amenable to treatment and tend to disappear without
treatment after age 30, both features which differ from true delusions. No doubt the clearest area of interest in this delusion versus
quasi-delusion differentiation lies in the diagnostic categories in
which there are delusions without personality deterioration or
thought disorder; that is, in the categories paranoia and, more particularly, in the recently delineated group of monosymptomatic hypochondriacal psychoses (MHP). We will now turn to an examination of these syndromes and compare them with Japanese/Korean
"third stage" TKS patients.

Paranoia in Western psychiatry was defined in ICD-9 in 1978 as
"a rare chronic psychosis in which logically constructed systema-
tized delusions have developed gradually without concomitant hallucinations or the schizophrenic type of disordered thinking. The
delusions are mostly of grandeur . . ., persecution or somatic abnormality" (Munro, 1982). Munro distinguished five subtypes of paranoia in the following terms: erotomania, the delusion that another
person has sexual feelings towards the patient (most often a female

patient); pathological jealousy, the fixed belief that one's sexual partner is unfaithful; monosymptomatic hypochondriacal psychosis (MHP), a single sustained hypochondriacal delusion; litigious paranoia, the endless delusional quest for restitution of real or imaginary wrongs; and megalomania, the preoccupation of the patient with his or her own extraordinary powers, importance, or wealth. In the context of social phobias, it is clear that the important types of paranoia to be considered from Munro's list are those types of MHP characterized by potential social censure of some type.

Once again we must turn to Munro (1980) for a classification of MHP syndromes. He distinguished several types on the basis of the nature of the hypochondriacal delusion involved: the delusion of infestation by parasites or worms of skin or internal organs; delusional lumps under the skin frequently leading to excoriations; convictions of personal ugliness, misshapenness, or prominence of body parts despite all evidence to the contrary; the delusion of emission of a foul odor; the conviction of an abnormal dental bite; and delusions about body image, as in anorexia nervosa.

It is evident from this analysis that convictions of personal ugliness and of the emission of bodily odors are highly reminiscent of some cases of TKS third-stage quasi-delusions described by Japanese and Korean psychiatrists. Other types of paranoia, including types of MHP, do not form part of the TKS constellation and, indeed, are unrelated to social situations; that is, although bodily odor and bodily deformity are potentially obvious to others, beliefs associated with erotomania, delusional jealousy, and megalomania are largely internally generated; and delusional parasitosis, dental bite, and body image among the subtypes of MHP are much less likely to refer to the social responses of others. The other elements comprising the TKS syndrome of the Japanese/Koreans (blushing, talking aloud to oneself, intensity of gaze, shakiness of limbs or voice, and the set of one's face) do not enter into MHP syndromes.

Because of its centrality in this debate, it is worthwhile to explore further Western writings on delusions of offensive bodily odors. Pryse-Phillips' (1971) pioneer study is of special significance. A Montreal neurologist, he collected data on some 137 patients who suffered olfactory hallucinations. He diagnosed 32 of these as schizophrenia, 50 as depressive disorders, and 11 as temporal lobe epilepsy. However, of the remaining, 36 patients constituted a special group which he labeled the "olfactory reference syndrome." A distinctive feature of olfactory reference patients as opposed to the other diagnostic categories was that they displayed the "contrite reaction," which Pryse-Phillips characterized as the "deeply ashamed, embarrassed, self-abasing, sensitive reactions of people who believed that their bodies stank and were a perpetual source of displeasure or disgust to people near them. Such patients tended to wash excessively, to change their clothes with more than usual frequency, to hide themselves away, and to restrict their social and domestic excursions to a greater or lesser extent" (Pryse-Phillips, 1971, p. 491). However, in his series, 66% continued in fulltime employment (78% were male and 75% were single). The following abbreviated case history is highly reminiscent of Japanese cases of TKS described earlier:

> A 39-year-old married male machinist with the complaint "I think I smell, body odour or something like that." He reported always having many friends but was sensitive, retiring and temperamental as well as "fanatically clean." At age 11 he was forced to wear clothes smelling of smoke and was ridiculed by his schoolmates. From that time on he feared that an unpleasant, sweaty body odor emanated from him. He was certain that others could smell it because remarks such as "old smelly" or "stinker" were continually made around him; and he had seen people around him making gestures of disdain. He agreed that neither he nor his family smelled anything unusual but found excuses why this should have been so. For example he argued that the smell only appeared when he sweated at work. He moved his job repeatedly on this account. He had no social life except at home where he seldom worried about the smell. He washed frequently and changed his clothes every day. Psychotherapy, tranquilizers and monoamine oxidase inhibitors were ineffective. Behavior therapy was of temporary benefit only. (Pryse-Phillips, 1971, p. 492)

Since the appearance of Pryse-Phillips' article, many others have described patients with similar symptom patterns: Riding and Munro (1975), Bishop (1980), Beary and Cobb (1981), Brotman and Jenike (1984), and Malasi, El-Hilu, Mirza, and El-Islam (1990). It is interesting that in these olfactory reference syndrome articles, the TKS syndromes of Japanese/Korean authors is never mentioned. There is frequent mention that olfactory reference syndrome patients (as well as most MHP patients) almost always first present themselves to surgeons, internists, dermatologists, or other physical medical specialists and strongly reject referral to psychiatrists. They frequently shop around from one physician to another. There is frequent discussion of whether the delusions of bad odor are always based on hallucinations of smell or sometimes only a delusional idea without a hallucinatory component. The consensus seems to be that both delusions with or without hallucinations may occur without implications for the severity of the illness. Patients often suffer secondary depressions and sometimes suicidal behavior. Although dysmorphophobic and olfactory reference syndrome patients commonly fear and avoid social situations, they are not mentioned in the Western literature in the context of social phobias (which, however, are of little importance in the West, or at least have received little attention).

It is interesting in view of the possible high frequency of social phobias in the Arab world mentioned above that, as far as I am aware, the only published paper on olfactory reference syndromes from culture areas other than the West, Japan, and Korea has been from the Arab world. Malasi, El-Hilu, Mirza, and El-Islam (1990), from the Department of Psychiatry, Kuwait University, have described six Arab cases (Egyptian, Kuwaiti, Palestinian, and Jordanian) of what they call olfactory delusional syndrome. Only two of these cases demonstrate olfactory delusions without other symptoms of psychosis.

Although most early authors viewed these chronic delusional states with well-preserved personalities as extremely difficult to treat, a number of studies now suggest that several modes of therapy may be effective: behavior therapy (Beary & Cobb, 1981); individual insight therapy (Bishop, 1980); and several psychopharmacological agents. The latter, because of their simplicity of administration, are perhaps of most interest. Riding and Munro (1975), in a letter to *Lancet*, first described the successful treatment of five cases of MHP (demonstrating quite diverse symptomatologies including offensive bowel odor, oddness of appearance, and delusional parasitic infestation) with the major tranquilizing drug pimozide (diphenylbutyl piperidine). Munro and Chmara (1982), on the basis of treatment experience with 50 cases of MHP, now believe that five out of six cases can be successfully treated with pimozide. Others have reported success with antidepressants (Brotman & Jenike, 1984) and sometimes cases which were unresponsive to pimozide were responsive to antidepressants (Fernando, 1988).

Discussion

Is TKS a culture-bound syndrome occurring in Japanese/Korean cultures but not in Western cultures? Or do the differences outlined above merely reflect differences in the ways Japanese and Western psychiatrists conceptualize psychiatric disorders? There does seem to be a consensus in these two culture areas that Stage I and Stage II TKS patients are highly similar to Western social phobics as described in DSM–III. Furthermore there is consensus that MHP delusions, particularly delusions of offending or being rejected by others because of offensive body odors or deformities, may occur as part of the picture of the major psychoses.

The major area of controversy has to do with Stage III TKS patients (see section on Social Phobias: Japan and Korea above). Many Japanese/Korean psychiatrists see these Stage III illnesses as differing from psychiatric disorders in the West. These Oriental patients are not like Western, self-centered, social phobics with stage fright, for example, but suffer an "other-centered" fear of a quasi-delusional character. Moreover, these pseudo-delusions are relatively easy to treat and are largely restricted to young males. But it is difficult to agree that there is a significant difference here. These TKS patients show symptomatology which is highly similar to some of Munro's monosymptomatic hypochondriacal psychoses (which he regards as a subtype of paranoia). It is of course true that whereas olfactory reference and dysmorphophobic beliefs occupy center stage in Western patients, Oriental patients have a much broader spectrum of delusions including blushing, speaking aloud of one's thoughts, piercing gaze, and hardness of facial expression that do not occur in the West (or at least have not been described).

It should be noted that in Oriental patients, the delusional concern has to do with causing other people discomfort or damaging them, while Western patients are preoccupied with disgust or rejection on the part of others. This is a subtle but important difference, which probably reflects cultural features. It is also of interest that in the Orient, the quasi-delusional disorders are seen as lying on a continuum with social phobias, while in the West, MHP cases are seen as lying on a continuum with paranoia, paranoid states, and paranoid schizophrenia (Munro, 1980). This tradition is maintained in DSM–III–R, which includes olfactory reference syndromes within a new category labeled "delusional states" and not within "anxiety disorders" (which includes the social phobias). This of course raises the question whether in the future these hypochondriacal delusions with social implications (bad odor and dysmorphophobia) should more properly be included with social phobias in the West as well as in Japan. This review also suggests that we in the West should use the word "delusion" in a more flexible way to include relatively short-lasting, false beliefs which may be amenable to treatment.

TKS and social phobias are much more prevalent in Oriental cultures than in the West, and although highly similar delusional phenomena are to be found within both culture areas, delusions are much less common in the West and without the ingenious proliferations of content found among Japanese and Koreans. The differences in categorization of these illnesses reflect the historical imprint of Shoma Morita in Japan and of Emil Kraepelin in Europe more than a difference in the natural forms of these illnesses. We may conclude that, in this Eastern/Western comparison at any rate, social phobias are influenced by culture much more in their epidemiology than in their form. On the basis of this limited comparison, it would appear that TKS is not a particularly clear-cut example of a culture-bound syndrome.

CONCLUSIONS

1. Recent advances in the definition of culture-bound syndromes have excluded many of the illnesses so designated. Excluded syndromes have been those which are distinctive not in their symptom patterns but on the basis of local etiological notions or labels.

2. Whereas previously the culture-bound label had been used only for syndromes in exotic cultures, it is now recognized that culture-bound syndromes (e.g., anorexia nervosa) are also to be found in the West or in cultures powerfully influenced by Western cultures.

3. In spite of the gross reduction in genuine culture-bound disorders through the use of a more stringent definition, a small number still warrant the label. Probable candidates include anorexia nervosa, latah, obsessive-compulsive disorders, and possibly social phobias, but even these may disappear after more detailed worldwide scrutiny.

4. Even if the quest for culture-bound syndromes proves chimerical, important culture-related differences in the epidemiology of many disorders will remain.

5. There should be continuing endeavors to broaden disease categories in international disease classifications (or even include new categories) so that all psychiatrists may employ them with intellectual integrity and comfort.

REFERENCES

Al-Radi, O. M., & Al-Mahdy, M. A. (1989). Group therapy: An Islamic approach (abstract) *Transcultural Psychiatric Research Review, 26,* 273–276.

Amies, P. L., Gelder, M. G., & Shaw, P. M. (1983). Social phobia: A comparative clinical study. *British Journal of Psychiatry, 142,* 174–79.

Beary, M. D., & Cobb, J. P. (1981). Solitary psychosis—three cases of monosymptomatic delusion of alimentary stench treated with behavioral psychotherapy. *British Journal of Psychiatry, 138,* 64–66.

Bishop, E. R. (1980). Monosymptomatic hypochondriasis. *Psychosomatics, 21,* 731–747.

Brotman, A. W., & Jenike, M. A. (1984). Monosymptomatic hypochondriasis treated with tricyclic antidepressants. *American Journal of Psychiatry, 141,* 1608–1609.

Buckley, A. D. (1985). *Yoruba medicine.* Oxford: Clarendon Press.

Cassidy, C. M. (1982). Protein-energy malnutrition as a culture-bound syndrome. *Culture, Medicine and Psychiatry, 6,* 325–345.

Chaleby, K. (1987). Social phobia in Saudis. *Social Psychiatry, 22,* 167–170.

Fernando, N. (1988). Monosymptomatic hypochondriasis treated with a tricyclic antidepressant. *British Journal of Psychiatry, 152,* 851–852.

Hinsie, L. E., & Campbell, R. J. (1970). *Psychiatric Dictionary,* Fourth Edition. London: Oxford University Press.

Homer. (1950). *The Iliad.* Translated from the Greek by E. V. Rieu. Harmondsworth, Middlesex: Penguin Books.

Honda, Y. (1983). DSM–III in Japan. In Spitzer, R. L., Williams, J. B. W., & Skodol, A. E. (Eds.). *International perspectives on DSM–III.* Washington, DC: American Psychiatric Press.

Hunter, R., & Macalpine, I. (1963). *Three hundred years of psychiatry 1535–1860.* London: Oxford University Press.

Kasahara, Y. (1988). Social Phobia in Japan. Abstracted in *Transcultural Psychiatric Research Review, 25,* 145–148.

Kasahara, Y., & Sakamoto, K. (1971). Ereuthophobia and Allied Conditions: A Contribution Toward the Psychopathological and Cross-cultural Study of Borderline State. Arieti, S. (Ed.). *The World Biennial of Psychiatry and Psychotherapy 1.* New York: Basic Books.

Lee, Si-hyung (1988). Social phobia in Korea. Abstracted in *Transcultural Psychiatric Research Review, 25,* 148–150.

Lee, Si-hyung, Lee, Sung-hee, & Kim, G. J. (1986). Group therapy of social phobias: Process and results (in Korean with English abstract). *Korean Journal of Neuropsychiatry, 25,* 618–627.

Littlewood, R., & Lipsedge, M. (1986). The "Culture-Bound Syndromes" of the Dominant Culture: Culture, Psychopathology and Biomedicine. In John Cox (Ed.), *Transcultural psychiatry.* (pp. 253–273). London: Croom Helm.

Malasi, T. H., El-Hilu, S. R., Mirza, I. A., & El-Islam, M. F. (1990). Olfactory delusional syndrome with various etiologies. *British Journal of Psychiatry, 156,* 256–260.

Marks, I. M. (1969). *Fears and phobias.* New York: Academic Press.

Marks, I. M. (1987). *Fears, phobias, and rituals/panic, anxiety and their disorders*. New York: Oxford University Press.

McNeill, W. H. (1976). *Plagues and peoples*. New York: Anchor Books.

Munro, A. (1980). Monosymptomatic hypochondriacal psychosis. *British Journal of Hospital Medicine, 24,* 34–38.

Munro, A. (1982). Paranoia revisited. *British Journal of Psychiatry, 141,* 344–349.

Munro, A., & Chmara, J. (1982). Monosymptomatic hypochondriacal psychosis: A diagnostic checklist based on 50 cases of the disorder. *Canadian Journal of Psychiatry, 27,* 374–376.

Murphy, H. B. M. (1982). *Comparative psychiatry.* (pp. 261–279). Berlin: Springer-Verlag.

Prince, R. H. (1985). The concept of culture-bound syndromes: Anorexia nervosa and brain-fag. *Social Science and Medicine, 21,* 197–203.

Prince, R. H., & Tcheng-Laroche, F. (1987). Culture-bound syndromes and international disease classifications. *Culture, Medicine and Psychiatry, 11,* 3–19.

Pryse-Phillips, W. (1971). An olfactory reference syndrome. *Acta Psychiatrica Scandinavica, 47,* 484–510.

Riding, J., & Munro, A. (1975). Pimozide in monosymptomatic psychosis. *Lancet, 1,* 400–401.

Sadi, L. M. (1935). The millenium of Ar-Razi (Rhazes) 850–932 A.D. *Annals of Medical History, 7,* 62–72.

Simons, R. C., & Hughes, C. C. (1985). *The culture-bound syndromes/folk illnesses of psychiatric and anthropological interest*. Dordrecht: Reidel.

Snaith, R. P. (1968). A clinical investigation of phobias. *British Journal of Psychiatry, 114,* 673–697.

Spitzer, R. L., & Williams, J. B. (1988). Basic Principles in the Development of DSM–III. In J. E. Mezzich and M. von Cranach (Eds.). *International Classification in Psychiatry.* Cambridge: Cambridge University Press.

Yamashita, I. (1977). *Taijin-Kyofu*. Tokyo: Kenehara (In Japanese). English review by S. C. Chang (1984). *Transcultural Psychiatric Research Review, 21,* 283–288.

Yap, P.-M. (1962). Words and things in comparative psychiatry, with special reference to the exotic psychoses. *Acta Psychiatrica Scandinavica, 38,* 163–169.

Chapter 5

The Postwar Generation and Depression

Gerald L. Klerman *

This chapter deals with an aspect of the social environment—the historical generation in which the individual is born and comes into maturity. We will highlight a specific generation, that born after World War II (often called the "Baby Boom" generation), to exemplify the larger issue, the importance of changing rates of mental illness.

The thesis we will put forth is that there has been a rise in depression, particularly among young female adults born since World War II (Weissman, Leaf, Holzer, Meres, & Tischler, 1984). This topic usually falls in the province of epidemiology where it is called "temporal effects" or "secular trends." As such, it is a specific example of a period effect, one particular form of a secular trend.

The chapter will review the current status of temporal trends in psychopathology and discuss the evidence for increased rates of depression, possible sources, and implications.

TEMPORAL TRENDS IN PSYCHOPATHOLOGY

Mental health professionals and the public have long been interested in changes in the rates of illness in general and mental illness

*deceased

Supported in part by grant UO1 MH43077 from the National Institute of Mental Health, U.S. Mental Health Service, Department of Health and Human Services, Rockville, Md.

Portions of this manuscript are derived from Klerman & Weissman (1989) and Wickramaratne (1989). Permission for reprint is being obtained from the *Journal of the American Medical Association* and the *Journal of Clinical Epidemiology*.

in particular (Weissman & Klerman, 1978; Robins, 1978). For example, in the last decade the rise in HIV infection resulting in acquired immunodeficiency syndrome (AIDS) has become a major public health concern. At the same time, rates of death from cerebro- and cardiovascular diseases have decreased, stimulating research and speculation about possible causes, such as reduction in cigarette smoking, changes in diet, and/or in life-style.

Changes in the rates of an illness are an epidemiologic problem, usually referred to as either temporal or secular effects. Historically, epidemiology has been primarily concerned with infectious diseases, but in recent decades the epidemiologic approach has been applied to the understanding of noninfectious and/or chronic diseases such as cancer, coronary arterial disease, and hypertension.

Epidemiologic approaches have been applied less frequently to the study of specific psychiatric disorders. However, recent improvements in psychiatric methods for diagnosis of disorders have made large-scale population and family studies possible (Weissman & Klerman, 1978).

Changes in rates of illness have been matters of long-standing public and professional concern. From the mid-19th century to current times there has been concern over the apparent increased rates of mental illness, particularly "lunacy" and "idiocy" (to use 19th century terms) in the growing urban centers of North America and Western Europe. This public concern was a response to the increase in numbers of hospitalized mental patients and the necessity for public construction of additional facilities for treatment—from schools for the mentally handicapped to asylums for the severely ill. This increase in patients needing care and treatment in public institutions stimulated debates about its possible causes. The adverse effects of urbanization and industrialization, and changes in the racial and ethnic composition of the population, (e.g., following immigration) were frequently invoked as explanations.

In recent decades two trends among adolescents and youth have come into public awareness: the increase in the rates of suicide deaths and suicide attempts (MacMahon, Johnson, & Pugh, 1963; Hollinger, Offer, & Zola, 1988), and the increase in the use of psychoactive drugs (Hollinger & Offer, 1982).

Changes in frequency of psychiatric illnesses are usually observed initially by clinicians reacting to changes in individuals seeking treatment (Klerman, 1978). However, there were significant biases in data from clinical studies because of the selection bias introduced by help-seeking behavior. For example, women and affluent persons were apt to seek treatment and were often over-represented in clinical studies relative to the true rate of the disorder in the general population. This pattern of treatment-seeking behavior characterizes many nonpsychiatric disorders as well. Therefore, it is imperative that studies of clinical samples of patients seeking treatment be supplemented by community surveys that sample individuals independent of whether they are seeking or have received psychiatric treatment. This design issue is of particular importance for studies of mental disorders, because many persons with these disorders do not seek treatment; and if they do, it is frequently from nonpsychiatric physicians or nonmedical professionals (Myers, Weissman, Tischler et al., 1984).

Basic Concepts

Epidemiologists usually distinguish a number of related effects:

Temporal (secular) effects are variations in rates over time. They are well established in hospitalization and treatment records for many medical conditions such as Parkinson's disease, cerebrovascular disease, and some forms of cancer. Temporal changes can be analyzed as age, period, or cohort effects and their interactions.

Age effects refer to the changes in age-specific rates of illness (usually age of the first onset of the disorder), and occur if the disease rate varies by age, regardless of the year of birth—for example, an increase in the rates of Alzheimer's disease after 65 years of age. Hypertension and most cancers also have strong age effects (Barrett, 1973; Day & Charney, 1982; Magnus, 1982). Pure age effects should be consistent across birth cohorts or time periods (Frost, 1989).

Period effects refer to changes in the rates of illness associated with a demarcated time period, which are best illustrated by epidemics of infectious diseases. Examples of psychiatric illnesses that have period effects would include the impact of unemployment cycles on suicide rates (Cormier & Klerman, 1986) or the decrease of alcoholic dementia during prohibition.

Cohort effects refer to changes in rates of illness among the individuals who are defined by some shared, continued temporal experience, usually the year or decade of their birth (Case, 1966). Persons born in certain years may carry relatively higher or lower risk of a disease throughout their lives. The concept of cohort is close to the popular idea of a "generation." An example would be the effect of being born after World War II—the Baby Boom generation.

Age-period interactions occur if the period effect varies with age-related vulnerability, as in the recent increases in substance abuse among adolescents.

CHANGING RATES OF DEPRESSION

Until recently the conventional wisdom has held that the risk of depression increased with age, that is, a pure age effect that would apply to rates of current depression, lifetime prevalence, and other indices of the depressive morbidity. This expected distribution would show that the rates of current depression, whether point prevalence or lifetime, increase with age (pure age effect). The cumulative rates would be higher because they represent the aggregation of current plus past events.

In the 1970s a number of reports of large-scale epidemiologic and family studies suggested that this expected distribution was not, in fact, the case. Weissman and Myers (1978) reported on the New Haven survey and Robins and associates (1984) reported on the Epidemiologic Catchment Area (ECA) studies on the lifetime prevalence rates in major depression. Klerman and associates (1985), using lifetime prevalence data from family studies of the National Institute of Mental Health (NIMH) Collaborative Program on the Psychobiology of Depression, found age distribution incompatible with "pure age effect," suggesting possible cohort effect. Contrary to expectation, rates of current and lifetime depression decreased with age. These effects are depicted in Figure 5.1.

Clinical Observations

At the same time, the hypothesis that the rates of depression were changing was suggested by the observations made in the 1960s and 1970s (Klerman, 1979; Hagnell, 1982; Klerman, 1988):

(a) admissions to hospitals for affective illness increased during 1950 to 1980, as compared with 1920 to 1950;

(b) the average age of onset for depression in large clinical samples was considerably younger than that reported before World War II;

(c) childhood depressions were being seen with increased frequency in pediatric and psychiatric settings;

(d) an increase in suicide attempts and deaths among adolescents was noted (Klerman, 1986);

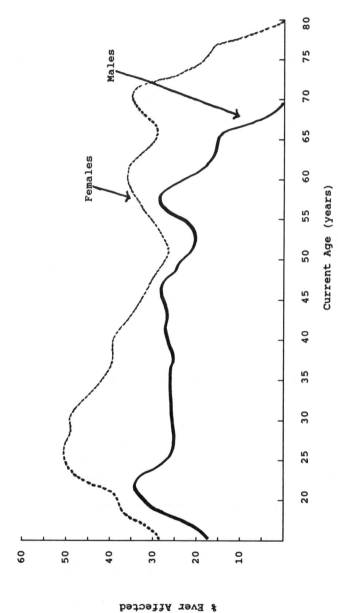

Figure 5.1. The percentage of relatives (affected with major depressive disorder, and bipolar illness (BPI and BPII) of probands with major depressive disorder, BPI, and BPII. Dashed line indicates females; solid line, males.

From Klerman and Weissman (1989).

(e) clinical and epidemiologic studies showed that depression did not increase with menopause (termed "involutional melancholia") (Weissman, 1979);

(f) rates of depression based on community studies in the elderly were low (Blazer & Williams, 1980);

(g) a decrease of suicide deaths among elderly persons was observed; and

(h) increased attention was given to depression in the lay press and professional literature.

Methodological Considerations

In order to test the hypotheses concerning increased rates of depression among young adults, a number of conditions must be met, which include:

1. Large data sets with samples of patients covering range of age groupings.
2. Consistent use of standardized diagnostic criteria such as DSM–III (APA, 1980) or RDC (Spitzer, Endicott, & Robins, 1978).
3. Standardized methods for reliable and valid information about past and current psychopathology, social functioning, age of onset, and treatment received (Endicott & Spitzer, 1981).

These considerations can be applied to community surveys, family studies, or studies of clinical samples in treatment.

Until recently, relatively few opportunities were available to test hypotheses using samples with the above characteristics. Most trends in mental illness were based upon hospitalization records or vital statistics. Survey methodology improved greatly during and after World War II with the development of structured interviews and diagnostic algorithms developed by Wing, Cooper, & Sartorius (1974), the World Health Organization use of the Present State Examination (PSE), and the methodology developed by Robins, Holzer, Croughan, & Ratcliff, (1979) at Washington University, St. Louis. Robins used the DSM–III (the most widely accepted diagnostic system), the Washington University Renard System as codified by Feighner et al. (1972), the Schedule for Affective Disorders and Schizophrenia (SADS) (Endicott & Spitzer, 1981), and the Research Diagnostic Criteria (RDC) (Spitzer et al., 1978). Furthermore, the availability of high-speed computers allowed for the storage of large amounts of data and the calculation of complex multivariant statistics, specifically the life-table method and logistic regression.

Similar observations were made of the increased rates of depression by the family studies component of the NIMH Collaborative Study of the Psychobiology of Depression (Katz & Klerman, 1979). In all age groups, females have higher rates than males, but the trend of decreasing prevalence with age was apparent (Figure 5.1). If a pure age effect were operating, the curve would have shown increased lifetime prevalence of depression among elderly persons. On the contrary, lifetime prevalence rates of elderly persons were lower than the rates of younger persons.

There are considerable statistical problems encountered in making independent estimates of age, period, and cohort effects. A major issue in the analysis of age-period-cohort effect is that they are logically confounded—for example, period can be defined as a function of the age cohort. Methods for making quasi-independent estimates have been developed and applied to the data regarding depression (Holford, 1983; Wickramaratne, Weissman, Leaf, & Holford, 1989).

Application of Life Table Methodology

A further advance in understanding these phenomena occurred with the application of life-table methodology to data from three studies. The first application of the methods was to the family data in the NIMH Collaborative Program. The sample was divided into birth cohorts based on decade of birth. The cumulative probability of having an episode that reached the criteria for major depression by sex up to a given point was calculated. The data indicated increasing rates of depression for cohorts born through the 20th century (Figure 5.2) (Klerman et al., 1985).

Similar statistical methods were applied to survey data from the New Haven, Connecticut, site of the Epidemiologic Catchment Area (ECA) study—a U.S. study of 18,000 adults (Regier, Meyers, & Kramer et al., 1984). Again, there were successive increases in each birth cohort and an earlier age of onset across the 20th century. Weissman and associates (1988) subsequently applied these analyses to all five sites (New Haven, Connecticut; Baltimore, Maryland; St. Louis, Missouri; Durham, North Carolina; and Los Angeles, California). The temporal findings were similar in all five sites (Figure 5.3).

Thirdly, these methods were also applied to data from the NIMH

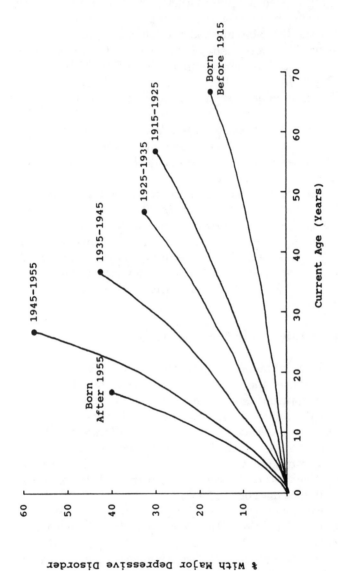

Figure 5.2. The cumulative probability of developing a diagnosable major affective disorder for relatives and controls by birth cohort (life-table method). From Klerman and Weissman (1989).

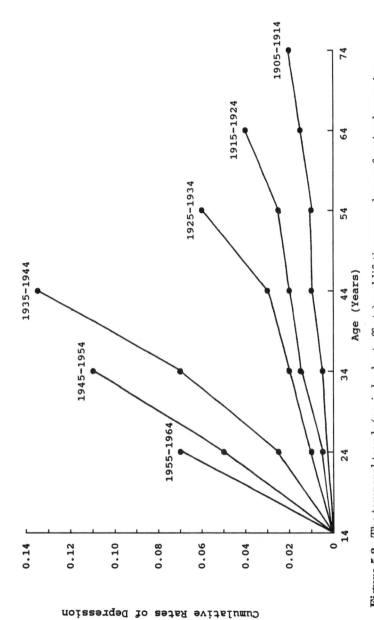

Figure 5.3. The temporal trends (period-cohort effects) and lifetime prevalence of major depression, from the National Institute of Mental Health and the Epidemiologic Area Catchment study at five sites. Includes both sexes, white only. From Wickramaratne et al. (1989).

study of relatives of bipolar and schizoaffective patients (Gershon, Hamovit, Guroff, & Nurnberger, 1987). Again, a significant difference was found in cumulative risk of major depression in relatives born after 1940, as compared with relatives born in earlier birth cohorts.

Evidence for Period Effect

Until 1987, most of the discussion focused on the evidence for some form of secular trend. Subsequent analyses by Lavori et al. (1987) and Wickramaratne et al. (1989) indicate that effect is more likely to be a specific period effect appearing in the 1960s and peaking in the 1970s and 1980s. This period effect has occurred for depression and for suicide attempts and suicide deaths.

The U.S. evidence comes from two sources: the NIMH Collaborative Program on the Psychobiology of Depression (Katz & Klerman, 1979; Klerman et al., 1985) and the NIMH epidemiology ECA study (Regier et al., 1984). Strong period effects are reported with age-period interaction, impacting most often on young adults, particularly on young females.

International Comparisons: Findings from Cross-national Studies

Further confirmation of these trends has come from international comparisons and findings from cross-national studies (Klerman & Weissman, 1989) (Table 5.1). The two reports from Sweden are of importance. In the study in Lund by Hagnell, based on a 25-year follow-up, a significant increase in rates of depression was found among the young adult group in the period 1967–1972 as compared with earlier cohorts in the period 1947–1957 (Hagnell, 1982; Hagnell, Lanks, Rorsman, & Ojesjo, 1982). Unfortunately, the life-table method and other statistical techniques have not been applied to these data. The existence of temporal trends in a community in Sweden has been reported by Hallstrom (1984).

CONCLUSIONS

Generational Identity

Having reviewed the available evidence, mainly from clinical and epidemiologic sources, we are now in a position to offer some inter-

TABLE 5.1 Studies Relevant to Temporal Trends of Depression

Investigator	Country	Type of Study	Sample Size	Diagnostic System*
Klerman et al. (1985)	United States	Family	2500	RDC
Gershon et al. (1987)	United States	Family	823	RDC
Weissman et al. (1988)	United States	Family	1300	RDC
Robins et al. (1979)	United States	Community	18000	DSM–III
Weissman & Meyers (1978)	United States	Community	511	RDC
Hagnell (1982)	Sweden	Community	2550	ICD
Hallstrom (1984)	Sweden	Community	453	ICD
Wittchen (1986)	Germany	Community	501	DSM–III
Oakley-Browne (1989)	New Zealand	Community	1496	DSM–III
Bland et al. (1988)	Canada	Community	2144	DSM–III
Lee et al. (1987)	Korea	Community	5100	DSM–III
Karno et al. (1987)	United States	Community	1243	DSM–III
Canino et al. (1987)	Puerto Rico	Community	1551	DSM–III

*RDC indicates Research Diagnostic Criteria; DSM–III, Diagnostic and Statistical Manual of Mental Disorders, edition 3; and ICD, International Classification of Diseases.
From Klerman and Weissman (1989).

pretation of these findings. The demonstration that the increase in depression and related phenomena involves a strong period effect and that it predominantly affects adults under the age of 35 is best understood by invoking the concepts of "generation" and "generational identity."

The concept of generation has been mainly applied to studies of trends in political and literary criticism. Thus, we talk about the "Lost Generation" following World War I, the Viet Nam generation, the "Me" generation of Baby Boomers. "Generational identity" refers to the sense of group consciousness and shared membership in a cohort, defined by a specific historical epoch.

Identity is usually formed in late adolescence and young adulthood, corresponding to clinical and developmental descriptions. Individuals, as they mature, identify with nodal historical events occurring during their adolescence and young adulthood. As they mature, they often orient their adult experience and the meaning they give to their lives in terms of these historical nodal points. Applied to the data on depression, it would appear that the Baby Boom generation, the one born after World war II and reaching its adolescence and young adulthood in the late 1960s, has been the source of a great deal of self-consciousness, public scrutiny and, at times, public curiosity and fascination. These effects seem to have had their greatest impact on young females (Guttentag & Secord, 1983; Weissman et al., 1984).

On the one hand, this was the healthiest generation in terms of physical health, and one that grew up in unprecedented economic prosperity in the United States and Western Europe (Easterlin, 1980). Yet, on the other, this generation experiences high rates of depression, suicide attempts and suicide deaths, and, concurrently, increased use of alcohol and psychoactive drugs. This would appear to be a paradox in what one might have expected from a generation with such good physical health and economic well-being.

REFERENCES

American Psychiatric Association. (1980). *Diagnostic and statistical manual of mental disorders.* 3rd Edition. Washington, DC: APA.

Barrett, J. C. (1973). Age, time and cohort factors in mortality from cancer of the cervix. *Journal of Hygiene, Epidemiology, Microbiology and Immunology, 2,* 253–269.

Bland, R. C., Newman, S. C., & Orn, H. (Eds.). (1988). Epidemiology of psychiatric disorders in Edmonton. *Acta Psychiatrica Scandinavica 77,* (suppl. 338).

Blazer, D., & Williams, C. D. (1990). Epidemiology of dysphoria and depression in an elderly population. *American Journal of Psychiatry, 137,* 439–444.

Canino, G. J., Bird, H. R., Shrout, P., et al. (1987). The prevalence of specific psychiatric disorders in Puerto Rico. *Archives of General Psychiatry, 44,* 727–735.

Case, R. A. M. (1966). Cohort analysis of mortality rates as a historical or narrative technique. *British Journal of Psychiatry, 10,* 159–171.

Cormier, J. H., & Klerman, G. L. (1986). Unemployment and male-female labor force participation as determinants of changing suicide rates of males and females in Quebec. *Social Psychiatry, 20,* 109–114.

Day, E., & Charney, B. (1982). Time trends, cohort effects and aging as influences on cancer incidence. In: Magnus, K. (Ed.), *Trends in cancer incidence.* Washington, DC: Hemisphere Publishing.

Easterlin, R. (1980). *Birth and fortune.* New York: Basic Books.

Endicott, J., & Spitzer, R. (1981). A diagnostic interview: The schedule for affective disorders and schizophrenia. *Archives of General Psychiatry, 135,* 837–844.

Feighner, J. P., Robins, E., Guze, S. B., Woodruff, R. A., Winokur, G., & Munoz, R. (1972). Diagnostic criteria for use in psychiatric research. *Archives of General Psychiatry, 26,* 57–63.

Frost, W. H. (1989). The age selection of mortality from tuberculosis in successive decades. *American Journal of Hygiene, 90,* 91–96.

Gershon, E. S., Hamovit, J. H., Guroff, J. J., & Nurnberger, J. I. (1987).

Birth cohort changes in manic and depressive disorders in relatives of bipolar and schizoaffective patients. *Archives of General Psychiatry, 44,* 314–319.

Guttentag, M., & Secord, P. F. (1983). *Too many women: The sex ratio question.* Beverly Hills, CA: Sage Publications.

Hagnell, O. (1982). The 25 year followup of the Lundby Study: incidence and risk of alcoholism, depression, and disorders of the senium. In: Barrett, J., & Rose, R. M. (Eds.) *Mental Disorders in the community.* New York: Guilford Press.

Hagnell, O., Lanks, J., Rorsman, B., & Ojesjo, L. (1982). Are we entering an age of melancholy? Depressive illnesses in a prospective epidemiological study over 25 years: The Lundby Study, Sweden, *Psychological Medicine, 12,* 279–289.

Hallstrom, T. (1984). Point prevalence of major depressive disorder in a Swedish urban female population. *Acta Psychiatrica Scandinavica, 59,* 52–59.

Holford, T. R. (1983). The estimation of age, period, and cohort effects for vital rates. *Biometrics, 39,* 311–324.

Hollinger, P., & Offer, D. (1982). Prediction of adolescent suicide: a population model. *American Journal of Psychiatry, 139,* 302–306.

Hollinger, P., Offer, D., & Zola, M. A. (1988). A prediction model of suicide among youth. *Journal of Nervous and Mental Disease, 176,* 275–279.

Karno, M., Hough, R., Burman, A., et al. (1987). Lifetime prevalence of disorders among Mexican Americans and non-Hispanic whites in Los Angeles. *Archives of General Psychiatry, 44,* 696–701.

Katz, M. M., & Klerman, G. L. (1979). Introduction: Overview of the clinical studies program. *American Journal of Psychiatry, 136,* 49–51.

Klerman, G. L. (1978). Age and clinical depression: Today's youth in the twenty-first century. *Journal of Gerontology, 31,* 313–323.

Klerman, G. L. (1979). Age of melancholy. *Psychology Today, 12,* 37–42, 88.

Klerman, G. L. (Ed.). (1986). *Suicide and depression among adolescents and young adults.* New York: Basic Books.

Klerman, G. L. (1988). The current age of youthful melancholia: Evidence for increase in depression among adolescents and young adults. *British Journal of Psychiatry, 152,* 4–14.

Klerman, G. L., & Weissman, M. M. (1989). Increasing rates of depression. *Journal of the American Medical Association, 261,* 2229–2235.

Klerman, G. L., Lavori, P. W., Rice, J., et al. (1985). Birth cohort trends in rates in major depressive disorders among relatives of patients with affective disorder. *Archives of General Psychiatry, 42,* 689–695.

Lavori, P. W., Klerman, G. L., Keller, M. B., Reich, T., Rice, J., & Endicott, J. (1987). Age-period-cohort analysis of secular trends in onset of major depression: Findings in siblings with patients with major affective disorders. *Journal of Psychiatric Research, 21,* 23–35.

Lee, K. C., Kovak, Y. S., & Rhee, H. (1987). The national epidemiological study of mental disorders in Korea. *Journal of the Korean Medical Society, 2,* 19–34.

MacMahon, B., Johnson, S., & Pugh, T. (1963). Relationship of suicide rates to social conditions. *Public Health Report, 78,* 285–298.

Magnus, K. (Ed.). (1982). *Trends in cancer incidence.* Washington, DC: Hemisphere Publishing.

Myers, J. K., Weissman, M. M., Tischler, G. L., et al. (1984). The prevalence of psychiatric disorders in three communities. 1980–1982. *Archives of General Psychiatry, 41,* 959–967.

Oakley-Browne, M. A., Joyce, P. R., Wells, E., Bushnell, J. A., & Hornblow, A. R. (1989). Christchurch psychiatric epidemiology study, part II: Six-month and other period prevalences of specific psychiatric disorders. *Australian and New Zealand Journal of Psychiatry, 23,* 327–340.

O'Malley, P., Bachman, J. G., & Johnston, L. D. (1984). Period, age, and cohort effects on substance use among American youth. 1976–1982. *American Journal of Public Health, 74,* 682–688.

Regier, D. A., Myers, J. K., Kramer, M., et al. (1984). The National Institute of Mental Health Epidemiologic Catchment Area (ECA) program. *Archives of General Psychiatry, 41,* 934–941.

Robins, L. N. (1978). Psychiatric epidemiology. *Archives of General Psychiatry, 35,* 697–702.

Robins, L. N., Holzer, J., Croughan, J., & Ratcliff, K. (1979). National Institute of Mental Health diagnostic interview schedule. *Archives of General Psychiatry, 135,* 49–51.

Robins, L. N., Holzer, J., Weissman, M. M., et al. (1984). Lifetime prevalence of specific psychiatric disorders in three sites. *Archives of General Psychiatry, 41,* 959–968.

Spitzer, R., Endicott, J., & Robins, E. (1978). Research diagnostic criteria (RDC): Rationale and reliability. *Archives of General Psychiatry, 35,* 773–782.

Weissman, M. M. (1979). Myth of involutional melancholia. *Journal of the American Medical Association, 242,* 742–744.

Weissman, M. M., & Klerman, G. L. (1978). Epidemiology of mental disorders. *Archives of General Psychiatry, 35,* 706–712.

Weissman, M. M., & Myers, J. K. (1978). Affective disorders in a U.S. urban community: The use of Research Diagnostic Criteria in a community survey. *Archives of General Psychiatry, 35,* 1304–1311.

Weissman, M. M., Leaf, P. J., Holzer, C., Meres, J. M., & Tischler, G. L. (1984). The epidemiology of depression: An update on sex differences in rates. *Journal of Affective Disorder, 7,* 179–188.

Weissman, M. M., Leaf, P. J., Tischler, G. L., et al. (1988). Affective disorders in five U.S. communities. *Psychological Medicine, 18,* 141–154.

Wickramaratne, P. J., Weissman, M. M., Leaf, P. J., & Holford, T. R. (1989). Age, period and cohort effects on the risk of major depression: Results from five United States communities. *Journal of Clinical Epidemiology, 42*(4), 333–343.

Wing, J. K., Cooper, J. E., & Sartorius, N. (1974). *Measurement and classification of psychiatric symptoms: An instructional manual for the PSE and CATEGO Program.* New York: Cambridge University Press.

Wittchen, H. U. (1986). Epidemiology of panic attacks and panic disorders. In: Hand, I., & Wittchen, H. U., (Eds.). *Panic and phobias.* (pp. 18–27). Berlin: Springer Verlag.

Chapter 6

Homelessness and Psychopathology

Rodrick Wallace, Elmer Struening, and Ezra Susser

"Homelessness" is an ill-defined term, emerging largely from discussions in the popular press, from funding agency requests-for-proposals and from service agency self-descriptions. The inevitable embedding of scientific analysis, and even basic problem definition, in this larger community discourse has, in our view, often resulted in an undue focus on the characteristics of individuals and families who are labeled as "homeless;" and in defining the causes of homelessness, rather than on larger processes or interactions which may express themselves through the increasingly widespread use of irregular forms of domicile.

Indeed, for some purposes the term "irregular forms of domicile" (IFD) may be of more use, involving a continuum of states ranging from living "doubled up" with a friend or relative, to occasional or regular use of an emergency shelter or similar institution, occupation of abandoned structures, to a lifestyle including sleeping on the streets, parks, or other public places. We envision, rather than a simple condition of homelessness, transitions between states of IFD, and between IFD and a more stable condition of "permanent" housing, resulting in a temporal dynamic of process largely driven by changes in time of availability and affordability of housing. We envision IFD as a response to an ongoing process of decreasing availability of low-income housing, a growing housing deficit with vulnerability to IFD structured by individual or family coping characteristics that may themselves be affected by the rigorous course of IFD (Wallace, 1989, 1990a; Wallace & Bassuk, 1991).

As is all too usual, it has proven popular in politically powerful circles to characterize those using, or more exactly forced to use, irregular forms of domicile as, by definition, defective, and to see a causal intersection between psychopathology and homelessness. Indeed, on first view, evidence seems to abound: Almost every study of "the homeless" finds widespread evidence of depression, psychosis, substance abuse, and their various interactions, so-called "dual-diagnoses." For example, our own recent study of some 800 persons using the New York City shelter system in 1985, and some 1,200 in 1987, found that about 25% of the shelter population sampled had a history of, or a current manifestation of, a serious mental disorder. Thirteen percent expressed moderate symptoms of mental disorder, 28% modest symptoms; and only about a third, few or no such symptoms (Struening, 1989). Rates of hospitalization for this relatively young population, average age about 33 years, were very high, particularly for dual substance abuse/mental disorder conditions.

These—our own—and many similar findings are sometimes taken as proof that homelessness and psychopathology, often involving substance abuse, are virtually identical, and as implying a certain direction for public policy intervention; for example, the necessity of reopening facilities for the involuntary incarceration of the mentally ill.

Here we are going to argue for another, a basically interactional, interpretation of these data, namely that on the one hand, those most vulnerable to the effects of large-scale loss or growing unavailability of low-income housing—what we shall ultimately characterize as a progressively worsening housing famine—will be individuals or families with truncated effective social networks, including, of course, the mentally ill. On the other hand, the rigorous experience of IFD itself may exacerbate, or even trigger, behavioral and other symptomatology. Basically we shall argue that the often-observed relationship between psychopathology and homelessness has led to a misidentification of the causal process, and that a larger perspective is required if proper interventions are to be designed and effectively implemented.

THE LOW-INCOME HOUSING FAMINE IN THE UNITED STATES: THE HOUSING CONTEXT

6. Wright and Lam (1986) describe the present state of housing availability in the United States most succinctly:

The past ten years have witnessed a virtual decimation of the low income housing supply in most American cities. During the same period, the poverty population of the cities has increased substantially. Less low income housing for more low income people predestines an increase in the numbers without housing. The coming of the new homeless, in short, has been 'in the cards' for years and will continue unabated so long as low income housing continues to disappear from the urban scene. (p. 48)

Data from Wright and Lam (1986) provide starkly confirming statistics for a number of American cities. For Philadelphia, between 1978 and 1983, the number of low-income housing units declined from 211,000 to 157,000 while the number of low-income individuals rose from 516,000 to 708,000. For Baltimore the numbers were 75,000 to 66,000 units and 152,000 to 233,000 individuals, and for San Francisco, 175,000 to 110,000 units and 234,000 to 288,000 individuals.

The decline in the number of low-income housing units in urban areas has, in turn, created economic incentive for the conversion of yet more low-income housing into high-income units through displacement of the poor, a process popularly termed "gentrification."

In addition, rapid processes of South Bronx-like contagious urban decay have resulted in the burning and abandonment of vast numbers of residential buildings in overcrowded poor neighborhoods of many cities, including New York (Wallace & Wallace, 1977, 1980, 1990); Philadelphia (Dear, 1976); and elsewhere (Odland, 1983; Odland & Balzer, 1979; Odland & Barff, 1982; Greenberg, Popper, & West, 1990). The rapidity of this massive housing loss, and the necessary wholesale evacuation of burned or "red-lined" and abandoned neighborhoods, results in a kind of forced migration shredding the personal, domestic, and community social networks of the poor at a time when strong social networks are essential to coping with the consequences of both migration and loss of community and housing (Wallace, 1988; Wallace & Wallace, 1990; Struening, Wallace, & Moore, 1990). This will be seen to have serious implications for homelessness and its mental disorder covariates.

Well before onset of this accelerating maelstrom of collapsing low-income communities, disappearing low-income housing, and decline in the real income of the poor, came the deinstitutionalization of the mentally ill. Between 1955 and 1984 the number of persons in state mental hospitals declined from 552,000 to about 119,000—a decrease of almost 80% (Torrey, 1988)—while the elaborate system community support services planned to provide needed services for these individuals were, largely, not put in place. However, while the deinstitutionalized mentally ill have been the focus of many analyses of homelessness, it is important to note that the most rapidly growing segment of those using emergency shelter systems is presently the displaced family (Bassuk & Rosenberg, 1988), while the crisis of homelessness, or more properly, of the growing use of IFD, became manifest only long after the most rapid period of deinstitutionalization. Clearly something else is happening.

We argue that the decline in the number of low-income housing units, and the rise in the number of low-income individuals and families, have created a kind of deadly game of musical chairs in which those without elaborate social networks are unable to compete. Wallace and Bassuk (1991) argue that:

> Most socially integrated people are surrounded by family and friends, by coworkers, and when necessary by professional caretakers from various social agencies. When they fall on hard luck they can mobilize some of these resources to buffer the stress and to help prevent a downward slide. . . . If times become difficult, for example, as during an economic recession or a severe housing crisis, and if they do not have a support network and/or the personal skills to enlist help, then it is more likely that they may become isolated and even lose their homes. The recent alarming rise in the number of homeless families suggests that many people increasingly lack adequate supports or have difficulty getting the help they need as social conditions deteriorate. We suspect that during the current accelerating housing famine, personal and domestic support networks have, of necessity and by default, become almost the only safety net helping to prevent homelessness. (p. 486)

Stack (1974) describes the geographically based social network structure of a poor Black community which has evolved over many years to buffer the pattern of severe, random resource deprivation, characteristic of the American system of poverty:

> Expectations are so elastic that when one person fails to meet another's needs, disappointment is cushioned. Flexible expectations and the extension of kin relations to non-kin allow for the creation of mutual aid networks which are not bounded by genealogical distance or genealogical criteria. Much more important for the creation and recruitment to personal networks are

the practical requirements that kin and friends live near one another. (Stack, 1974, p. 60)

The loss of social networks, through massive displacement of population, as occurred in New York City following widespread "South Bronx" burnout or through personal inability to form or maintain sharing relationships, or for a variety of reasons, will clearly place a poor person at greater risk for IFD under the circumstances of a declining stock of affordable housing. We argue, in fact, that the condition of low-income housing loss in the United States constitutes a famine in the sense of a profound deficit in a resource essential for the general well-being of a population. The impacts of this famine have, as usual, expressed themselves according to what we will term a "structure of vulnerability," here involving social network resources rather than the dual age structure of the traditional famine, a food deficit.

Carlson (1982) provides a context for an assertion that the housing deficit constitutes a famine in his description of a classic food famine:

> Famine usually happens when many elements of the biological and social ecosystems have been profoundly disturbed and altered. The human physical stigmata are well known . . . Psychological effects are less obvious but important . . . Interpersonal relationships may be broken down . . . completely . . . Infants, children, and the elderly suffer first; young and middle-aged adults are usually able to travel to food sources, leaving the young and old to fend for themselves and possibly die . . . Social chaos is evident everywhere, as refugees flock to cities or roads seeking food . . . Food shortages have the most severe impact on the lower economic classes, less on the advantaged. In a time of famine, the urban working classes . . . are often the first and most severely hit, because their fixed wages and salaries do not keep pace with grossly inflated food prices. (p. 17)

For residents of poor communities of the United States, successful coping strategies must focus on maintenance of elaborate, geographically based personal and domestic social networks whose breadth and depth are sufficient so that almost any reasonable need can be met within or through the resources of associated kin or friend-kin. Thus loss of social networks through loss of housing stock, through forced migration from disintegrating communities, or the failure to establish such networks in the first place, can seriously compound housing unavailability, placing both individuals and families at risk for the

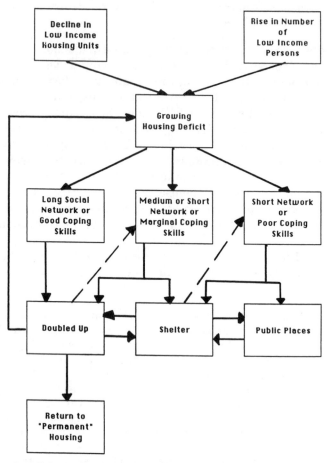

Figure 6.1. Schematic showing interaction between rising numbers of the poor, declining numbers of low income housing units, and a "Structure of Vulnerability" to the resulting housing famine based on the ability to maintain a large "effective" social network.

more extreme forms of IFD. That is, under conditions of a low-income housing deficit, failure to maintain an elaborate, geographically focused, social-network-based coping structure among those stressed by that deficit, expresses itself as use of the more extreme forms of IFD, including shelters and public places.

Figure 6.1 is a schema showing our hypothesis of the interaction between a rising low-income housing deficit—onset of a housing famine—and a structure of vulnerability to that deficit based on effective social network length and related coping skills. A combination of declining numbers of low-income housing units and rising numbers of low-income persons creates a growing housing deficit, the first three boxes at the top of Figure 6.1.

At the second level, the effects of that deficit parcel out according to the effective social network length and coping skills of the affected low-income individuals and families. Those with long effective nets and good skills are able to live for long periods doubled-up with friends or relatives.

Those with medium or short nets and marginal skills either become doubled-up or directly enter the shelter. The doubling-up process itself contributes to the housing deficit by consuming a possible housing space in someone's spare bedroom or living room. Those with short nets or poor coping skills either go directly to the shelter or into public spaces—waiting rooms, parks, streets, and so on.

The dashed lines going backwards from the "doubled-up" to "medium net/marginal coping" and from "shelter" to "short net/poor coping" boxes indicate that the demoralizing experience of IFD itself—doubling-up or using a shelter—may erode coping skills or truncate effective social network length. This takes place through a variety of mechanisms including intensification of interpersonal conflicts or exacerbation of individual or family behavioral pathologies.

The horizontal lines connecting the "doubled-up" and "shelter" boxes indicate the likelihood of transitions between these states for those with medium nets, while those between "shelter" and "public places" are likely transitions for those with short nets or poor coping skills.

The transition from "doubled-up" to "return to permanent housing," in the absence of increasingly unlikely or increasingly overwhelmed social intervention programs, is most probable only for those with long effective nets and good coping skills who find new housing before doubled-up living conditions erode those resources. By contrast, those with short social networks or poor coping skills, in time become "permanently homeless." That is, they become stalled in the two interacting boxes labeled "Shelter" and "Public Places."

HOUSING FAMINE AND PSYCHOPATHOLOGY

What, then, is the connection between homelessness and psychopathology, according to the paradigm of Figure 6.1? A classic literature (Leighton, 1990), which we cannot adequately review here, describes how the mental health of individuals is itself highly dependent on the strength and stability of personal, domestic, and community social networks. Indeed, the massive loss of housing and displacement of population which occurred in New York City between 1970 and 1980, and which other studies show occurred in other urban areas of the United States, can be classified as a disaster, in the classic sense of Kinson and Rosser (1974), with all that implies for psychosocial functioning.

Kinson and Rosser (1974, p. 437) define disaster as " . . . a situation of massive collective stress . . . [in which] the psychic distress and behavioral disturbance of an individual cannot be fully understood or managed unless . . . analyzed as elements in the disruption of the equilibrium social system."

Melick, Logue, and Frederick (1982) describe disasters as:

> . . . situations of massive collective stress . . . A growing body of [evidence] indicates that disasters may give rise to a variety of psychological symptoms, including grief, anxiety, anger, hostility, resentment, depression, and loss of ambition among adults . . .
>
> Other indicators of psychological disturbance include marital and family discord, increase in the use of tranquilizers and psychoactive medications, excessive consumption of alcohol . . . In children, mental health effects may include phobias, prolonged sleep disturbances and nightmares, loss of interest in school, and lack of responsibility . . . (p. 623)

Some time ago Fried (1963) examined the impact on individuals of a community's destruction, the "urban renewal" of West Boston. The words of the affected individuals are truly riveting:

> 'I felt as though I had lost everything,' 'I felt like my heart was taken out of me,' 'I felt like taking the gaspipe,' 'I lost all the friends I knew,' 'I always felt I had to go home to the West End and even now I feel like crying when I pass by,' 'Something of me went with the West End,' 'I felt cheated . . .' 'I threw up a lot,' 'I had a nervous breakdown.' (p. 151)

Fried states "Altogether . . . at least 46 percent [of those displaced] give evidence of a fairly severe grief reaction or worse."
Kasl (1977) puts it:

> . . . involuntary physical relocation has adverse consequences because it precipitates a severe disruption of the existing social

networks and relationships, i.e., a profound change in the social environment. And individuals who are particularly well embedded in these social networks and dependent on them, appear to suffer the most adverse consequences . . . (p. 65)

John Cassel (1974, p. 480) argues:

> A remarkably similar set of social circumstances characterizes people who develop tuberculosis . . . and schizophrenia, alcoholics, victims of multiple accidents, and suicides. Common to all these people is a marginal status in society. They are individuals who for a variety of reasons (e.g. ethnic minorities rejected by the dominant majority in their neighborhood; high sustained rates of residential and occupational mobility; broken homes or isolated living circumstances) have been deprived of meaningful social support.

These considerations provide a more proper context for the examination of IFD and psychopathology, particularly in the devastated and disintegrating inner cities of the United States.

Whatever the particular resource deficit, or system of deficits, mitigation for the poor in the United States is highly dependent on an elaborate repertoire of social and interpersonal skills, on existence of a geographically focused social network upon which to exercise those skills, and on considerable ability to navigate an increasingly inadequate, and hence increasingly unfriendly, social service bureaucracy. Clearly, the poor with impaired social skills, or otherwise deprived of long effective social networks, will be increasingly vulnerable to the effects of a growing deficit of low-income housing.

It is important to understand that lack of low-income housing is just one facet of a larger, indeed interacting, and often self-reinforcing nexus of deprivation and social disintegration within which the poor are often embedded—a nexus which may perhaps be characterized as a "slow disaster." Lack, or destruction, of physical resources is often compounded by a resulting social disintegration affecting the strength and viability of personal, domestic, and community social networks.

Outcomes may be similar to those seen more commonly in acute disaster situations, including rising levels of community and interpersonal violence, often coupled with intensified substance abuse, school failure, and rising rates of both physical illness and psychopathology. Acute disaster experiences may, in fact, also be relatively common in such populations; for example fires, murders, muggings, and the results of infrastructure deterioration and building collapse, along with catastrophic occupational illness and injury. The lives of the American poor are unquiet indeed.

Disaster experience, whether slow or acute, may seriously impair the ability to form and maintain the kind and intensity of interpersonal relationships needed to successfully mitigate the impact of an accelerating housing famine. This impairment may be further compounded by the rapidity of community disintegration associated with onset of the housing famine. Even those with proper social skills may then become bereft of the very social networks those skills are designed to navigate.

If, to the general disaster of life in a physically or socially disintegrating community, is added the direct experience of loss of domicile, of sleeping in parks or other public places, the particularly degrading necessity of repeated intimate contact with social service bureaucracies, of life in emergency shelters, with their violence and turmoil, then the resulting symptomatology may become quite complex. This may be particularly true for those who suffered overt psychopathology before loss of domicile: No one has ever been made healthier by being made homeless. Indeed, in a study of homeless men in New York City shelters, we found a high prevalence of severe distress. A plausible interpretation is that much of this distress was related to the experience of entering the shelter system (Susser, Struening, & Conover, 1989).

Various studies have shown that female-headed households in emergency shelters have experienced higher rates of violent victimization than similar families not in such shelter (Bassuk & Rosenberg, 1988). Assault by male intimates, or by family members, may significantly impair the ability to form close relationships in the long term, and thus inhibit formation of the kind of social nets needed to avoid use of emergency shelter under conditions of deteriorating housing availability and intensification of poverty.

Young, substance-abusing, violent males may have special difficulty forming and maintaining attachments to resource-sharing social networks and family, especially when younger children are seen as being exposed to a "bad influence." Indeed, a disjoint subculture of young males may develop into a kind of "floating crap game" including life on the streets, city jails, hospitals, emergency shelters, and, occasionally, with family and friends—all held together with a glue of substance abuse and petty crime.

Results from the 1987 Homeless Survey (Struening, 1989) show that over one-third of male respondents had been arrested one or more times in the previous 3 years and some 42% had been incarcerated one or more times in the past. Some 23% had been hospitalized three or more times in a population with an average age of 33 years; some 11% had been hospitalized for a drug problem and the same percentage for an alcohol problem. In addition this population is marked by exceedingly high rates of victimization, with some 26% having been robbed in the last year, 59% having had property stolen, 24% threatened with a gun or knife, and 18% beaten. Of course, such experiences may be consequences as well as causes of homelessness.

Clearly this population is deeply enmeshed in a nexus of violence, illness, criminality, and substance abuse which might be expected to strain interpersonal relationships and erode interpersonal skills; that is, to place the participants at increasing risk of IFD under circumstances of declining availability of low-income housing.

If inadequacy or disruption of social networks, interacting with a growing deficit of low-income housing, increases rates of IFD, then certainly IFD itself may have a further, and progressive, feedback effect on the ability to maintain social connectedness and on individual psychopathology itself. Loss of self-esteem and confidence, labeling, loss of intimates, strain on existing intimate relationships, loss of social support, may all express themselves in onset or exacerbation of various symptoms of psychopathology.

Evidently our view of the relation between psychopathology and homelessness has significant implications for public policy. Expectations that (nonetheless necessary) case-by-case interventions will have large-scale impact in decreasing the more extreme forms of IFD are unwarranted, as the progressive housing famine structures its effects according to an inverse interaction between income and real social network length (Wallace & Bassuk, 1991). (Until there is more empirical data on the social networks and supports within the IFD population, we rely upon the term "network length" to cover a variety of possible dimensions.)

In order for the poor to avoid the more extreme forms of IFD as the supply of available low-income housing declines, they must have long effective social networks, able to provide temporary or even long-term shelter under doubled-up conditions. Because these conditions stress even the best of relationships, they must involve "chaining," or using a series of temporary residences. Repeatedly living with different friends or relatives in overcrowded conditions in one temporary residence will lead to conflicts. Those who "run out" of friends or family to stay with must use public spaces or public shelters.

Schematically speaking, if p is the probability of homelessness for an individual or a family, then, crudely,

$$p = C \text{ (Housing Deficit Size)/[(Effective Social Net Length)} \times \text{(Income)],}$$

where C is a scaling constant. Social networks are, in this view, the riches of the poor.

If, as seems increasingly likely, the housing deficit becomes so large that virtually everyone who can house a homeless relative or friend is actually doing so, then the effective social network length of even those without overt psychopathology will become truncated, leading to high rates of IFD even among the psychologically healthy (Wallace & Bassuk, 1991). As the low-income housing famine in the United States becomes more acute, we thus expect a lower and lower fraction of the homeless to show Axis I diagnoses.

Our analysis also has serious implications for intervention. First, and most clearly, is the need to stabilize housing circumstances for affected individuals and families; that is, to provide adequate levels of independent or (various kinds of) supervised housing. There is little debate on this matter. Less clearly, but of equal importance for long-term stability, that is, for interrupting a possible recurrent cycle of homelessness, according to our analysis, is the necessity of re-knitting individual, family, and community social networks either weak to begin with or riven by the rigorous odyssey of homelessness and housing destruction. This may require community organizing programs, possibly supplemented by time-limited programs of individual or family therapy. Finally there seems a clear need to embed mentally ill users of IFD in a long-term therapeutic community— particularly those suffering the effects of dual diagnosis of substance abuse and mental disorder.

There will, of course, always remain a relatively small number of severely mentally ill individuals who will require overt hospitalization at any given time. But the intensity and duration of crises requiring such hospitalization may well be affected by proper contextual management as well. These kinds of interventions, however, will become more and more difficult as the low-income housing famine progresses in the United States, and as social and treatment services are increasingly overwhelmed.

Wallace and Bassuk (1991) summarize the relation between housing availability and the individual characteristics of those using IFD as follows:

> . . . it is the nature and progression of the low-income housing famine which directly produces homelessness, and not the characteristics of those who become homeless. For any famine affecting an essential resource, the most vulnerable sectors of the population are stricken hardest: during a food famine the very young and the very old suffer most, and during a housing famine . . . it is those who are poor and have inadequate social support networks who may be most and first affected. Although the exact structure of population vulnerability depends on the particular resource lack, certainly any claim of vulnerability to famine as cause of the effects of famine is a blaming-of-the-victim . . . it is famine which produces distress among the vulnerable, but not that vulnerability of itself.

Until provision of low-income housing is again made a serious national priority, in conjunction with programs to stem the continued loss of housing in congested urban areas subject to outbreaks of contagious urban decay, there will be growing interaction between housing famine and social network truncation, what the media, public officials and funding and service agencies term "rising homelessness." This outcome is intertwined with, affected by and affecting, but is not driven by, individual and family psychopathology. On the contrary, it is the mentally ill, the isolated, brutalized, and despairing poor who are the first victims of rising housing famine in the United States. It is time, in our view, to begin focusing our attention at least as much on the process of victimization as on the characteristics of the victims.

REFERENCES

Bassuk, E., & Rosenberg, L. (1988). Why does family homelessness occur? A case-control study. *American Journal of Public Health, 78*, 783–788.

Bassuk, E,. Rubin, L., & Lauriat, A. (1988). Characteristics of sheltered homeless families. *American Journal of Public Health, 76*, 1097–1101.

Carlson, D. (1982). Famine in history. In *Famine*, K. Cahill (Ed.). Maryknoll, NY: Orbis Books.

Cassel, J. (1974). Psychosocial processes and "stress": Theoretical formulation. *International Journal of Health Services, 4*(3), 471–482.

Dear, M. (1976). Abandoned housing. In *Urban policy making and metropolitan development*, J. Adams (Ed.). Cambridge: Ballanger.

Fried, M. (1963). Grieving for a lost home. In *The urban condition.* L. Duhl (Ed.). New York: Simon & Schuster.

Greenberg, M., Popper, F., & West, B. (1990). The TOADS: a new American epidemic. *Urban Affairs Quarterly, 25*(3), 435–454.

Kasl, S. (1977). The effects of the residential environment on health and behavior. In Hinkle & Loring (Eds.). *The effect of the man-made environment on health and behavior.* U.S. DHEW.

Kinson, W., & Rosser, R. (1974). Disaster: Effects on mental and physical state. *Journal of Psychosomatic Research, 18*, 437–456.

Leighton, A. H. (1990). Community mental health and information underload. *Community Mental Health Journal, 26*(1), 49–67.

Melick, M., Logue, J., & Frederick, C. (1982). Stress and disaster. In Goldberger & Breznitz (Eds.). *Handbook of stress.* New York: The Free Press, Macmillan & Co.

Odland, J. (1983). Conditions for stability and instability in spatial diffusion processes. *Modeling and Simulation, 14*, 627–633.

Odland, J., & Balzer, B. (1979). Localized externalties, contagious processes and the deterioration of urban housing: An empirical analysis. *Socio-Economics and Planning Science, 13*, 87–93.

Odland, J., & Barff, R. (1982). A statistical model for the development of special patterns: Applications to the spread of housing deterioration. *Geographic Analysis, 14*(4), 326–339.

Stack, C. (1974). *All our kin: Strategies for survival in a Black community.* New York: Harper & Row.

Struening, E. (1989). *A study of residents of the New York City shelter system for homeless adults.* Epidemiology of Mental Disorders Research Dept., Box 47, NY Psychiatric Institute, 722 W. 168 St., NY, NY 10032.

Struening, E., Wallace, R., & Moore, R. (1990). Housing conditions and the quality of children at birth. *Bulletin of the New York Academy of Medicine, 66*(5), 463–478.

Susser, E., Struening, E., & Conover, S. (1989). Psychiatric problems in homeless men: Lifetime psychosis, substance use and current distress. *Archives of General Psychiatry, 46*(9), 845–850.

Susser, I. (1984). *Norman Street: Poverty and politics in an urban neighborhood.* New York: Oxford Univ. Press.

Torrey, E. (1988). *Nowhere to go: The tragic odyssey of the homeless mentally ill.* New York: Harper & Row.

Wallace, R. (1988). A synergism of plagues: "Planned Shrinkage," contagious housing destruction, and AIDS in the Bronx.

Wallace, R., & Wallace, D. (1977). *Studies on the collapse of fire service in New York City 1972–1976: The impact of pseudoscience in public policy.* Washington, DC: University Press of America.

Wallace, R., & Wallace, D. (1980). Rand-HUD fire models. *Management Science, 26*, 418–422.

Wallace, R. & Wallace, D. (1990). Origins of public health collapse in New York City: The dynamics of planned shrinkage, contagious urban decay and social disintegration. *Bulletin of the New York Academy of Medicine, 66*(5), 391–434.

Wallace, R. (1989, 1990a). 'Homelessness,' contagious destruction of housing and municipal service cuts in New York City: Part 1, Demographics of a housing deficit, and Part 2, Dynamics of a housing famine. *Environment and Planning Analysis, 21*, 1585–1603; *22*, 5–15.

Wallace, R., & Bassuk, E. (1991). Housing famine and homelessness: How the low-income housing crisis affects families with inadequate supports. *Environment and Planning Analysis, 23*, 485–498.

Wright, J., & Lam, J. (1986). The low-income housing supply and the problem of homelessness. *Social Policy, 17*(4), 48–53.

Chapter 7

Psychoactive Substance Abuse and Psychopathology

Abdu'l-Missagh A. Ghadirian

Substance abuse has emerged in recent years as one of the most common psychiatric disorders. In many parts of the world this problem, which has been called "the plague of our time," has affected a critical proportion of the population, causing considerable alarm to health professionals and families.

Substance abuse, as a broad term, is no longer confined to those with "addictive personality," although such a character pathology is most conducive to its development. Nor is it limited to specific socioeconomic classes or cultural environments. Societal attitudes play an important role in its appearance, as do environmental stressors and genetic vulnerability. The presence of certain psychopathologies can also precipitate alcoholism and other substance abuse disorders. In turn, psychoactive drug abuse itself can lead to other types of psychopathologies.

Substance abuse and psychopathology are interrelated; however, the interface between them is complex. The co-existence of these types of psychopathology, although widely documented, raises questions as to which one began first. It is, moreover, necessary to distinguish symptoms caused by drug intoxication or withdrawal from those symptoms which are manifestations of a comorbidity. Approximately 30% to 50% of substance abusers who enter treatment suffer from a concurrent non-drug psychopathology. In most cases this additional psychopathology is affective disorder and in some others, panic or anxiety disorder (Rounsaville, Weissman, Kleber, & Wilber, 1982; Weissman, Pottenger, Kleber et al., 1977).

Certain societies have assimilated particular drugs into their cultural activities in such a way that behavioral problems associated with mild to moderate intoxication caused by those drugs is not a matter of special concern. Some cultural groups, in fact, choose certain drugs for their cultural-congruent pharmacological effects (Westermeyer, 1985). As an example, communities that value emotional and behavioral control may reinforce the use of opium rather than alcohol (Singer, 1974; Westermeyer, 1971).

There is a substantial body of evidence to indicate relationships between substance abuse and other psychopathologies (Alterman, 1985). Some have been known for a long time while others have only recently been explored. This chapter reviews the current literature on the subject.

METHODOLOGICAL ISSUES

In examining the relationships between substance abuse and psychopathology, the etiological and developmental aspects of this relationship should be explored and certain methodological issues should be taken into consideration. One of these issues is the type of measurement instrument used for the evaluation of psychopathology. In their review of the prevalence of depression among alcoholics, Keeler, Taylor, and Miller (1979) noted that the prevalence range of depression varied between 3% and 98%. These authors then conducted a study of the prevalence of depression among a group of recently detoxified alcoholics, using different measurement instruments on the same population. They reported the following prevalence rates for depression on the basis of their measurement instruments: 8.6% by clinical interview, 28% by the Hamilton Depression Rating Scale, 43% by the Minnesota Multiphasic Personality Inventory (MMPI), and 66% by the Zung Self-Rating Depression Scale.

Another methodological problem is a lack of valid and reliable diagnostic criteria for substance abuse. In the DSM–III (American Psychiatric Association, 1980), the categorical and diagnostic criteria for this disorder are primarily based on pathological use of these substances. This pathological pattern is characterized by impairment of social functioning and negative social or psychological consequences of drug use. The DSM–III–R (American Psychiatric Association, 1987) criteria stress the substance-seeking and substance-using behavior more than the development of tolerance and withdrawal symptoms. To this end, Bukstein, Brent, &

Kaminer (1989) argue that the application of DSM–III or DSM–III–R criteria to the classification of substance abuse in adolescents creates certain problems. They indicate that "the inclusion of criteria for impairment in social functioning assumes that negative social consequences are the result of substance abuse and not due to pre-existing factors, including another psychiatric disorder, or the coexistence of substance use and other psychopathology. Substance use by adolescents is almost always illicit and certain negative consequences follow from this proscription rather than necessarily from the properties of the substance being used or from the behavior of the substance user." However, depending on the type, duration, and quantity of substance of abuse, the pre-existing functional impairment can be intensified.

Another methodological issue concerns studies conducted on hospitalized substance abusers. The diagnostic impression immediately after admission can be misleading because the acute pharmacological effect of these substances may present symptoms which would initially suggest a major psychiatric syndrome. But several days later the clinical picture will change as the drug effects dissipate. As an example, the depressive symptoms in a majority of hospitalized alcoholic patients may disappear within 2 weeks of abstinence and without further treatment (Schuckit, 1983). Likewise, psychotic symptoms, including hallucination and paranoid delirium appearing in alcoholic patients (with clear sensorium), will disappear in days or weeks without treatment (Bukstein et al., 1989).

In general the issue of primary or secondary diagnosis presents another challenge in the identification of psychopathology. Within this system of classification a diagnosis is primary if the signs and symptoms appear first. The value of this form of diagnosis lies in the reduction of diagnostic heterogeneity. On the other hand, such hierarchical diagnostic ranking, based on the chronological appearance or severity of diseases, may obscure the interrelationship between the coexisting disorders. Different researchers, based on their individual orientation, have used various terminologies to identify the same group of psychoactive substances. The term "hallucinogenic" or "illusionogenic" substance is used to emphasize the perceptual effects. Other researchers have used the term "psychotomimetic" or "psychotogen" because of their interest in the psychotic effects of these drugs. The term "psychedelic" was used by Osmond in 1957 in an attempt to use a nonjudgmental expression for this group of substances (Leikin, Krantz, & Zell-Kanter, et al., 1989).

CULTURAL ENVIRONMENT AND SUBSTANCE ABUSE

Cultural environment plays an integral role in the development and pattern of substance abuse in a society. Psychoactive substances provide a chemical environment conducive to behavioral changes. In certain societies consumption of alcohol in any form is forbidden, but attitudes toward other psychoactive substances are less stringent. In other societies the opposite attitude prevails. Westermeyer (1985) stated:

> The relationship between culture and drugs is a dynamic one. A given society may have no difficulty with one drug and considerable trouble with another drug. Or the society may have no problems with a drug at one point in time and subsequently develop problems. Some of these problems could be due to non-medical use of drugs.
>
> Even psychopathological conditions with probable pharmacological and neurophysiological bases (such as alcoholic psychosis and alcoholic amnesia) can vary considerably across cultural boundaries. This variance appears to be related to such factors as different drinking patterns as well as different expectations or secondary gain from intoxication.
>
> Genetic and epidemiological data suggest that substance abuse and certain other psychopathological conditions (e.g., major depression, generalized anxiety) may be pathoplastic variants of each other. The violence and criminality associated with substance abuse are probably related to substance abuse *per se*, at least to some extent. But violence and criminality associated with substance abuse are also influenced by social class, legal codes, the cost of drugs and their licit or illicit status in the society, and cultural norms and mores. (p. 63)

RELATIONSHIP BETWEEN SUBSTANCE ABUSE AND PSYCHOPATHOLOGY

The relationship between psychoactive drug abuse and psychopathology has long been the subject of considerable debate. Meyer (1986) identified the following types of relationships between substance abuse and other psychiatric disorders:

1. Psychopathology as a risk factor for substance abuse
2. Psychopathology as a consequence of substance abuse

3. Psychiatric disorders which may alter the course and outcome of substance abuse and vice versa
4. Coexistence of substance abuse and other psychopathologies which are not specifically related
5. Psychopathology and substance abuse stemming from a common vulnerability.

In addition, certain psychiatric disorders may appear after the cessation of substance abuse. However, the clinical and biological sequences of these relationships are generally not clear. Although new patterns are emerging, more research is needed to clarify the interrelationship of substance abuse and other psychopathologies. There are a number of factors which may influence this relationship, such as ethnic and cultural values, societal norms and expectations, environmental factors, biological vulnerability, and genetic predisposition. For practical purposes the term "substance abuse" is intended here to include alcohol and illicit drugs. Drug dependence or addiction is an advanced stage of abuse in which psycho-physiological characteristics include tolerance and withdrawal reaction.

PSYCHOPATHOLOGY AS A RISK FACTOR FOR SUBSTANCE ABUSE

It has been traditionally presumed that substance abuse and addictive behavior are the consequences of certain psychiatric disorders. Some researchers contend that "addictive-prone personality" characterizes individuals who will eventually get involved in substance abuse and become drug addicts. However, there has been no clearly established etiological link between addictive disorders and specific antecedent psychopathology (Meyer & Hesselbrock, 1984). Nevertheless, the presence of an antecedent psychopathology may not only facilitate the development of substance abuse but it may also modify the course of this disorder. It is also quite possible that these two types of psychopathology may occur concurrently, with no etiological linkage or consequential relationship.

Although certain psychopathologies may serve as possible predictors of the subsequent development of drug addiction, the attitude of the individual and availability of psychoactive substances also play an important role. In a society where use of certain drugs or heavy drinking are part of the normative values of that society, psychopathology as a risk factor or predictor of alcoholism or drug addiction loses its significance. On the basis of this hypothesis Meyer and Hesselbrock (1984) contend that psychopathology may be more of a significant determinant factor for alcoholism among Jews than among Irish people in the United States.

SUBSTANCE ABUSE AS A RISK FACTOR FOR OTHER PSYCHOPATHOLOGIES

Psychopathological consequences may arise as a result of acute or chronic use of addictive drugs. According to Mendelson and Mello (1966), chronic use of alcohol would lead to symptoms such as increased withdrawal, depression, anxiety, and low self-esteem. Wikler (1952) reported that opiate dependence was associated with hostility, paranoid thinking, and general dysphoria, while Haertzen and Hooks (1969) found that the increased euphoria in the early stage of a 3-month addiction cycle later subsided and patients showed greater hypochondriacal and irritable behavior. Heroin addicts showed increased hostility, somatic concern, depression, uncooperativeness, suspicion, blunted affect, and emotional withdrawal (Meyer & Mirin, 1979).

Transient paranoid state is reported to be a common feature of cocaine dependence. In one study, 34 (68%) of the 50 cocaine-dependent men reported distressing paranoid states in the context of cocaine use. Individual vulnerability and limbic sensitization may underline this phenomenon (Satel, Southwick, & Gawin, 1991). Affective disorders are prevalent among cocaine abusers but reports on the extent of this prevalence are conflicting. In one study of 30 cocaine abusers matched with a control group, 16 (53%) met DSM–III criteria for affective disorders as compared to 24.2% of the control. It is believed that some of these patients used cocaine to treat their depression or potentiate manic episodes (Weiss & Mirin, 1984).

Generalized anxiety or panic disorder has been observed among substance abusers. Statistics vary but a review of two studies shows that generalized anxiety disorder was found in 9% to 11% and panic disorder in 3% to 5% of addicts (Weissman, Meyers, & Harding, 1980; Rounsaville, Rosenberger, Wilber, Weissman, & Kleber, 1980).

Psychopathological symptoms which may persist after the cessation of alcohol and other substance abuse are: A) cognitive impairment; B) depression; and C) personality changes (Meyer & Hesselbrock, 1984). All of these are found to be associated with alcoholism and opiate addiction (Meyer, 1986).

Cognitive Impairment

Chronic alcoholics may show three types of cognitive impairment: deficits in abstraction, impairment of short-term memory, and impairment of visual-spatial performance (Eckhardt & Ryback, 1981). Some of the cognitive functions may return to normal after one year of abstinence from alcoholic drinks; however, other cognitive deficits may persist (Meyer & Hesselbrock, 1984). Some of these cognitive disorders, such as Korsakoff syndrome, are well-known.

Depression

Depression is another area of psychopathology caused by addictive disorder. However, depression can be primary or secondary. While secondary depression may be the result of psychoactive substance abuse or other psychiatric disorders, primary depression usually prevails in the absence of other significant psychopathology or organic factors. Various researchers report different rates of prevalence of depression secondary to substance abuse. Hesselbrock, Hesselbrock, Tennen, Meyer, & Workman (1983) reported that in their study of 250 male and female alcoholic inpatients, 50% were found to be depressed based on the Beck Depression Inventory but only 27% of this population fulfilled the criteria for the DSM–III Diagnosis of Major Affective Disorders. These authors concluded that depressive symptoms found in alcoholic patients are not the same as those observed in the diagnosis of Major Affective Disorders based on the DSM–III criteria. Weissman et al. (1977), in their review of the literature, found that 59% of 61 alcoholic outpatients showed depressive symptoms.

Secondary depression may not be associated with a family history of mood disorders in alcoholics or opiate addicts (Cadoret, 1981). Primary depression is generally more frequent in women alcoholics than in men (Winokur, Rimmer, & Reich, 1971). Diagnosis of depression in alcoholics will have certain implications in the treatment and prognosis of this disorder. Alcoholic patients metabolize tricyclic antidepressants more rapidly and therefore the blood levels of antidepressants should be more closely monitored (Ciraulo & Jaffe, 1981).

A number of researchers have indicated that alcohol consumption usually decreases during depressive episodes and increases during manic states (Allen & Frances, 1986). Although this finding may be debatable, it carries certain implications regarding the relationship between bipolar cycles and alcohol consumption. Rounsaville, Weissman, Crits-Christoph, Wilber, and Kleber (1982), in their study of 157 opiate addicts who entered treatment, reported that 48% of the sample had a lifetime diagnosis of major depression. Of these, 94.5% suffered from a depression secondary to opiate addiction.

Personality Deterioration

The third type of psychopathology resulting from alcoholism and other substance abuse is personality changes. The issue of alteration of personality as a result of substance abuse is quite controversial. For example, there is no consensus on the development of the "amotivational syndrome" as a result of chronic marijuana use. There is a scarcity of longitudinal studies to examine personality changes before and after the development of substance abuse behavior (Meyer, 1986). Vaillant and Milofsky (1982), in a follow-up study of alcoholics, noted that personality deterioration was a consequence of drinking behavior. The most common type of personality disorder encountered in these patients is antisocial (sociopathic) personality. Some researchers are of the opinion that secondary sociopathy in alcoholics tends to have a different prognosis and treatment response as compared to primary sociopathy (Meyer & Hesselbrock, 1984).

Antisocial personality disorder may affect the onset and course of alcoholism. Its presence may cause an earlier onset, a more rapid development, and a poorer treatment outcome as compared to alcoholism without antisocial personality disorder. Substance abuse may also serve as a risk factor in the development of conduct disorder. Intoxication with alcohol or other substances leads to behavioral disinhibition and consequently lowers the threshold to antisocial behavior (Bukstein et al., 1989). There is a statistical relationship between crime rate and illicit use of drugs such as cocaine and opioid in the United States. The arrest rate for nondrug offenses and property crimes rises 1.5- to 3-fold after the onset of opioid addiction. Although this may be partly due to a number of factors, including the addict's struggle to generate income, there are indications that the premorbid life-style also plays an important role. Indeed, more than 50% of heroin addicts have been arrested prior to their opioid use (Jaffe, 1985).

CONCURRENT PSYCHOPATHOLOGY

There seems to be a relationship between the drug of choice and the concurrent psychopathology in the population of drug abusers. For example, affective disorder is found to be a more prevalent concurrent psychopathology in those who also abuse central nervous system (CNS) stimulants (Mirin, Weiss, Sollogub, & Michael, 1984). On the other hand, schizophrenic patients are reported to have a greater tendency to abuse psychotomimetics and will rarely use CNS depressants (Hekimian & Gershon, 1968).

Concurrent nondrug psychopathologies may complicate the clinical evaluation and diagnosis of these patients. Antisocial behavior of substance abusers could be a consequence of their drug abuse or an expression of the underlying antisocial personality disorder. Withdrawal from CNS stimulants may lead to symptoms which often become difficult to differentiate from symptoms of psychiatric disorders such as panic or generalized anxiety disorder and depression. A number of approaches have been suggested to distinguish a concurrent psychopathology from withdrawal symptoms. One approach is clinical evaluation after detoxification, when the patient has remained abstinent for an extended period of time. In opiate addicts depressive symptoms of the withdrawal period usually disappear in a drug-free environment unless there is a concurrent major depression which would require pharmacological intervention.

Nace, Davis, & Gaspari (1991) evaluated 100 substance abusers admitted consecutively to a psychiatric hospital, using the DSM–III criteria for personality disorders, and found that 57% of them had at least one personality disorder. Patients with character disorders showed significantly greater lifetime use of marijuana, amphetamines, cocaine, LSD, and opiates.

Rounsaville and Kleber (1986) reported that of 533 opiate addicts seeking treatment, 70.3% suffered from a current psychiatric illness, and 86.9% fulfilled diagnostic criteria for at least one psychiatric disorder other than drug abuse at some time during their lives. The authors used a standard interview schedule, the SADS-Lifetime Versions (Endicott & Spitzer, 1978) and the highly specific Research Diagnostic Criteria (Spitzer, Endicott, & Robins, 1978).

They noted that certain specific psychiatric disorders were much more prevalent in addicts as compared to a community survey population. Most of these specific disorders involved major depression, antisocial personality, and alcoholism. Of these three groups, major depression was the most common diagnosis; 23.8% of the patients were currently depressed and 53.9% had a lifetime diagnosis of depression. Alcoholism was the second most common diagnosis, accounting for 13.7% of the addicts who met RDC criteria for current episodes, and 34.5% had a lifetime diagnosis of alcoholism. Most alcoholics had an alcohol problem before developing opium or other drug dependencies. Views on antisocial personality among opiate addicts differed as some of them were primary and some secondary antisocial addicts.

ALCOHOLISM AND DEPRESSION

The relationship between alcoholism and depression has been explored extensively. Alcoholism in individuals prone to depression is thought to follow a malignant course of illness. But this notion has been challenged by a number of investigators who found no difference between the course of illness in alcoholics with depression and those without depression (Hesselbrock et al., 1983; Woodruff, Guze, Clayton, & Carr, 1979). Alcoholics with depression, however, appear to become more receptive to seeking out treatment as a result of their depression.

Although it was previously assumed that depressive symptoms would play a causal role in the genesis of alcoholic behavior, more recent studies show that genetic predisposition to alcoholism can be independent from depression or other psychiatric disorders. Some of the depressive symptoms observed during heavy drinking, or shortly after its cessation, may be related to the toxic effect of alcohol. Evidence to that effect comes from a number of studies which show that the initial disinhibition after the ingestion of alcohol is gradually replaced by increasing irritability, dysphoria, and depression (Freed, 1978). However, Jaffe and Ciraulo (1986) indicated that in a patient with alcoholism and depression there are no reliable methods to distinguish which depressive symptoms stem from personality disorder, which originate from the toxic effects of alcohol, and which are the result of a primary depression.

ALCOHOLISM AND SUICIDE

The suicide rate rises significantly with alcoholism. Approximately 5% to 27% of all deaths among alcoholics are attributed to suicide, as compared to almost 1% in the general population. About 5% to 25% of all suicides are committed by alcoholics (Jaffe & Ciraulo, 1986). This high rate of suicide, however, is not necessarily associated with severe depression. Although depression contributes to suicide, it may not be a universal factor in suicidal alcoholics. Based on coroners' reports, suicide may manifest itself as a late complication of a long history of drinking (Allen & Frances, 1986). Murphy, Armstrong, Hermele, Fisher, & Clendenin (1979) stated that 11 out of 50 completed suicides occurred in uncomplicated alcoholism. In this sample only 8% were suffering from primary affective disorder with secondary alcoholism and the majority of the rest had alcoholism with secondary depression.

In another study, 47% of alcoholics who later committed suicide were only slightly depressed, but many of them had symptoms of "irritability, dysphoria and aggressiveness" (Burgland, 1984). Suicide in alcoholics is probably associated with a number of factors, including the toxic and disinhibiting effects of alcohol, social losses, personality traits, and depression (Jaffe & Ciraulo, 1986). Impulsivity may play as important a role in suicide as depression.

Alcohol has been found empirically and experimentally to facilitate the expression of aggressive behavior. Its role in facilitating suicide, homicide, and other violent behavior has been well documented (Goodwin, 1973; Tinklenberg, 1973).

FAMILY ENVIRONMENT AND PSYCHOPATHOLOGY

Although the theory of genetic transmission has been gaining popularity in the study of alcoholism, environment also plays an important role in this and other substance abuse disorders. As an example, in the families of alcoholics, when the biological sons were removed from the original family and were adopted elsewhere at an early age, they showed a higher frequency of alcoholism but not antisocial personality or affective disorders as compared to biological sons of nonalcoholic individuals (Goodwin et al., 1974). On the other hand, biological daughters of alcoholics who were reared away from their parents manifested an excess of alcohol consumption but not depression (Goodwin, Schulsinger, Knop, Mednick, & Guze, 1977).

More evidence of the role of the environment on alcoholism comes from the work of Vaillant (1984). He found that of 57 men who grew up in families with an alcoholic parent, 27% became alcohol-dependent. On the other hand, of 56 men with nonalcoholic parents, only 5% developed alcohol dependency in spite of psychosocial stressors. Mendelson, Johnson, and Stewart (1971) studied 83 hyperactive children aged 12 to 16 years, many of whom showed antisocial behavior. Among those with the most antisocial problems, 22% had fathers who were problem drinkers as compared to 4% who had mothers with the same problem.

SUBSTANCE ABUSE AND PSYCHOSIS

There are several factors that contribute to the manifestations of psychopathology in substance abusers: preexisting psychopathology, genetic vulnerability, environmental factors, and the type and potency of substance of abuse. Certain drugs are more conducive to psychosis than others in vulnerable individuals. However, a distinction should be made between the toxic symptoms of substance abuse and psychosis resulting from regular drug use. High doses of amphetamine for an extended period of time are reported to be associated with psychosis (Ellinwood & Petrie, 1976; Griffith, Cavanaugh, Held, & Oates, 1972). Antisocial personality is reported to have been present in an average of 45% of cases who developed amphetamine psychosis (Ellinwood, 1969). But there has been controversy over the adverse reactions such as psychosis following LSD ingestion. According to some reports, such a psychosis occurs infrequently under controlled circumstances (Cohen, 1960; Glass & Bowers, 1970).

The role of pre-existing psychosis in drug users has been the subject of many studies. Hekimian and Gershon (1968) reported that 50% of psychotic drug abusers manifested symptoms of schizophrenia and 9% had schizoid features prior to their involvement with drugs. Vardy and Kay (1983), in their study of 52 LSD psychotics matched with 29 first-break schizophrenics, reported that these two groups were fundamentally similar in genealogy, phenomenology, and course of illness. However, LSD patients showed markedly fewer delusions but more depressive traits.

Manschreck, Allen, & Neville (1987) found that freebase smoking of cocaine accounted for 98% of the cocaine psychiatric referrals to a hospital (freebase: the pure alkaloid). Cocaine is believed to increase dopamine activity considerably. However, with chronic use, dopamine activity falls below normal. The psychopathological effects of cocaine use comprise the following symptoms: anxiety, irritability, illusions, hallucinations, and increasing desire to continue smoking cocaine. Heavy doses over hours and days will lead to progressive symptoms of euphoria, dysphoria, hallucinations, and acute paranoid psychosis. When a clinical pattern of this psychosis appears, its duration can last from days to weeks.

Psychosis attributed to khat (catha edulis) has been reported in Somalia. It is estimated that approximately 18% of the population of the south and 55% of the population of the north of Somalia are consumers of khat (Pantelis, Hindler, & Taylor, 1989). In the surveyed cases, psychosis developed after a heavy consumption of khat. The episode usually resolved within 1 to 2 weeks of the cessation of the use of this substance.

CONCLUSION

A growing body of evidence indicates a relationship between psychoactive substance abuse and other psychopathology. Substance abuse may precipitate a psychiatric disorder in vulnerable individuals. Substance abuse may also develop as a result of an antecedent psychopathology. The developmental and psychobiological sequence of the interrelationship between substance abuse disorder and other psychopathology, however, is unclear at present. More research is warranted for a clear understanding of this relationship.

REFERENCES

Allen, M. H., & Frances, R. J. (1986). Varieties of psychopathologies found in patients with addictive disorders: A review. In R. E. Meyer (Ed.), *Psychopathology and addictive disorders* (pp. 17–38). New York: Guilford Press.

Alterman, A. I. (1985). Relationships between substance abuse and psychopathology. In A. I. Alterman (Ed.), *Substance abuse and psychopathology* (pp. 1–12) New York: Plenum Press.

American Psychiatric Association. (1980). *Diagnostic and statistical manual of mental disorders* (3rd ed.) Washington, DC: Author.

American Psychiatric Association. (1987). Diagnostic and statistical manual of mental disorders (3rd ed.), (revised). Washington, DC: Author.

Burglund, M. (1984). Suicide in alcoholism. *Archives of General Psychiatry, 41*, 888–891.

Bukstein, O. G., Brent, D. A., & Kaminer, Y. (1989). Comorbidity of substance abuse and other psychiatric disorders in adolescents. *American Journal of Psychiatry, 146*, 1131–1141.

Cadoret, R. J. (1981). Depression and alcoholism. In R. E. Meyer, T. F. Babor, B. C. Glueck et al. (Eds.), *Evaluation of the alcoholic: Implications for research theory and treatment* (pp. 59–68). Washington, DC: U.S. Department of Health and Human Services.

Castellani, S., Petrie, W. M., & Ellinwood, Jr., E. (1985). Drug-induced psychosis: Neurobiological mechanisms. In A. I. Alterman (Ed.), *Substance abuse and psychopathology* (pp. 173–210). New York: Plenum Press.

Ciraulo, D. A., & Jaffe, J. H. (1981). Tricyclic antidepressants in the treatment of depression associated with alcoholism. *Journal of Clinical Psychopharmacology, 1*, 146–149.

Cohen, S. (1960). Lysergic acid diethylamide: Side effects and complications. *Journal of Nervous and Mental Disease, 130*, 30–40.

Day, N., & Leonard, K. (1985). Alcohol, drug use, and psychopathology in the general population. In A. I. Alterman (Ed.), *Substance abuse and psychopathology* (pp. 15–43). New York: Plenum Press.

Eckhardt, M. J., & Ryback, R. S. (1981). Neuropsychological concomitants of alcoholism. *Currents in Alcohol, 8*, 5–27.

Ellinwood, E. H. (1969). Amphetamine psychosis: A multi-dimensional process. *Seminars in Psychiatry, 1*, 208–226.

Ellinwood, E. H., & Petrie, W. M. (1976). Psychiatric syndromes induced by non-medical use of drugs. In R. J. Gibbons, Y. Israel, H. Kalant, R. E. Popham, W. Schmidt, & R. C. Smart (Eds.), *Research advances in alcohol and drug problems* (Vol. 3, pp. 177–222). New York: Wiley.

Endicott, J., & Spitzer, R. L. (1978). A diagnostic interview: The schedule for affective disorders and schizophrenia. *Archives of General Psychiatry, 37*, 837–844.

Freed, E. X. (1978). Alcohol and mood: An updated review. *International Journal of the Addictions, 13*, 173–200.

Glass, G. S., & Bowers, M. B. (1970). Chronic psychosis associated with long-term psychotomimetic drug abuse. *Archives of General Psychiatry, 23*, 97–103.

Goodwin, D. W., Schulsinger, F., Knop J., Mednick, S., & Guze, S. B. (1977). Alcoholism and depression in adopted-out daughters of alcoholics. *Archives of General Psychiatry, 34*, 751–755.

Goodwin, D. W. (1973). Alcohol in suicide and homicide. *Quarterly Journal of Studies on Alcohol, 34*, 144–156.

Goodwin, D. W., Schulsinger, F., Miller, N., Hermansen, L., Winokur, G., & Guze, S. B. (1974). Drinking problems in adopted and nonadopted sons of alcoholics. *Archives of General Psychiatry, 31*, 164–169.

Griffith, J. D., Cavanaugh, J., Held, J., & Oates, J. A. (1972). Dextroamphetamine: Evaluation of psychotomimetic properties in man. *Archives of General Psychiatry, 26*, 97–100.

Haertzen, C. A., & Hooks, N. T. (1969). Changes in personality and subjective experience associated with the chronic administration and withdrawal of opiates. *Journal of Nervous and Mental Disease, 148*, 606–614.

Hekimian, L. J., & Gershon, S. (1968). Characteristics of drug abusers admitted to a psychiatric hospital. *Journal of the American Medical Association, 205*, 125–130.

Hesselbrock, N. M., Hesselbrock, V. M., Tennen, H., Meyer, R. E., & Workman, K. L. (1983). Methodological considerations in the assessment of depression in alcoholics. *Journal Consulting Clinical Psychology, 51*, 399–405.

Jaffe, J. H. (1985). Opioid dependence. In H. I. Kaplan & B. J. Sadock, (Eds.), *Comprehensive textbook of psychiatry* (Vol. 1, 4th Edition, pp. 987–1003). Baltimore: Williams and Wilkins.

Jaffe, J. H., & Ciraulo, D. A. (1986). Alcoholism and depression. In R. E. Meyer, (Ed.), *Psychopathology and addictive disorders* (pp. 293–320). New York: Guilford Press.

Keeler, M. H., Taylor, C. I., & Miller, W. C. (1979). Are all recently detoxified alcoholics depressed? *American Journal of Psychiatry, 136*, 586–588.

Leikin, J. B., Krantz, A. J., Zell-Kanter, M. et al. (1989). Clinical features and management of intoxication due to hallucinogenic drugs. *Medical Toxicology and Adverse Drug Experience, 4*, 324–350.

Manschreck, T. C., Allen, D. F., & Neville, M. (1987). Freebase psychosis: Cases from a Bahamian epidemic of cocaine abuse. *Comprehensive Psychiatry, 28*, 555–564.

Mendelson, J. H., & Mello, N. K. (1966). Experimental analysis of drinking behavior of chronic alcoholics. *Annuals of New York Academy of Science, 133*, 828–845.

Mendelson, W., Johnson, N., & Stewart, M. A. (1971). Hyperactive children as teenagers: A follow-up study. *Journal of Nervous and Mental Diseases, 153*, 273–279.

Meyer, R. E. (1986). How to understand the relationship between psychopathology and addictive disorders: Another example of the chicken and egg. In R. E. Meyer, (Ed.), *Psychopathology and Addictive Disorders* (pp. 3–16). New York: Guilford Press.

Meyer, R. E., & Hesselbrock, M. N. (1984). Psychopathology and addictive disorders revisited. In S. M. Mirin, (Ed.), *Substance abuse and psychopathology* (pp. 2–17). Washington, DC: American Psychiatric Press.

Meyer, R. E., & Mirin, S. M. (1979). Operant analysis. In *The heroin stimulus: Implications for a theory of addiction* (pp. 61–91). New York: Plenum Press.

Mirin, S. M., Weiss, R. D., Sollogub, A., & Michael, J. (1984). Psychopathology in the families of drug abusers. In S. M. Mirin (Ed.), *Substance abuse and psychopathology* (pp. 80–101). Washington, DC: American Psychiatric Press.

Mullaney, J. A., & Trippett, C. J. (1979). Alcohol dependence and phobias:

Clinical description and relevance. *British Journal of Psychiatry, 135,* 565–573.

Murphy, G. E., Armstrong, J. W., Hermele, S. L., Fisher, J. R., & Clendenin, W. W. (1979). Suicide in alcoholism. *Archives of General Psychiatry, 35,* 65–69.

Nace, E. P., Davis, C. W., & Gaspari, J. P. (1991). Axis II comorbidity in substance abusers. *American Journal of Psychiatry, 141,* 118–120.

Pantelis, C., Hindler, C. G., & Taylor, J. C. (1989). Use and abuse of khat *(Catha edulis)*: A review of the distribution, pharmacology side effects and a description of psychosis attributed to khat chewing. *Psychological Medicine, 19,* 657–668.

Robins, L. N., Bates, W. N., & O'Neil, P. (1962). Adult drinking patterns of former problem children. In D. J. Pittman & C. R. Snyder, (Eds.), *Society, culture and drinking patterns.* New York: John Wiley & Sons.

Rounsaville, B. J., & Kleber, H. D. (1986). Psychiatric disorders in opiate addicts: Preliminary findings on the course and interaction with program type. In R. E. Meyer, (Ed.), *Psychopathology and addictive disorders* (pp. 140–168). New York: Guilford Press.

Rounsaville, B. J., Rosenberger, P., Wilber, C., Weissman, M. M., & Kleber, H. D. (1980). A comparison of the SAD/RDC and the DSM–III. *Journal of Nervous and Mental Disease, 168,* 90–97.

Rounsaville, B. J., Weissman, M. M., Crits-Christoph, K., Wilber, C., & Kleber, H. (1982). Diagnosis and symptoms of depression in opiate addicts: Course and relationship to treatment outcome. *Archives of General Psychiatry, 39,* 151–156.

Rounsaville, B. J., Weissman, M. M., Kleber, H. D., & Wilber, C. H. (1982). Heterogeneity of psychiatric diagnosis in treated opiate addicts. *Archives of General Psychiatry, 39,* 161–166.

Satel, S. L., Southwick, S. M., & Gawin, F. H. (1991). Clinical features of cocaine-induced paranoia. *American Journal of Psychiatry, 148,* 495–498.

Schuckit, M. A. (1983). Alcoholic patients with secondary depression. *American Journal of Psychiatry, 140,* 711–714.

Singer, K. (1974). The choice of intoxicant among the Chinese. *British Journal of Addiction, 69,* 257–268.

Spitzer, R. L., Endicott, J., & Robins, E. (1978). Research diagnostic criteria: Rationale and reliability. *Archives of General Psychiatry, 35,* 773–782.

Tinklenberg, J. R. (1973). Alcohol and violence. In P. Bourne & R. Fox (Eds.), *Alcoholism: Progress in research and treatment* (pp. 195–210). New York: Academic Press.

Vaillant, G. E. (1984). The course of alcoholism and lessons for treatment. In L. Grinspoon (Ed.), *Psychiatry update, III* (pp. 311–319). Washington, DC: American Psychiatric Press.

Vaillant, G. E., & Milofsky, E. S. (1982). The natural history of male alcoholism: Paths to recovery. *Archives of General Psychiatry, 39,* 127–133.

Vardy, M.M., & Kay, S. R. (1983). LSD psychosis or LSD-induced schizophrenia? *Archives of General Psychiatry, 40,* 877–883.

Weiss, R. D., & Mirin, S. M. (1984). Drug, host and environmental factors in the development of chronic cocaine abuse. In S. M. Mirin (Ed.), *Sub-*

stance abuse and psychopathology (pp. 42–53). Washington, DC: American Psychiatric Press.

Weissman, M. M., Myers, J. J., & Harding, P. S. (1980). Prevalence and psychiatric heterogeneity of alcoholism in a U.S. urban community. *Journal of Studies on Alcohol, 41,* 672–681.

Weissman, M. M., Pottenger, M., Kleber, H. D. et al. (1977). Symptom patterns in primary and secondary depression: A comparison of primary depressives with depressed opiate addicts, alcoholics, and schizophrenics. *Archives of General Psychiatry, 34,* 854–862.

Westermeyer J. (1971). Use of alcohol and opium by the Meo of Laos. *American Journal of Psychiatry, 127,* 110–123.

Westermeyer, J. (1985). Substance abuse and psychopathology—sociocultural factors. In A. I. Alterman (Ed.), *Substance abuse and psychopathology* (pp. 45–68). New York: Plenum Press.

Wikler, A. (1952). Psychodynamic study of a patient during experimental self-regulated readdiction of morphine. *Psychiatric Quarterly, 26,* 270–293.

Winokur, G., Reich, T., Rimmer, J., & Pitts, F. (1970). Alcoholism III: Diagnosis and familial psychiatric illness in 259 alcoholic probands. *Archives of General Psychiatry, 23,* 104–111.

Winokur, G., Rimmer, J., & Reich, T. (1971). Alcoholism IV. Is there more than one type of alcoholism? *British Journal of Psychiatry, 118,* 525–531.

Woodruff, R. A., Guze, S. B., Clayton, P. J., & Carr, D. (1979). Alcoholism and depression. In D. W. Goodwin and C. K. Erickson (Eds.), *Alcoholism and affective disorders* (pp. 39–48). New York: Spectrum.

PART III

Catastrophic Forces

Chapter 8

Natural and Technological Disasters: Evidence of Psychopathology

Robert Bolin

The physical environment is becoming increasingly hazardous. Events such as Hurricane Hugo, the Loma Prieta earthquake, the Chernobyl nuclear disaster, and the Exxon Valdez oil spill are a few of the better-known recent examples. That humans and their societies are increasingly exposed to hazards and disasters is a result of conscious human choices, the unanticipated consequences of those choices, and ineluctable environmental processes. At the most obvious level, more people are exposed to environmental disasters because of the unchecked growth of human societies. With rapid population growth, people increasingly are forced, or choose, to live in disaster-prone areas. Whether those areas are unstable mountainsides of many Latin American shanty towns, or the upper-class condominiums of the hurricane-prone Florida coast, the result is the same—more people living in hazardous areas (Wijkman & Timberlake, 1988).

Natural hazards such as landslides, earthquakes, and hurricanes have been a consistent feature of human societies for millennia. However, only in the last century has the emergence of technological systems given rise to the complex and far more dangerous hazards to which humans have had to adjust. Many complex technological systems are failure-prone, not by intent, but by virtue of their very complexity (Perrow, 1984). The periodic failure of these systems, and the resultant technological disasters, are having an increasing impact on societies.

When humans are exposed to a disaster, whether from natural

forces or from the failure of human technological systems, they are subjected to stressors which they must try to cope with, adjust to, and recover from. The psychological sequelae of natural and technological disaster are an area of increasing concern for researchers and mental health practitioners alike (Lystad, 1988).

This chapter will present an overview of recent literature on the psychosocial impacts of natural and technological disasters. This brief introduction to the field will examine and contrast the characteristics of natural and technological disasters in order to identify the event features associated with psychosocial sequelae. In the course of the review, a number of theoretical and methodological issues will be identified to illustrate certain current debates in the field. The evidence for psychopathological responses to disaster will be discussed in the context of both event characteristics and victim vulnerabilities.

DEFINITIONAL ISSUES

The term technological disaster is used here to refer to a broad range of events caused by the failure of technological systems and devices that humans have made and ostensibly control. These disasters can run the gamut from transportation accidents to urban fires, from nuclear power plant failures to the collapse of dams. Such events may be catastrophic, or they may be hidden and insidious. Some may be clearly identifiable as a disaster at the moment of occurrence because of ensuing destruction, injury, and death. Others, such as the intentional exposure of thousands of Americans to nuclear radiation in the West (Wasserman & Solomon, 1982; Miller, 1986; Millpointer, 1987), become socially defined disasters only years after toxic exposure occurred (Ball, 1986).

In contrast to technological disasters, natural disasters present less ambiguous threats, produce immediately visible impacts, and are likely to have acute rather than chronic effects. Further, natural disasters typically impact a community, while technological disasters may victimize other types of collectivities, as with building fires or airplane accidents. However, even when technological disasters impact communities, they can engender social processes and psychosocial impacts that sometimes differ significantly from natural disasters (Kasperson & Pijawka, 1985; Baum & Davidson, 1985).

The distinction between natural and human-caused disasters is not always clear. Natural disasters, as agents of psychosocial stress, are typically referred to as "acts of God," a phrase that eliminates human agency or culpability from consideration. Technological disasters imply human negligence, willfulness, or incompetence as causal or contributing factors. Natural disasters are presumed to be uncontrollable, while technological disasters are caused by the loss of control of a human-built system (Baum, Fleming, & Davidson, 1983; Baum & Davidson, 1985). Of course, many natural disasters, in fact, would not be disasters if people didn't choose to live in hazardous areas or build hazardous structures. For example, in earthquakes, collapsed buildings are the major source of death. While the earthquake itself is a natural force, the susceptibility of a building to collapse during a quake is a consequence of human decisions about siting and building construction (Bolin, 1989).

In discussing the psychosocial impacts of a disaster, it is necessary to consider the physical properties of the disaster agent. Typologically these would include speed of onset, duration of impact, scope of impact, predictability, intensity, length of forewarning, and threat of recurrence (Barton, 1970; Bolin, 1988; Drabek, 1986; Quarantelli, 1985; Warheit, 1985). The second dimension that influences psychosocial outcomes is the nature of the individuals and human settlements that the disaster agent impacts. The third area that affects psychological impacts, particularly over the long term, involves the characteristics of organized social responses to the disaster (Quarantelli, 1985).

Natural and Technological Impact Disasters

Much of the available research on the mental health impacts of disaster focuses on natural disasters, although there is a burgeoning body of clinical literature concerning several notable technological disasters (e.g., Smith, North, & Price, 1988). Of technological disasters, those with acute physical impacts appear to engender the most significant incidence of posttraumatic morbidity (Gleser, Green, & Winget, 1981; Green et al., 1985; Lindy & Titchener, 1983). For both technological and natural disasters, major factors associated with psychopathological outcomes are the exposure of victims to life-threatening situations and to the death of others (Bolin, 1985). In contrast, disasters involving toxic exposure or its threat (e.g., Three Mile Island) are associated with subclinical levels of psychological distress, as they often lack any clear and tangible traumatic impact (Baum, 1987; Bromet & Schulberg, 1986).

Technological disasters differ from most types of natural disasters in a number of qualitative dimensions (Kasperson and Pijawka, 1985). While both types of disasters have relatively sudden onset (the exception being hurricanes), technological disasters are almost always unpredictable and unexpected. While natural disasters usually have a clearly delimited impact period, lasting from a few seconds (earthquakes) to a few days (floods), technological disasters vary widely. In the case of toxic exposures, the impact period can be a matter of decades.

The perception of controllability of the event differs between disaster types as well (Hohenemser, Kasperson, & Kates, 1982). Natural disasters are seen by victims as uncontrollable while technological disasters represent a breakdown of control. Many technological disasters, once they begin, are typically uncontrollable. It has been argued that it is precisely the perception of the *loss* of control over something previously under control that makes technological disasters inherently more stressful (Baum & Davidson, 1985).

Some types of technological disasters resemble natural disasters in terms of physical forces and the impact of the event. Of technological disasters, dam collapses (e.g., Buffalo Creek, West Virginia, and the Teton Dam, Idaho) are most physically similar to natural disasters. Dam collapses differ from other technological disasters in that they do not involve toxic contamination, and the destruction they cause is produced by a familiar substance. Unlike naturally occurring floods, issues of culpability and blame assignation are important parts of the psychological sequelae of dam failures (Erikson, 1976; Golec, 1983; Gleser et al., 1981).

Baum and his colleagues (1983) have suggested that one characteristic of natural disasters not shared with many technological disasters is an identifiable low point. After the low point of a natural disaster, there is a shift in victim appraisal from that of the agent's impact to the physical losses it caused. Following the low point, victims conclude that the "worst is over," restoration activities begin, and environmental conditions start to improve.

Technological disasters involving hazardous substances (e.g., chemical and nuclear plants) often lack such a low point. The impact of the disaster is often unclear, the threats posed by exposure are subject to debate, the threat of recurrence is constant, and the stressors can become chronic (Smith et al., 1988). As recent risk-perception research documents, the general public views nuclear and chemical hazards with dread. The risks are seen as unknown, uncontrollable, posing a threat of catastrophe, and likely to negatively affect future generations (Slovic, 1987; Covello, 1983).

When considering the psychosocial effects of disaster events, it bears noting that certain impact characteristics, irrespective of their cause, can traumatize victims. Sudden, violent events, particularly those that heavily impact large segments of a community, killing or injuring significant numbers of persons, have a high probability of producing psychopathological outcomes in *some* victims (Bolin, 1988). In addition, events for which there is little or no warning and those that involve agents unfamiliar to victims, as in the case of many technological disasters, are likely to produce psychological sequelae. The exposure of survivors to the disfigurement and death of others has been clearly linked to significant posttraumatic morbidity in a number of disasters (Gleser et al., 1981; McFarlane, 1989; Madakasira & O'Brien, 1987).

These generalizations are necessarily subject to significant qualification. The interpersonal and community contexts of the victims, including the availability of social support (Kaniasty et al., 1990) and how the larger society responds to the disaster, can affect post-event morbidity (Quarantelli, 1985). In addition, victims will vary considerably in their vulnerability to disaster-related stress, whether the stressors are acute or chronic.

POST-EVENT STRESSORS

Disasters that impact communities create a complex of effects that, in turn, may produce new stresses on victims. These post-event stresses can generate psychological impacts of a chronic nature, ones that may be only tangentially related to the traumas of impact. Quarantelli (1985, 1985A) has argued that the psychological distress caused by natural disasters may be more a consequence of societal responses to the event than the actual physical event of the disaster.

Typical social responses to natural disasters include evacuations, staying in mass shelters, search and rescue, restoration/reconstruction of homes, extended stays in temporary housing camps, seeking recovery assistance, and forced or voluntary relocation (Bolin & Bolton, 1986). These "response generated demands" (Quarantelli & Dynes, 1985) may also accompany technological disasters, although there are significant post-event differences between technological and natural disasters (Kasperson & Pijawka, 1985).

Sociologists have found that after natural disasters, communities go through periods of heightened altruism, social support, and solidarity, a phase sometimes referred to as the "therapeutic community" (Barton, 1970; Drabek & Key, 1984). Some sociologists maintain that it is precisely this altruistic response to natural disasters that mitigates potential negative psychological impacts of the event (Quarantelli, 1985A).

If natural disasters create post-event solidarity, technological disasters frequently lack this therapeutic response (Sorensen, Soderstrom, Coperhaver, Carnes, & Bolin, 1987; Bolin, 1988). Technological disasters are more likely to create divisiveness and are rarely accompanied by a post-event consensus. Political and ideological conflicts often erupt between victims and corporate/governmental entities in the aftermath. Corporations and governments may argue that no harm has been done, particularly in the case of toxic exposures and nuclear accidents (Levine, 1982; Sorensen et al., 1987). The burden is thus shifted to the victims to prove that effects are present and that they were caused by exposure (Miller, 1986). When people who feel victimized have to then prove they are victims, the stress they experience can increase. Even if the consequences of technological disaster are manifested clearly (e.g., explosions, dam breaks), these can be followed by extended periods of dispute over issues of blame and responsibility, which in turn politicizes and divides neighborhoods and communities (Erikson, 1976; Perrow, 1984; Walsh, 1984).

Disasters can be followed by "secondary disasters" (Golec, 1983, p. 265) created by the exclusion of some victims from aid and recovery programs in the impacted community. For these victims, disaster stress may become chronic and they will ". . . experience loss and disruption as an enduring and possibly permanent condition of existence" (Golec, 1983, p. 265). Protracted stays in temporary housing facilities, particularly mobile homes in hastily constructed camps, can also be a continuing source of stress for victims (Gleser et al., 1981; Bolin, 1982).

Victims of technological disaster are unlikely to receive the support and assistance that natural disaster victims typically receive from the nonvictim community (Kasperson & Pijawka, 1985; cf. Bolin, 1990). Studies on Love Canal (Levine, 1982), Times Beach, Missouri (Smith et al., 1988), and Three Mile Island (Sorensen et al., 1987) found that victims were sometimes stigmatized as troublemakers and resented by those in surrounding areas.

In certain community-wide technological disasters, the very concept of "victim" is itself disputed. Questions may be raised about whether damage or harm was actually done. Victims, in turn, have to confront the problem of what types of delayed health impacts their exposure might have created. Those who remain in areas of questionable safety have to cope with the possible chronic health threats that may be present. Evidence from both Love Canal and Three Mile Island indicates that these uncertainties produced general anxieties, depression, feelings of anger, and despair (Levine, 1982; Baum & Davidson, 1985; Bromet & Dunn, 1981).

Both natural and technological disasters can require the evacuation of at-risk populations. Evacuation is seldom associated with psychological distress as long as families can evacuate as a unit, and especially when abetted by a warning period (e.g., Drabek, 1986). Evacuations in response to technological hazards, owing to the frequent lack of warning, can be more conflict-ridden and stressful on the evacuees. In the case of nuclear accidents there is a clear record of corporate/government interest in suppressing information and attempting to minimize the threats posed (Millpointer, 1987; Wasserman & Solomon, 1982). The result is an atmosphere of confusing and contradictory information about the nature of the risks posed to residents. In such circumstances evacuations can be stressful because of the ambiguity of hazard information provided (Sorensen et al., 1987; Drabek, 1986).

Both natural and technological disasters may result in the temporary or permanent relocation of victims. Relocation has been clearly identified as a significant source of prolonged psychosocial stress and may produce subclinical and clinical levels of dysfunction (Parker, 1977; Milne, 1977; Wettenhall, 1979). Relocation produces significant existential demands on victims including employment problems, establishing new homes, disruption of previous social support networks, living in unfamiliar surroundings, and lack of social support in relocation centers (Raphael, 1986; Garrison, 1985). Parker (1977, p. 385) refers to such phenomena as "relocation stressors." Relocation cuts victims off from the stress-buffering effects of the therapeutic community while subjecting them to a host of new stressors. The result is increased vulnerability to stress-related morbidity (Milne, 1977).

Permanent relocation of victims is relatively rare after natural disasters (cf. Wijkman & Timberlake, 1988; Oliver-Smith, 1986). Technological disasters that involve toxic substances often require relocation of neighborhoods (Kasperson & Pijawka, 1985), irrespective of the level of observable physical damage (Levine, 1982). The nature of contamination in some technological disasters may be so profound and persistent that entire areas are abandoned permanently (Flavin, 1987).

The negative impacts of relocation are intensified when victims do not feel they control the relocation process (Garrison, 1985). After technological disasters, victims often have to engage in protracted efforts to be compensated for their lost homes and relocation expenses. Depression, demoralization, and feelings of helplessness are common sequelae (Levine, 1982; Milne, 1977). The psychological impacts of loss of home and neighborhood, combined with fragmentation of social support, can create grief reactions and bereavement in those relocated (Bolin, 1985; Garrison, 1985; Fried 1982).

In sum, technological disasters tend not to produce the therapeutic environment of social support for victims that natural disasters produce (Kasperson & Pijawka, 1985). Victims of technological disasters often must respond to and recover from the event in a social context characterized by conflict and uncertainty (Levine, 1982). Technological disasters are also accompanied by uncertainties over continuing and future threats posed by the source of the event, resulting in conditions of chronic stress (Smith et al., 1988; cf. Adams & Adams, 1984; Leik, Leik, Ekker, & Gifford, 1982). Victims of natural disaster do not have to worry about exposure-related health problems emerging a decade after the event (e.g., Beigel & Berren, 1985).

BHOPAL AND CHERNOBYL

Two technological disasters stand out as archetypical examples of industrial accidents with major psychological, social, economic, and ecological consequences: Bhopal, India, and Chernobyl, the former U.S.S.R. Each symbolizes a specific major technological threat to humans—pesticides and nuclear power. Likewise, each involves major political-economic forces with vested interests in concealing risks from the general public. While detailed psychological studies are not available on the impact of either of these disasters, each event embodied characteristics well-documented as producing trauma.

The Bhopal, India, chemical plant disaster of December 3, 1984, occurred when up to 40 tons of methyl isocyanide, a lethal chemical used in pesticide manufacture, leaked from a Union Carbide plant into the atmosphere. The leak was a direct consequence of technological failure against a background of corporate negligence (Shrivastava, 1987). Residents of the town of Bhopal (population 800,000) were immediately affected by the toxic cloud. Lacking any warning system or means of mass evacuation, flight on foot was the only available response for tens of thousands of those exposed. The toxicity of the chemical was such that an estimated 3,000 died and several hundred thousand were exposed, many suffering blindness, gynecological problems, and other serious internal disorders (Weir, 1987; Shrivastava, 1987). The transgenerational effects of the disaster include birth defects, which appeared within a year of the disaster, and major disruption of family life through death and injury (Weir, 1987). The lack of medical facilities along with preexisting illnesses among the poor have exacerbated the long-term negative health consequences of the disaster. The exposure to death, disabling injuries, the fear of long-term negative health effects, and corporate denial of culpability and liability for the disaster can be viewed as significant traumatic stressors.

The Chernobyl nuclear power plant disaster of April 26, 1986, is possibly the watershed technological disaster of the century, precisely because it involved atomic energy and nuclear contamination. As a consequence of human errors while conducting experiments with one of the reactors at the Chernobyl nuclear complex in the Ukraine, a series of explosions destroyed a reactor and released record levels of radioactive materials into the atmosphere (Dudley, 1986). Europe, particularly Scandinavia and Poland, were showered with nuclear contaminants that polluted crops, water supplies, milk products, wildlife, and livestock (Flavin, 1987). In addition, millions of residents were exposed to varying, often significant, levels of radioactivity and experienced high levels of anxiety over personal health and safety (Park, 1989).

In the former Soviet Union more than 30 plant workers and emergency response personnel died from acute radiation poisoning in the immediate aftermath of the Chernobyl disaster. More than 1,000 were injured from high exposure rates, 200,000 received potentially dangerous exposure, and an estimated 135,000 were evacuated from their homes in the "danger zone" established around the damaged reactor (Park, 1989). (U.S. press estimates of 2,000 dead have been proved both alarmist and wholly false.) Billions of dollars in direct financial losses were incurred through relocation, the building of thousands of homes for evacuees, decontamination costs, losses to agricultural production, and increased electrical costs in the former

Soviet Union and Eastern Europe (Dudley, 1986; Flavin, 1987; Park, 1989).

In a fashion reminiscent of Three Mile Island, Soviet authorities waited 2 days before announcing that an accident had occurred. Further, recent evidence suggests full disclosure of the facts of the event and its impact has yet to be made (Marples, 1988; Medvedev, 1990). It now appears that the Chernobyl disaster was more serious than official reports have indicated and that the International Atomic Energy Agency has been complicating the situation by underreporting impacts, possibly to protect the international nuclear industry (Marples, 1988).

The potential sources of traumatic stress in the Chernobyl disaster are many. Because of significant cultural differences between the former Soviet Union and the United States it is difficult to estimate to what extent fear and dread (Slovic, 1987) of nuclear radiation and its health effects may have created distress among those exposed to contamination from the event. Although Chernobyl lacked the large death toll and acute health impacts of the Bhopal disaster, it did result in massive evacuations and relocation of victims. During the course of these evacuations families were often split up and relocated in different evacuation centers (Park, 1989), a potential source of significant stress.

The mass evacuation of tens of thousands, the permanent relocation of many of those evacuees, the loss of homes and possessions due to nuclear contamination, the forced cessation of agricultural occupations, are all major "response-generated" stresses on victims. The psychological costs of such dislocations and losses can only be speculated on, but experience from other disasters suggest they will be a prolonged source of psychological distress (Gleser et al., 1981). The fact that the highly contaminated 30-kilometer danger zone around the Chernobyl reactor (Medvedev, 1990) may not be re-inhabited permanently within the lifetimes of its former occupants can only add to the sense of loss and grief experienced by victims.

Both Chernobyl and Bhopal are signal events, illustrating the types of technological catastrophes that will likely occur with increasing frequency in the future. With the proliferation of complex technological systems with a tendency to fail systemically (Perrow, 1984) and the burgeoning of a global population increasingly exposed to the consequences of technological failures, technological hazards will only increase. Correspondingly, the social dislocations and psychological traumas associated with such hazards can be expected to increase.

VICTIM VULNERABILITY

The discussion to this point has focused on event characteristics and post-event conditions as factors in the etiology of psychosocial sequelae. The personal characteristics of the victims are the third dimension involved in explaining psychological impacts of disaster events. These characteristics include the individual's biological constitution, basic psychological profile, interpersonal relationships/resources, family characteristics, and social class-related factors (Warheit, 1988; Bolin & Bolton, 1986). The evidence for certain categories of persons being more vulnerable to traumatic stress than others is uneven and ostensibly contradictory (Quarantelli, 1985).

A number of studies have found that persons having an existing psychiatric condition are vulnerable to disaster-related trauma (Bromet & Schulberg, 1986; Lopez-Ibor, Canas, & Rodriguez-Gamazo, 1985; McFarlane, 1986). As McFarlane (1986, p. 10) observed of victims presenting for psychiatric treatment after an Australian bushfire: "The importance of trait and/or constitutional factors was suggested by the observation that a majority of patients had either a family or personal history of major psychiatric illness."

A number of sociological and psychological studies have looked at demographic characteristics as vulnerability factors. Age has been identified as a risk factor, although conclusions are difficult to draw. Some researchers have found older persons not to be at risk from disaster-related psychological trauma (Melick & Logue, 1986). Others have found that elders have lower rates of psychological sequelae than younger victims (Bolin & Klenow, 1983). Conversely, a number of studies have found that elders tend to have higher rates of impairment after disaster (Cleary & Houts, 1984; Kaniasty et al., 1990). Given the variability in samples, research designs, and instrumentation in the preceding studies, it is not possible to conclude that age is *prima facie* a risk factor in either natural or technological disasters.

At the other end of the age spectrum, there are inconsistencies in findings on levels of disaster trauma in children by age and sex (Smith et al., 1988). There is evidence that some children are vulnerable to posttraumatic disorders (Kinzie, Sack, Angell, Manson, & Rath, 1986). Others have suggested (Rutter, 1981; McFarlane, 1988) that post-disaster emotional problems in children may be influenced more by psychological distress in parents than by the disaster itself.

Other demographic characteristics associated with various levels of post-disaster psychological sequelae include social class factors, marital status, and family size. Education and income are negatively related to posttraumatic morbidity. That is, victims with higher education levels and incomes tend to report fewer stress-related symptoms and appear to recover more quickly from them (Bolin, 1982; Bolin & Bolton, 1986; Green et al., 1985). These findings appear to hold across both natural and community-wide technological disasters.

The research findings on the effects of marital status on psychological symptomatology are mixed, with marital status effects often subsumed under social support measures (Green et al., 1985). While Cleary and Houts (1984) found unmarried persons less subject to psychological stress after Three Mile Island than those who were married, Bolin (1982) found the opposite after a tornado. In a recent study of earthquake-related stress (Bolin, 1989), divorced women were found to have significantly higher rates of posttraumatic stress symptoms one year after impact than any other group (see also Madakasira & O'Brien, 1987).

The presence of children may be a risk factor for adults in the household, although the exact mechanisms for this are not clear. Bolin and Bolton (1986) found family size to be a significant predictor of post-disaster emotional distress. Family size was a "proxy" for the presence of younger children in the household, as well as the overall dependency load on the parents. Dohrenwend, Dohrenwend, Kasl, and Warheit (1979) found that the presence of young children in the home was a risk factor for parents after a nuclear accident.

From the range of findings covered in this brief review, it should be apparent that the issue of vulnerability to disaster-related trauma is complex and subject to significant variation in findings and interpretation. Further, the findings do not consistently vary by disaster type. Rather, psychiatric outcomes appear to be determined by a complex of disaster characteristics, experiential factors, risk factors, response-generated demands, and related, often idiosyncratic, situational elements (Warheit, 1988). To complicate the picture, variations in research findings may reflect disciplinary differences among researchers.

DISASTER-RELATED PSYCHOPATHOLOGY

The evidence that natural and technological disasters produce a significant rate of psychiatric disorders is limited and disputed

(Warheit, 1988). That disasters produce a wide variety of subclinical sequelae among some victims is, however, amply documented (Lystad, 1988). What is at issue is the severity, rate, and persistence of psychopathological responses.

A significant body of evidence that documents psychopathologies among technological disaster victims comes from the Buffalo Creek flood (Erikson, 1976; Lifton & Olson, 1976; Titchener & Kapp, 1976; Gleser et al., 1981). Psychoanalytic assessment of victims of the flood found 80% to have traumatic "neuroses" 2 years after the dam break (Titchener & Kapp, 1976). Follow-up studies on the victims 4 years post-impact found psychiatric impairment in approximately one-third of the victims (Gleser et al., 1981). A number of authors (Quarantelli, 1985; Bolin, 1985) have suggested that the Buffalo Creek disaster, due to a convergence of stress factors and social response factors, is a unique and extreme case of disaster. Studies on other community-wide natural and technological disasters do not report the levels of psychiatric impairment found in the Buffalo Creek victims (Green et al., 1985; Bromet, Parkinson, & Schulberg, 1982; McFarlane 1985).

Comparing levels of impairment across studies is difficult because of the variability in reporting as well as in instruments used in assessment. It is common in much of the literature to find reporting rates for symptoms of psychological distress and emotional problems. Fewer studies utilize specific DSM–III (American Psychiatric Association, 1980) criteria for identifying diagnosable psychiatric syndromes such as Posttraumatic Stress Disorder (PTSD) (Green et al., 1985; McFarlane, 1989).

PTSD is an increasingly common diagnosis for post-disaster psychological morbidity in both natural and technological disasters. Because it is concerned directly with psychological responses to traumatic events (acute, chronic, or delayed), PTSD would appear to be particularly relevant for disasters. However, as with other post-disaster sequelae, its incidence as reported in the literature appears to be highly variable, whether as a consequence of actual rates of morbidity or of measurement and diagnostic differences. The diagnostic picture is complicated by the evolution of diagnostic criteria as reflected in differences between the DSM–III and DSM–III–R (APA, 1980; APA, 1987). As Laufer (1988, pp. 117–118) has noted, significant shifts in these criteria include the addition of "enduring circumstances" of stress to the existing category of acute stressors, the new emphasis on the avoidance of stimuli rather than on psychic numbing, the addition of several new symptoms as part of Criterion C diagnoses and the dropping of survivor guilt (Lifton & Olson, 1976) as a criterion, and various quantitative changes in scoring the diagnosis. Consequently, what literature has reported as PTSD after disasters may not be comparable across studies, depending on whether DSM–III or DSM–III–R criteria were used. This is significant because of the tendency of the literature to report the presence of symptoms rather than severity or endurance of sequelae (Smith et al., 1988). There is the further question of whether the presence of symptoms is indicative of post-disaster morbidity or more normal short-term reactions to disaster trauma (McFarlane, 1986; Quarantelli, 1985).

What, then, is the evidence for PTSD following natural and technological disaster, given some of the methodological and diagnostic issues noted above. In a study of survivors of an Australian bushfire, McFarlane (1986) noted a significant incidence of clinically diagnosed acute and chronic PTSD among cases presenting for psychiatric treatment. Few studies exist of unsolicited cases presenting for treatment, thus comparable data are not readily available. However, what is significant about McFarlane's study is that those presenting with PTSD did not do so until 2 months into the post-disaster period. This suggests that initial screenings may miss when diagnosing the disorder (McFarlane, 1986, p. 11).

Shore, Tatum, and Vollmer (1986) discuss PTSD following the volcanic eruption at Mount St. Helens (Washington State). That study, conducted 38 months after impact, reported "Mount St. Helens disorders" (which included PTSD) at a rate of 11% of all male subjects for the high-exposure group. While the research makes a case for a clear "dose-response" pattern for post-disaster disorders, the combining of separate syndromes into a single disorder category obscures the exact prevalence of PTSD by itself. It does point to the importance of specific exposure factors in the etiology of morbidity following.

Madakasira and O'Brien (1987), using DSM–III criteria for the diagnosis of PTSD, examined the consequences of a tornado disaster in the southeastern United States. They reported a rate of 59% of respondents with acute PTSD, 16% of those with a "severe form" (Madakasira & O'Brien, 1987, p. 287). While this is a high rate for natural-disaster victims, the reported incidence is problematic because of a 42% response rate on the self-administered questionnaire. Sampling biases could be significant; thus comparison to morbidity rates in other studies is problematic.

Compared to these rates, other studies have reported significantly lower incidence. For example, after a flood disaster in Missouri that involved dioxin exposure, Smith et al. (1988) reported diagnosable PTSD in approximately 5% of the victims, with somewhat higher individual symptom rates. Although Smith's study involved a natural disaster (flood) and a technological hazardous agent (dioxin), the disaster lacked severe impact characteristics, possibly accounting for the relatively low PTSD rate in contrast to studies discussed above. Studies of the Three Mile Island (TMI) nuclear accident have reported psychiatric diagnoses among 14% of a high-risk population (mothers with young children) (Bromet & Dunn, 1981). While a chronic threat suffused with the dread and uncertainty of nuclear power (Slovic, 1987), TMI lacked any visible physical impacts, again influencing the levels of impairment. However, significant evidence exists for persistently elevated subclinical levels of psychological distress following the event (Dew, Bromet, & Schulberg, 1987).

The Buffalo Creek disaster, with its convergence of extremely stressful impact characteristics (exposure to death and grotesque sights, destruction of community) and social response stressors (temporary housing camps, relocation) has been associated with high levels of diagnosed psychiatric morbidity. Because much of the research preceded DSM–III definitions of PTSD, studies report rates of "posttraumatic neuroses" (Titchener & Kapp, 1976). Diagnosed disorder rates for Buffalo Creek approached 80% for victims 2 years after the flood. Other research on Buffalo Creek has documented similar persistently high rates of disorder among survivors (Gleser et al., 1981).

CONCLUSION

Although space limitations preclude a comprehensive review of the intricate interplay of factors in the etiology of psychopathology following natural and technological disaster, this review has highlighted significant findings from the literature. It is important to remember that the etiology of post-disaster psychosocial stress and psychiatric disorder is complex and event characteristics alone are not sufficient to account for morbidity (McFarlane, 1988). The qualitative and quantitative differences among disaster events, including both human-caused and natural, are complex and interact with social dimensions and victim psychological and experiential background.

At the social level, two essential variables are the stressfulness of social responses to the event, and the availability of social support to assist victims in coping with stress. In this regard, it may be suggested that technological disasters are more stressful than natural disasters because of their divisive nature in communities and their potential for disrupting social support networks (Baum, 1987).

At the psychological level, existing morbidity is clearly a vulnerability factor in subsequent disorder (McFarlane, 1988). The uncertainties of technological disasters may be experienced as more stressful than the unambiguous impact dimensions of natural disasters. On the other hand, because many technological disasters lack clear impacts resulting in death or injury, the result may be fewer overt cases, but more subclinical symptomatology. Thus, in anticipating psychological impacts of disaster it is necessary to consider the complex interplay of such factors in the disaster event and aftermath, recognizing the likelihood of idiosyncratic factors that may result in higher or lower levels of morbidity than in other ostensibly similar events.

REFERENCES

Adams, P., & Adams, G. (1984). Mount Saint Helen's ashfall: Evidence for a disaster stress reaction. *American Psychologist, 39*(3), 252–260.

American Psychiatric Association. (1980). *Diagnostic and statistical manual of mental disorders.* (3rd ed.). Washington, DC: Author.

American Psychiatric Association. (1987). *Diagnostic and statistical manual of mental disorders.* (3rd ed., rev.). Washington, DC: Author.

Ball, H. (1986). *Justice downwind: America's atomic testing program in the 1950s.* New York: Oxford University Press.

Barton, A. (1970). *Communities in disaster.* Garden City, NY: Doubleday.

Baum, A., Fleming, R., & Davidson, L. (1983). Natural disaster and technological catastrophe. *Environment and Behavior, 15*(3), 333–354.

Baum, A., & Davidson, L. (1985). A suggested framework for studying factors that contribute to trauma in disaster. In B. Sowder (Ed.), *Disasters and mental health: Selected contemporary perspectives* (pp. 29–40). Washington, DC: DHHS Publication No. 85–1421.

Baum, A. (Ed.). (1987). *Cataclysms, crises and catastrophes.* Washington, DC: American Psychological Association.

Beigel, A., and Berren, M. (1985). Human induced disaster. *Psychiatric Annals, 15*(3), 143–150.

Bolin, R. (1982). *Long-term family recovery from disaster.* Boulder: Institute of Behavioral Science, University of Colorado.

Bolin, R. (1985). Disaster characteristics and psychosocial impacts. In B. Sowder (Ed.), *Disasters and mental health: Selected contemporary perspectives* (pp. 3–28). DHHS Publication No. 85–1421, Washington, DC.

Bolin, R. (1988). Response to natural disaster. In M. Lystad (Ed.), *Mental health response to mass emergencies: Theory and practice* (pp. 22–52). New York: Brunner-Mazel.

Bolin, R. (1989a). *Temporary sheltering after the Whittier Narrows earthquake.* Final Report to the National Science Foundation. New Mexico State University: Las Cruces.

Bolin, R. (1989b). Families in Disaster: Theory and Research. In Quarantelli and Pelanda (Eds.), *Preparations for, response to, and recovery from major community disasters* (pp. 56–91). Disaster Research Center: University of Delaware, Newark.

Bolin, R. (Ed.). (1990). *The Loma Prieta earthquake: Studies of short-term impacts.* Institute of Behavioral Science Monograph Series. University of Colorado: Boulder.

Bolin, R., & Bolton, P. (1986). *Race, religion, and ethnicity in disaster recovery.* Boulder: Institute of Behavioral Science, University of Colorado.

Bolin, R., & Klenow, D. (1983). Response of the elderly to disaster: An age-stratified analysis. *International Journal of Aging and Human Development, 16*, 283–296.

Bromet, E., & Dunn, L. (1981). Mental health of mothers nine months after the Three Mile Island accident. *The Urban and Social Change Review, 14*, 12–15.

Bromet, E., Parkinson, D., & Schulberg, H. (1982). Mental health of residents near the Three Mile Island reactor: A comparative study of selected groups. *Journal of Preventative Psychiatry, 1*, 225–276.

Bromet, E., & Schulberg, H. (1986). The Three Mile Island disaster: A search for high risk groups. In J. Shore (Ed.), *Disaster Stress Studies: New Methods and Findings.* New York: American Psychiatric Press.

Cleary, P., & Houts, P. (1984). The psychologic impact of the Three Mile Island incident. *Journal of Human Stress, 10*, 28–34.

Covello, V. (1983).The perception of technological risk: A literature review. *Technological Forecasting and Social Change, 23*, 285–297.

Dew, M., Bromet, E., & Schulberg, H. (1987). Comparative analysis of two community stressor's long-term mental health effects. *American Journal of Community Psychology, 15*(2), 167–184.

Dohrenwend, B., Dohrenwend, B., Kasl, S., & Warheit, G. (1979). *Report of the Task Force on Behavioral Effects of the President's Commission on the Accident at Three Mile Island.* Washington, DC.

Drabek, T. (1986). *Human system responses to disaster.* New York: Springer-Verlag.

Drabek, T., & Key, W. (1984). *Conquering disaster: Family recovery and long-term consequence.* New York: Irvington.

Dudley, E. (1986). In the aftermath of Chernobyl: Contamination, upheaval, and loss. *Nucleus, 8*(3), 3–5.

Erikson, K. (1976). *Everything in its path.* New York: Simon & Schuster.

Flavin, C. (1987). Reassessing Nuclear Power. In L. Brown (Ed.), *The State of the world 1987*, (pp. 57–80). New York: Norton.

Fried, M. (1982). Endemic stress: The psychology of resignation and the politics of scarcity. *American Journal of Orthopsychiatry, 52*, 4–19.

Garrison, J. (1985). Mental health implications of disaster relocation in the

United States. *Journal of Mass Emergencies and Disasters, 3*(2), 49–66.

Gleser, G., Green, B., & Winget, C. (1981). *Prolonged psychosocial effects of disaster: A study of Buffalo Creek.* New York: Academic Press.

Golec, J. (1983). A contextual approach to the social psychological study of disaster recovery. *Journal of Mass Emergencies and Disasters, 1*(August), 255–276.

Green, B. (1985). Conceptual and methodological issues in assessing the psychological impact of disaster. In B. Sowder (Ed.), *Mental health and disaster: Selected contemporary perspectives.* Washington, DC: DHHS Publication No. 85-1421.

Green, G., Grace, M., & Lindy, J. (1983). Levels of functional impairment following a civilian disaster: The Beverly Hills Supper Club fire. *Journal of Consulting and Clinical Psychology, 51,* 573–580.

Green, B., Wilson, J., & Lindy, T. (1985). Conceptualizing post-traumatic stress disorder. In C. Figley (Ed.), *Trauma and its wake,*(pp. 53–72). New York: Brunner/Mazel.

Hohenemser, C., Kasperson, R., & Kates, R. (1982). Causal structure: A framework for policy formulation. In Hohenemser & Kates, (Eds.), *Risk in Technological Society,* (pp. 109–139). Boulder, CO: Westview Press.

Kaniasty, K., Norris, F., & Murrel, S. (1990). Received and perceived social support following natural disaster. *Journal of Applied Social Pathology, 20*(2), 85–114.

Kasperson, R., & Pijawka, D. (1985). Societal response to hazards and major hazard events: Comparing natural and technological hazards. *Public Administration Review, 45,* 7–18.

Kinzie, J., Sack, W., Angell, R., Manson, S., & Rath, B. (1986). The psychiatric effects of massive trauma on Cambodian children. *Journal of the American Academy of Child and Adolescent Psychiatry, 25,* 370–376.

Laufer, R. (1988). Human response to war and war-related events in the contemporary world. In M. Lystad (Ed.), *Mental health response to mass emergencies.* New York:Brunner-Mazel.

Leik, R. K., Leik, S. A., Ekker, K., & Gifford, G. A. (1982). *Under the threat of Mount St. Helens: A study of chronic family stress.* University of Minnesota: Family Study Center, Minneapolis.

Levine, A. (1982). *Love Canal: Science, politics and people.* Toronto: Lexington.

Lifton, R. J., & Olson, E. (1976). The human meaning of total disaster. *Psychiatry, 39,* 1–18.

Lindy, J., & Titchener, J. (1983). Acts of God and man: Long-term character change of survivors of disasters and the law. *Behavioral Science and the Law, 1*(3), 16–21.

Logue, J., Hansen, H., & Struening, E. (1981). Some indications of the long-term effects of a natural disaster. *Public Health Reports, 96*(1), 67–79.

Lopez-Ibor, J., Canas, S., & Rodriguez-Gamazo, M. (1985). Psychopathological aspects of the toxic oil catastrophe. *British Journal of Psychiatry, 147,* 352–365.

Lystad, M. (1988). *Mental health response to mass emergencies.* New York: Brunner-Mazel.

Madakasira, S., & O'Brien, K. (1987). Acute posttraumatic stress disorder in victims of a natural disaster. *Journal of Nervous and Mental Disease, 175*, 286–290.

Marples, D. (1988). *The social impact of the Chernobyl Disaster.* New York: St. Martin's.

McFarlane, A. (1985). The effects of stressful life events and disasters: Research and theoretical issues. *Australia-New Zealand Journal of Psychiatry, 19*, 409–421.

McFarlane, A. (1986). Posttraumatic morbidity of a disaster: A study of cases presenting for psychiatric treatment. *The Journal of Nervous and Mental Disease, 174*, 4–13.

McFarlane, A. (1988). Relationship between psychiatric impairment and a natural disaster: The role of distress. *Psychological Medicine, 18*, 129–139.

McFarlane, A. (1989). The aetiology of post-traumatic morbidity: predisposing, precipitating and perpetuating factors. *British Journal of Psychiatry, 154*, 221–228.

Medvedev, Z. (1990). *The legacy of Chernobyl.* New York: Norton.

Melick, M., & Logue, J. (1986). The effect of disaster on the health and well-being of older women. *International Journal of Aging and Human Development, 21*, 27–38.

Miller, R. (1986). *Under the cloud.* New York: Free Press.

Millpointer, K. (1987). Accidents—nuclear ones—will happen. *These Times, 11*(186), 7.

Milne, G. (1977). Cyclone Tracy: Some consequences of the evacuation for adult victims. *Australian Psychologist, 12*(1): 39–54.

Oliver-Smith, A. (1986). *The martyred city.* Albuquerque: University of New Mexico Press.

Park, C. (1989). *Chernobyl: The long shadow.* London: Rutledge.

Parker, G. (1977). Cyclone Tracy and Darwin evacuees: On the restoration of the species. *British Journal of Psychiatry, 130*, 548–555.

Perrow, C. (1984). *Normal accidents: Living with high-risk technologies.* New York: Basic Books.

Quarantelli, E. (1985). Social support systems: Some behavioral patterns in the context of mass evacuation activities. In B. Sowder (Ed.), *Disasters and mental health: Selected contemporary perspectives* (pp. 158–168). Washington, DC: DHHS Publication No. 85–1421.

Quarantelli, E. (1985A). Conflicting views on mental health: The consequences of traumatic events. In C. Figley (Ed.), *Trauma and its wake* (pp. 173–218). New York: Brunner-Mazel.

Quarantelli, E., & Dynes, R. (1985). Community responses to disaster. In B. Sowder (Ed.), *Disasters and mental health: Selected contemporary perspectives* (pp. 158–168). Washington, DC: DHHS Publication No. 85–1421.

Raphael, B. (1986). *When disaster strikes.* New York: Basic Books.

Rutter, M. (1981). Stress, coping and development: Some issues and questions. *Journal of Child Psychology and Psychiatry, 22*, 323–356.

Shore, J., Tatum, E., & Vollmer, W. (1986). The Mount St. Helens stress response syndrome. In Shore (Ed.), *Disaster stress studies: New methods and findings.* Washington, DC: American Psychiatric Press.

Shrivastava, P. (1987). *Bhopal: Anatomy of a Crisis.* Cambridge, MA: Ballinger.

Slovic, P. (1987). Perception of risk. *Science, 236,* 280–285.

Smith, E. (1984). Chronology of disaster in Eastern Missouri. Report for the National Institute of Mental Health, contract No. 83md525181.

Smith, E., North, C., & Price, P. (1988). Response to Technological Accidents. In M. Lystad (Ed.), *Mental health response to mass emergencies* (pp. 52–95). New York: Brunner-Mazel.

Sorensen, J., Soderstrom, J., Coperhaver, E., Carnes, S., & Bolin, R. (1987). *The impacts of hazardous technology: The psychosocial effects of restarting TMI–1.* Albany, NY: SUNY Press.

Titchener, J., & Kapp, F. (1976). Family and character change at Buffalo Creek. *American Journal of Psychiatry, 133,* 795–799.

Walsh, E. (1984). Local community vs. national industry: The TMI and Santa Barbara protests compared. *Mass Emergencies and Disasters, 2*(1), 147–164).

Warheit, G. (1985). A propositional paradigm for estimating the impact of disasters on mental health. *Mass Emergencies and Disasters, 3*(2), 29–48.

Warheit, G. (1988). Disasters and their mental health consequences: Issues, findings and future trends. In M. Lystad (Ed.), *Mental health response to mass emergencies* (pp. 3–21). New York: Brunner-Mazel.

Wasserman, H., & Solomon, N. (1982). *Killing Our Own.* New York: Delta.

Weir, D. (1987). *The Bhopal syndrome.* San Francisco: Sierra Club Books.

Wettenhall, R. (1979). Disaster and social science in Australia. *Disasters, 2*(4), 241–245.

Wijkman, A., & Timberlake, L. (1988). *Natural disasters: Acts of God or acts of man?* Santa Cruz, CA: New Society Publishers.

Chapter 9

Terrorism and Torture
Federico A. Allodi

DEFINITIONAL ASPECTS

From a medical and psychological point of view, terrorism and torture are closely related phenomena with important similarities and differences. The main points in common are their violent nature, the personality and motivation of their agents, terrorists, or torturers, and the effects that such acts may have on the victims. The differences bear on the political aspects of the situation and on the ethical dilemmas that occasionally may face the physicians and mental health professionals involved.

There is considerable agreement on the definition of torture and on the role of the physician facing this phenomenon. Torture is defined as pain or suffering, intentional and avoidable, whether caused by physical or psychological means, inflicted by a party or parties or their agents on a person or persons for the purpose of punishment, obtaining information, coercing the will, or for any other purpose (Amnesty International, 1984). In torture the role of the physician is quite explicit: He/she cannot participate or support it in any active or passive form, or condone it or be present on the premises in which it may be practiced or threatened (World Medical Association, 1975).

The motivation of the agent does not change the nature of the act: Whether the victim is innocent or guilty of any crime, or whatever the political context, any act of torture is a violation of the rights of the victims, as granted by Article 5 of the Universal Declaration of Human Rights of the United Nations (United Nations, 1948). All countries in all continents officially repudiate torture, and even those who covertly practice it or condone its practice as a tool of

141

state policy have signed charters or conventions to this effect (Amnesty International, 1990).

No such agreement exists on the definition of terrorism. It is clear that terrorism is "any act of violence which endangers or takes innocent human lives or jeopardizes fundamental freedoms" and it is "to be condemned as criminal" (Sofaer, 1987, pp. 370–371). However, those acts cannot be finally judged, it is claimed, without reference to their motivation or causes, as there is wide acceptance in the international community that "terrorist acts can be lawful in the pursuit of proper goals," such as in wars of national liberation or "in struggles against colonial and racist regimes and other forms of alien domination" (Sofaer, 1987, pp. 370–371). Thus, any agent of terrorism who may have killed, even innocent victims, in the pursuit of political goals in a national or international context may not be considered a criminal but may be granted the status of political refugee or of prisoner of war. The result is that in our daily newspaper reports "one man's terrorist is another man's freedom fighter" (Johnson, 1987, p. 271). In other words, the definition of the violent act as terrorism or sabotage or as a legitimate attack by "guerrillas," "commandos," or "freedom fighters" will depend on the political stance of who is defining the act. Within this controversy the "USA's Draft Convention on Terrorism of 1972 failed in the United Nations, largely because of definitional problems" (Johnson, 1987, p. 267).

However, the guidelines for ethical behavior for a physician involved in treating victims of terrorism are clear if we understand his or her role in the narrow sense of a healer ministering to the sick and wounded. In this case physicians must have the courage to plead for the recognition of their patients' rights as patients and for their own rights to treat them regardless of ideology. But even their patients' rights have limits insofar as confidentiality must not jeopardize the safety of the community, as was ruled in the Tarasoff's decision. (In 1974 the Supreme Court of California ruled that a psychologist was negligent in not informing a member of the community that a patient of his might possibly have represented a danger to her [Sharpe, 1987]).

More controversial is the wider role of the psychiatrist or psychologist who may advise police or other organs of state security during conditions of siege, hostage taking, and on other technical matters in the fight against "terrorism." In this case professional behavior must be guided by traditional and broader ethical principles. When the doctor feels that an organization's principles and objectives are incompatible with health ethics, that his or her advice is to be misused, or that he or she lacks the clinical autonomy to insure a clear ethical stand, he or she should comment on the ethics of the situation and refuse to collaborate (Gunn, 1983).

Various typologies of terrorism have been used (Johnson, 1987, pp. 274–277). Schematically, terrorism can be classified in two major categories—political and nonpolitical. Political terrorism can be state repressive or revolutionary, that is, against the state, which in turn can be ethnic, nationalist, or ideological, according to its main motivation. Nonpolitical terrorism occurs in wars or out of pathological individuals or groups. Both state and revolutionary terrorism have a lengthy and well-documented history. State terrorists include the emperor Caligula, the Spanish inquisitors, the Committee of Public Safety of the French Revolution under Robespierre, Hitler, Stalin, and many of the recent crop of totalitarian regimens and dictators in Latin America, the Middle East, Asia, and Africa.

Revolutionary terrorism began with the early conspiracies against tyrants and despots. The most direct act was tyrannicide, or the assassination or deposition of the head of state. This was the motivation of the saboteurs, anarchists, urban guerrillas, and insurgent groups of the late 19th and 20th centuries. From Aristotle's time to modern days, moral philosophers have argued in favor of the legitimacy of tyrannicide and the forceful removal of unpopular and undemocratic leaders. The difficulty lies in getting the contending parties to agree upon who is a democratic ruler and what is the proper process for the expression of the popular will.

Taking into account the motivational aspects of terrorism, one can propose a narrower definition: violence directed against political targets of a sporadic or clandestine nature with primary coercive and psychological dimensions to induce a state of fear or terror in the victim (Johnson, 1987, pp. 269–270). The true aims of modern revolutionary terrorism (psychological and propaganda advantages) are evidenced by epidemiological analysis, which shows that resources and casualties are disproportionately small compared to the psychological and propaganda gains. In the 1960s and 1970s, between 50 and 200 international incidents of terrorism were reported each year, with an annual death rate ranging from 111 to 460 (Johnson, 1987, pp. 269–270). In the United States the number of casualties of terrorism was two for the year 1985. At an international level, for the period 1973–1985, the United States lost 169 lives to terrorism (Laqueur, 1987, p. 379). In other countries, for example Spain, West Germany, Italy, or the Middle East, the number of terrorist agents involved and the number of attacks are also disproportionately small in relation to the propaganda and political gains.

On the other hand, in terms of casualties, state terrorism is a phenomenon of an entirely different magnitude. In recent history it suffices to mention the millions sacrificed by Hitler and Stalin in pursuit of state policies. And in Latin America, since 1966, in a single modality of state terrorism, it is estimated that 100,000 people have been made to "disappear" by organs of the state (ACAFADE, 1989). The practice of illegally and secretly detaining, often torturing, and finally killing a person is aimed at removing the opposition to the political program of a totalitarian state, using violence and fear as a deterrent (Amnesty International, 1981; Independent Commission, 1986). Similar statistics of abuse against a state's own subjects can be found in human rights reports on the Middle East, Asia, and Africa (Amnesty International, 1983). At this point state terror and torture appear to be synonymous because the means and ends are identical and the targets are not only the individual victims, but also the family, the community, or a whole political or population sector.

CONSEQUENCES OF TERRORISM

The study of the personality, selection, training, and motivation of terrorists and torturers is beyond the scope of this paper. However, the psychological effects of terrorism and torture have been well documented in the last decade and will be summarized here. In a study of 500 victims of 8 hostage-taking episodes in the Netherlands, followed-up and re-examined 9 years after the incidents, it was found that about half of the victims and 29% of the families experienced symptoms of posttraumatic stress disorder (PTSD), general anxiety, phobias, and psychosomatic manifestations. In general, these symptoms decreased with time. A slightly lower proportion of victims saw positive value in their experiences (Van der Ploeg & Kleijn, 1989).

Of special interest is a psychological reaction called the "Stockholm syndrome," which hostages may present under stress. The Stockholm syndrome is named after the 1973 incident in Sweden in which Kristin, a hostage victim, fell in love with Olsson, a bank robber. She later berated the Swedish prime minister for his failure to understand Olsson's point of view. This pathological reaction of identification with the aggressor has been reported frequently in hostages and in brutalized or isolated prisoners for whom death is the only alternative to the surrender of their minds. Such were the cases of Patty Hearst, as prisoner of the Symbionese Liberation movement, and the United States prisoners of war in North Korean concentration camps in the 1950s (Farber, Harlow, & West, 1957). The Stockholm syndrome is adaptive, in the sense that falling in love with Olsson may have saved Kristin's life (Ochberg, 1983). This, however, can be avoided altogether, as in the case of train hostages taken by the South Moluccans in Holland, none of whom fraternized with the terrorists, whom they correctly perceived as the enemy.

The plight of children involved in armed conflicts in which violence is directed indiscriminately against civil populations has also been recently documented. In some instances the circumstances are indistinguishable from war. Bombings, assassinations, shootings, kidnappings, hijacking, illegal imprisonment, and torture are used to terrorize both adults and children.

That has been the case in Northern Ireland since 1968. The association between political violence and mental health has been reviewed with the conclusion that it has produced no increase in major mental illness. It has, however, caused moderate and brief reactions in most of the adults and children (Cairns & Wilson, 1989). Children showed symptoms of stress and anxiety, somatoform and behavioral reactions, and chronic phobic symptoms (Fraser, 1973, pp. 60–87). Other stressors (unemployment, financial hardship) had more significant effects. How the Northern Irish coped so well is not known, although it can be speculated that environmental factors, namely family cohesiveness, employment, religion, and ideology, as part of the social network of support, played an important role. The increased use of benzodiazepine tranquilizers in the general population and, as individual factors, denial of the violence as well as habituation, have also been postulated (Cairns & Wilson, 1989).

In the Middle East, attacks on Israeli and Palestinian communities by "soldiers," "guards," or "terrorists" have had adverse effects on the psychological status of children since 1948. Both groups showed signs of emotional distress including anxiety, intense fears, and nightmares about soldiers and terrorists. Similar to the Irish "child guerrillas" (Fraser, 1973), Israeli and Palestinian boys and girls expressed the belief that war was a means to resolve conflicts and the children showed a willingness to die for their own country (Punamaki, 1987).

Perhaps it is too early to know the extent of the psychological damage and the true cost of the Irish "troubles" and of the Israeli/ Palestinian conflict. As with war, it is not during the actual experience, but afterwards that the number of orphans and widows, the latent effects on prisoners, and the underground guerrilla and security forces can be fully assessed.

In a nonpolitical kidnapping incident in Chowchilla, California, in which a group of 25 children were involved and followed-up for 4 years, all showed fear as the main manifestation of PTSD. Other symptoms were denial of their vulnerability and anxiety at the time of the incident, daydreaming and visualization, repetitive playing and re-enactment, magical explanations, and blaming themselves or their parents rather than accepting the randomness and helplessness of the incident. Treatment, it was shown, did not prevent the presence of symptoms (Terr, 1983).

In general, the prevention and management of PTSD following acts of terrorism, whether state created or revolutionary, or whether against large or small groups, have become part of the expanding field of PTSD. A wide variety of events, some originated by man and some not, but all characterized by their potential for major stress and trauma, have been studied with common conceptual tools and methodology (Malt & Weisaeth, 1989). Terrorism and torture are included in this field of study.

STUDIES AND CONCEPTS OF TORTURE

Although torture is an early companion of the human species, medical concern with torture is a recent phenomenon. In 1977 a group of physicians associated with Amnesty International in Copenhagen published a report titled "Evidence of Torture" (Amnesty International, 1977). It represented the medical profession's response to this particular form of human rights abuse, which was by then denounced as a modern epidemic. It was followed by similar publications in Canada, the United States, the United Kingdom, other European countries, South Africa, Australia, and various countries in the Third World, mainly Chile, Argentina, and the Philippines (Allodi, 1980; Allodi & Cowgill, 1982; Cathcart, Berger, & Knazan, 1979; Foster, Davis, & Sandler, 1987; Kordon & Edelman, 1986; Lira et al., 1984; Mollica & Lavelle, 1988; Protacio-Marcelino, 1989;

Reid & Strong, 1988; Stover & Nightingale, 1985). Those reports, for the most part, were clinical descriptions and frequency counts of the various methods of torture and the consequent clinical psychological signs and symptoms.

Later studies on the clinical consequences of torture were based on the same concepts of trauma and related response, but included progressive methodological refinements. These refinements consisted of the use of standard protocols and specific measurements and scales of trauma and torture and of the consequent distress and disability. Sophisticated techniques of statistical analysis were applied and representative population samples and control groups were used (Allodi & Rojas, 1985; Mollica & Lavelle, 1988; Rasmussen, 1990; Weisaeth, 1989). Population groups considered at risk were studied, specifically women and children, and significant findings reported (Allodi, 1989; Allodi & Stiasny, 1990; Lunde & Ortman, 1990). Finally, the systematic application of strict criteria for the diagnosis of PTSD in torture victims (Allodi & Fareau-Weyl, 1991) and victims of other forms of state terrorism (Allodi & Rousseau, 1989) showed that these subjects fit the criteria for this diagnosis.

Over the years variations and controversy concerning the general concept of torture have appeared. Originally, in countries where victims took refuge (mostly the industrialized nations of Europe, North America, and Australia—"The North"), torture was considered a trauma that has more or less specific consequences of a medical and psychological nature and treatment was, logically, medical and psychological. On the other hand, wherever torture was taking place (most countries with totalitarian governments in the Third World— "The South"), it was viewed as part of a political and social process that required preventive measures and, by implication, social changes and active participation of the health professions in bringing about those changes. In the south the concepts were more global, the approach broader, and the proposed solutions more dynamic and holistic. In the North, particularly in English-speaking countries, the concepts were neat, narrow, and stress oriented, the methods empirical or rationalist, and the treatment specific and organic. Of course, both approaches were criticized on the grounds that the broad and preventive approach went beyond the traditional bounds of the medical and health fields in which physicians and psychologists could claim expertise. It was also argued that a narrow medical or psychological approach is reductionist and ignores the basic and complex social issues implicit in the phenomenon of torture, without which no proper understanding or solution is possible. In fact, when groups of professionals from countries of origin and regions of exile (that is, from the South and the North), got together, there was no clear-cut distinction concerning approach; it was more a matter of emphasis and priorities than a difference in views.

Both in the North and in the South the two approaches are merging as, indeed, a broad conceptual framework is compatible with sociometric methods and the experimental design. A review of the literature will show that sociological, humanistic, and psychoanalytical insights can generate bold and novel hypotheses that can be tested and complemented with rational and rigorous methods.

The Vietnam War and the Jewish Holocaust, as fundamental examples of man-made stress, have stimulated much thinking and produced results that are available to the study of torture and state and revolutionary terrorism. A plethora of studies on the Vietnam War contributed significantly to the development of the concept of posttraumatic stress disorder (PTSD) (Figley, 1986; Sonnenberg, Blank, & Talbott, 1985). Although the concept of traumatic stress was implicit in the diagnoses of "shell shock," "combat exhaustion," or "combat neurosis" of the First and Second World Wars, Vietnam studies led to the refinement of the diagnosis of PTSD with specific criteria or symptoms clustered under four headings: re-experiencing, hyperarousal or hyperalertness, denial and avoidance (also including psychic numbing), and miscellaneous (American Psychiatric Association, 1980).

The Vietnam War literature also contributed to the controversy between the role of traumatic stress, be it combat or POW experience (Ursano, Boydstun, & Wheatley, 1981), and personality factors (Hendin, 1984). In extreme cases it would seem that stress and personality predisposition are negatively correlated and both would have considerable predicting weight. However, in most cases personality would be difficult to assess reliably, trauma has a subjective component of meaning and interpretation, and demographic variables (education, rank in the military), related to social support play a modulating role in the psychological impact of trauma. Moreover, a recent critical review relates soldiers' exposure to "atrocities" (a pre-Amnesty International term for torture), both as witnesses and as agents, to symptoms of PTSD and takes into account the variable of dehumanization of the enemy among soldiers (Van Putten & Yager, 1984). This, of course, touches upon sensitive issues of ethics and politics of military conduct and warfare, so far faced mostly by political and social scientists (Sanford & Comstock, 1971). Thus, the studies on Vietnam War veterans proved that sociometric and categorical approaches do not deter from a broad conception and further exploration of the issue of stress, with innovative models and variables.

The wave of South East Asian refugees generated by the collapse of the regime in Vietnam supported by the United States in 1975 has been studied in Australia, Canada, and in the United States. Many of the refugees had also been victims of torture. In addition to clinical studies of populations in treatment (Mollica & Lavelle, 1988), epidemiological studies of community samples have permitted an understanding of the roles that torture or persecution, the stress of traveling, concentration camp experience, and the strain of exile and immigration play in the final psychological and social adaptation of victims and refugees (Rumbaut, 1991). They confirm that, in refugees, whether from South East Asia or Latin America, the trauma of political persecution, including torture, was related to subsequent psychological distress and social maladaptation (Allodi & Rojas, 1985).

The Jewish Holocaust, as a paradigm of the horror that man can inflict upon man, has had a major impact on our culture and has had a qualitatively different influence on the field of stress or trauma. It has become part of the language, imagery, and metaphor of our time; it is used as a standard or model to judge racism and genocide; it has shown the overwhelming importance of environmental factors in the breakdown of psychological functioning and its recovery and has brought home, specifically to physicians, the awesome moral dimensions of their work with victims of terror and/or trauma.

Early reports on survivors from the Holocaust and Nazi concentration camps emphasized the biological effects of malnutrition and chronic stress on their psychological and physical resistance and their increased vulnerability to illness in later life (Eitinger & Strom, 1973). The symptoms exhibited by camp survivors immediately after liberation or in a delayed presentation were reviewed as a medicolegal necessity to compensate victims in postwar Germany (Meerloo, 1969). They included all the criteria later listed in the DSM–III for the diagnosis of PTSD. Psychoanalytical reports have been particularly helpful in understanding the impact of massive trauma on the individual and collective psyches of the victims in the process of long-term treatment and recovery (Krystal, 1984). The Holocaust finally provided unique studies on the effects of the original trauma into subsequent generations (Sigal, Silver, Rakoff, & Ellin, 1973). (More indepth analysis of the effects of concentration camps is offered in the following chapter).

SYMPTOMS AND TREATMENT OF TORTURE VICTIMS

Victims of torture assessed in open or semistructured interviews or with screening and diagnostic scales have repeatedly shown symptoms of distress and specifically of PTSD. Symptomatology depended on the severity of trauma, time elapsed between trauma and assessment, individual characteristics and coping style (elusive as they may be) and, above all, on environmental conditions of added stress or safety and support. Possibly two categories of symptoms can be distinguished: those related directly to stress and threat to life, manifested by anxiety; and a second cluster less frequent and of briefer duration secondary to the depleting effect of anxiety and to losses incurred, manifested by depression, withdrawal, irritability, shame, and guilt (Weisaeth, 1989). Psychotic symptoms are rarely reported and usually related to pre-trauma history and organic precipitating factors. Although paranoid psychotic reactions are rare, ideas of influence and suspiciousness are frequent in the context of persecution or soon after (Allodi & Fareau-Weyl, 1991).

It is generally accepted that the needs of torture victims, either in their country of origin or in exile, are multiple. In their home country the victims' first needs are safety, protection, and emergency care, both medical and psychological. In exile, often after the harrowing experiences of exit and travel, their first needs are of a material and informational nature. Affective support in the form of human concern and reassurance is essential in every contact with the survivor of torture, but as a rule specialized psychological or medical services are not the first priority. Most often, symptoms of psychological distress will surface and require attention once the primary needs of food, shelter, and secure employment are satisfied.

It is also generally accepted in countries of origin and exile that services must be comprehensive and provided in an integrated manner. Many countries helping torture victims follow this comprehensive approach (Gruschow & Hannibal, 1990). The Canadian Centre for Victims of Torture (CCVT) is one of the earliest to have operated in this field. It was organized informally in 1977, and since 1983 has functioned on an ambulatory basis, receiving torture victims and assessing their needs and problems. It provides crisis intervention service, group therapy and support for specific problems, a large volunteer support program, and referrals to a professional network of over 30 physicians, 6 psychiatrists, and 30 lawyers. These doctors provide consultation, medical/legal reports, and treatment for selected cases. The majority of CCVT cases (85% to 90% of some 500 new cases per year) show signs of psychological strain and distress, but they are supported within the Centre's programs. Only a minority (10% to 15%) with more severe disorders require referral to the medical network for further assessment and treatment.

Pharmacological treatment of victims with acute or delayed symptoms of PTSD is empirical, though a rationale is available from studies of Vietnam veterans. PTSD implies a state of sympathetic or adrenergic system hyperactivity or a permanent state of alertness. Very few biological studies have been conducted with torture victims. The disturbed sleep pattern has been found to be similar to other PTSD subjects (Hefez, Allodi, & Moldofsky, 1987). Benzodiazepines have been used widely, both in acute and chronic stages and tricyclic antidepressants (desipramine and clomipramine) have been tried in patients with depression, somatoform symptoms, and re-experiencing. Haloperidol and Thioridazine at low doses have been prescribed temporarily to individuals with severe agitation and reactive paranoid symptomatology (Allodi, 1991; Allodi & Fareau-Weyl, 1991). No drug trials have been reported with torture victims.

At the level of assessment, crisis intervention, brief counseling, or psychotherapy, the basic issues are the same: trust, denial and avoidance of the theme or memories of torture, loss and consequent grief, acceptance and integration of their experiences, and the attempts to reconstruct a new view of themselves and their world which was shattered by torture. At the early stages of treatment of the post-torture syndrome the most frequent approaches reported have been cognitive (Somnier & Genefke, 1986), and self-theory oriented (Lira et al., 1984). Those approaches have in common a rational emphasis on acknowledging that the trauma of torture and victimization have triggered a response that leads to symptom formation and maladaptive behavior. Symptoms and behaviors might be altered through rational understanding or appraisal, affective integration and appropriate social support, and through experience. Some variants of the cognitive approach emphasize relationship aspects and the rituals of therapy as befits people coming from different cultures, or the political aspects of the context of torture and the ideology of the victims (Cienfuegos & Monelli, 1983; Agger & Jensen, 1990).

A PSYCHOANALYTIC APPROACH

The psychoanalytical approach has been reported with exiled groups (Amati, 1980) and in countries of origin (Kordon & Edelman, 1986). The most helpful writings, however, still belong to the domain of the Holocaust: In therapy with victims a number of stages have been outlined that are characterized by denial, acceptance, and reintegration (Fogelman, 1988). They also represent ego states in the process of recovery from trauma and loss (Lindy, 1986). In our own studies with families of "disappeared" people in Central America (Allodi & Rousseau, 1989), and in our current practice with torture victims in exile in Toronto, the same stages and themes can be recognized. The themes commonly encountered in analytically oriented therapy of torture victims are:

1. Denial, as the most common and first defense. The variations of denial are avoidance, forgetfulness, shifting themes, silences, confusion, etc. It applies to both patient and therapist.
2. Fearfulness, anxiety, sexual and castration anxiety, overidentification, anger, ambivalence, and confusion towards the aggressor and related figures.
3. Feelings of vulnerability, alienation, distress, helplessness, and apocalyptic fear.
4. Narcissistic omnipotence.
5. Escapist and counterphobic defenses.
6. Depression and inability to experience a range of emotions, particularly love or pleasure, to give love or to accept it. (These ego states are called alexithymia and anhedonia.)
7. Acting out in the form of alcohol abuse, anti-authoritarian attitudes, drug dependence, family and relationship problems, and violent outbursts. In the transference situation, acting out can be commonly manifested as seductive and manipulative behavior, non-compliance, missing appointments, or withdrawal from treatment.

CONCLUSION

The field of study of victims of state and revolutionary terrorism, torture, and refugees and concentration camp experience is so large and varied that it may become fragmented if we cannot find common elements which integrate it in a valid form. Massive or unusual stress and its psychological and physiological consequences upon the victims are the fundamental concepts. Any general model should concentrate on refining the assessment of those two and other intervening variables, of which the environmental sources of support or added stress seem most promising. PTSD has been proven to be a valid unifying clinical concept. An analysis of refugees, torture victims, and immigrants from Chile in Canada were interviewed with a list of PTSD criteria and a large and comprehensive list of symptoms of psychopathology revealed that PTSD criteria discriminated validly between traumatized and non-traumatized groups (Guerino, 1991).

In summary, the evidence is that victims of terrorism and torture fit the criteria for the diagnosis of PTSD. The application of the standard criteria of the DSM–III for PTSD would permit a more reliable diagnosis and the comparison of various groups of victims with each other and across international boundaries. Moreover, the analysis of symptom clusters might permit more specificity in the diagnosis and selective response to treatment. On the other hand, though the provision of support systems for victims has improved in the past 2 decades, and some specific empirical knowledge has been gained in the treatment of torture and terrorism victims, very little of it has been tested in an experimental design or with sophisticated methodology.

The narrative history of trauma and simple, precise descriptions of clinical consequences of terrorist attacks and torture continue to be the most valuable tools to document cases, treat victims, and eventually to educate professionals and the public in the phenomenon and medicopsychological consequences of terrorism and torture. Epidemiological and refined methods of clinical analysis and research should be applied, while maintaining respect for the right of victims to confidential and unconditional service and treatment. Scales to measure the nature and severity and the impact on psychological functioning, the control of other intervening family or social variables, and of other context-related or unrelated life events, should be taken into consideration in appropriate research designs. Conceptual models of study and treatment must remain open and flexible. A narrow clinical focus will have the advantages of simplicity and an easier public and political acceptance; on the other hand, a broad conceptual framework will increase our knowledge of the phenomena of terrorism and torture and permit testing of hypotheses with treatment and preventive implications.

REFERENCES

ACAFADE (Association Central Americana de Familias de Desaparecidos). (Nov, 1989). *Our search* (p. 5). San Jose, Costa Rica: Author.

Agger, I. (1989). Sexual torture of political prisoners: An overview. *Journal of Traumatic Stress, 2*(3), 305–318.

Agger, I., & Jensen, S. B.. (1990). Testimony as ritual and evidence in psychotherapy for political refugees. *Journal of Traumatic Stress, 3*, 115–130.

Allodi, F. (1980). The psychiatric effects in children and families of victims of political persecution and torture. *Danish Medical Bulletin, 27*, 229–232.

Allodi, F. (1989). The children of victims of political persecution and torture: A psychological study of a Latin American refugee community, Toronto, *International Journal of Mental Health, 18*, 3–20.

Allodi, F. (1990). Refugees as victims of torture and trauma. In W. H. Holtzman & T. H. Bornemann (Eds.), *Mental health of immigrants and refugees*. Austin, TX: Hogg Foundation for Mental Health Publications.

Allodi, F. (1991). Assessment and treatment of torture victims. *Journal of Nervous and Mental Disease, 179*(1), 4–11.

Allodi, F., & Cowgill, G. (1982). Ethical and psychiatric aspects of torture: A Canadian study. *Canadian Journal of Psychiatry, 27*, 98–103.

Allodi, F., & Fareau-Weyl, J. (1991, Jan. 31–Feb. 2). Posttraumatic stress disorder in torture victims and paranoid reaction. Paper presented at the Annual Meeting of the Ontario Psychiatric Association, Toronto.

Allodi, F., & Rojas, A. (1985). The health and adaptation of victims of political violence in Latin America. In P. Pichot, P. Berner, R. Wolf, et al. (Eds.). *Psychiatry, the state of the art: Vol 6. Drug dependency and alcoholism, forensic psychiatry, military psychiatry*. New York: Plenum.

Allodi, F., & Rousseau, C. (1989, Oct. 25–27). The trauma of forced disappearance in the families of victims as post-traumatic stress disorder. An analysis of fifteen cases in Central America. Paper presented at the Fifth Annual Meeting of the Society for Traumatic Stress Studies, San Francisco.

Allodi, F., & Stiasny, S. (1990). Women as torture victims. *Canadian Journal of Psychiatry, 35*, 144–148.

Amati, S. (1980). Aportes psicoanaliticos al conocimiento de los efectos de la violencia institucionalizada. In Riquelme, H. (Ed.), *Era de Tinieblas. Derechos Humanos, terrorismo de Estado y salud psicosocial en America Latina* (pp. 17–30). Caracas: Editorial Nueva Sociedad.

American Psychiatric Association. (1980). Diagnostic and statistical manual, III Revision. Washington, DC: Author.

Amnesty International. (1977). *Evidence of torture* (Studies by Amnesty International's Danish Medical Group). London: Author.

Amnesty International. (1981). *Disappearances: A workbook*. New York: Author.

Amnesty International. (1983). *Political killings by governments*. Amnesty International Publications. London: Author.

Amnesty International. (1984). Torture in the Eighties. An Amnesty International report (pp. 253–255). London: Author.

Amnesty International. (1990). An Amnesty International report. New York: Author.

Cairns, E., & Wilson, R. (1989). Mental health aspects of political violence in Northern Ireland. *International Journal of Mental Health, 18*(1), 38–56.

Cathcart, L., Berger, P., & Knazan, B. (1979). Medical examination of torture victims applying for refugee status. *Canadian Medical Association Journal, 121*, 179–184.

Cienfuegos, A. J., & Monelli, C. (1983). The testimony of political experiences as a therapeutic instrument. *American Journal of Orthopsychiatry, 53*, 43–51.

Eitinger, L., & Strom, A. (1973). *Mortality and morbidity after excessive stress: A follow-up investigation of Norwegian concentration camp survivors.* New York: Humanities Press.

Farber, I. E., Harlow, H. F., & West, L. J. (1957). Brainwashing, conditioning and debility, dependency and dread. *Sociometry, 20*, 271.

Figley, C. (Ed.). (1986). *Trauma and its wake. Vol II: Traumatic stress, theory, research and intervention.* New York: Brunner/Mazel.

Fogelman, E. (1988). Therapeutic alternatives for Holocaust survivors and second generation. In R. L. Braham (Ed.), *Stress disorder among Vietnam veterans.* New York: Brunner/Mazel.

Foster, D., Davis, D., & Sandler, D. (1987). *Detention and torture in South Africa.* Cape Town, South Africa: David Philip Publications.

Fraser, M. (1973). *Children in Conflict* (pp. 60–87). New York: Basic Books.

Gruschow, J., & Hannibal, K. (Eds.). (1990). *Health services for the treatment of torture and trauma survivors.* Washington, DC: American Association for the Advancement of Science.

Guerino, D. M. (1991). *Cross Cultural Validation of post traumatic stress disorder in Chilean political refugees.* M.A. thesis, Vancouver, BC: Simon Fraser University, Department of Psychology.

Gunn, J. (1985). The psychiatrist and the terrorist. In *Terrorism. Interdisciplinary perspectives.* Washington, DC: American Psychiatric Association.

Hendin, H. (1984). Combat adaptations of Vietnam veterans without posttraumatic stress disorder. *American Journal of Psychiatry, 141*(8), 956–960.

Hefez, A., Allodi, F., & Moldofsky, H. (1985). Nightmares, sleep and symptoms in survivors of torture. *Sleep Research, 14*, 129.

Independent Commission. (1986). *Disappeared! Technique of Terror.* A report of the Independent Commission on International Humanitarian issues. Introduction by Simone Veil. London: Vez.

Johnson, C. (1987). Perspectives on Terrorism. In W. Laqueur, & Y. Alexander (Eds.), *The terrorism reader.* New York: Meridiam.

Kardiner, A. (1947). *War stress and neurotic illness.* New York: Hoeber.

Kordon, D., & Edelman, L. I. (Eds.). (1986). *Efectos psicologicos de la represión politica.* Buenos Aires: Editorial Sudamericana-Planeta.

Krystal, H. (1984). Integration and self-healing in posttraumatic states. In

S. Luel & P. Marcus, (Eds.), *Psychoanalytic reflections on the Holocaust: Selected essays* (pp. 113–134). New York: Ktav.

Laqueur, W. (1987). Reflections on terrorism. In W. Laqueur & Y. Alexander (Eds.), *The terrorism reader*. New York: Meridiam.

Lindy, J. D. (1986). An outline for the psychoanalytic psychotherapy of PTSD. In C. R. Figley, (Ed.), *Trauma and its wake. Vol. II: Traumatic stress, theory, research and intervention*. New York: Brunner/Mazel.

Lira, E., Weinstein, E., Dominguez, R., et al. (1984). *Psycoterapia y represion politica*. Mexico City: Editores Siglo Veintiuno S.A.

Lunde, I., & Ortman, J. (1990). Prevalence and sequelae of sexual torture. *The Lancet, 336*, 289–291.

Malt, U. F., & Weisaeth, L. (1989). Disaster psychiatry and traumatic stress studies in Norway. History, current state and future. *Acta. Psychiat. Scand. Suppl. 355, 80*, 7–12.

Meerloo J. (1969). Persecution trauma and the reconditioning of emotional life: A brief survey. *American Journal of Psychiatry, 125*(9), 1187–1191.

Mollica, R., & Lavelle, J. (1988). The trauma of mass violence and torture: An overview of the psychiatric care of the South East Asian refugees. In L. Comes-Diaz & E. E. Griffith, (Eds.), *Clinical practice in cross-cultural mental health*. New York: Wiley.

Ochberg, F. (1983). Hostage Victims. In B. Eichelman, D. Joskis, & W. Reld, (Eds.), *Terrorism. Interdisciplinary perspectives*. Washington, DC: American Psychiatric Association.

Protacio-Marcelino, E. (1989). Children of political detainees in the Philippines. Sources of stress and coping patterns. *International Journal of Mental Health, 18*, 71–86.

Punamaki, R. L. (1987). Childhood under conflict. The Attitudes and Emotional Life of Israeli and Palestinian Children. *Research Report No. 32*. Tampere, Finland: Peace Research Institute.

Punamaki, R. L. (1989). Factors affecting the mental health of Palestinian children exposed to political violence. *International Journal of Mental Health, 17*, 63–79.

Rasmussen, O. V. (1990). Medical aspects of torture. *Danish Medical Bulletin, 37*, 1–88.

Reid, J. C., & Strong, T. (1988). Rehabilitation of refugee victims of torture and trauma: Principles of service provision in New South Wales. *Medical Journal of Australia, 148*, 340–346.

Rumbaut, R. (1991). The agony of exile: A study of the migration and adaptation of Indochinese refugee adults and children. In F. L. Ahearn & J. Garrison (Eds.), *Refugee children*. Baltimore: Johns Hopkins University Press.

Sanford, H., & Comstock, C. (Eds.). (1971). *Sanctions for evil: Sources of social destructiveness*. San Francisco: Jossey Bass.

Sigal, J. J., Silver, D., Rakoff, V., & Ellin, B. (1973). Some second-generation effects of survival of the Nazi persecution. *American Journal of Orthopsychiatry, 43*, 320–327.

Sofaer, A. D. (1987). Terrorism and the law. In W. Laqueur & Y. Alexander, (Eds.), *The terrorism reader*. New York: Meridiam.

Somnier, F., & Genefke, I. K. (1986). Psychotherapy for victims of torture. *British Journal of Psychiatry, 149,* 323–329.

Sonnenberg, S. M., Blank, A. S., & Talbott, J. A. (Eds.). (1985). *The trauma of war: Stress recovery in Vietnam veterans.* Washington, DC: American Psychiatric Press.

Stover, E., & Nightingale, E. O. (Eds.). (1985). *The breaking of bodies and minds. Torture, psychiatric abuse and the health professions.* New York: WH Freeman.

Terr, L. C. (1983). Chowchilla revisited: The effects of psychic trauma four years after a schoolbus kidnapping. *American Journal of Psychiatry, 140,* 1543–1550.

United Nations (1948) Universal declaration of Human Rights (OP 1/15–18574, September 1973). New York: Author.

Ursano, R. J., Boydstun, J. A., & Wheatley, R. D. (1981). Psychiatric illness in US Air Force Vietnam prisoners of war: A five-year follow-up. *American Journal of Psychiatry, 138*(3), 310–314.

Van Der Ploeg, H. M., & Kleijn, W. C. (1989). Being held hostage in the Netherlands: A Study of long term after effects. *Journal of Traumatic Stress, 2*(3), 153–169.

Van Putten, T., & Yager, J. (1984). Posttraumatic stress disorder. *Emerging from the rhetoric. Archives of General Psychiatry, 41,* 411–413.

Weisaeth, L. (1989). Torture of a Norwegian ship's crew. *Acta Psychiatrica Scandivanica, Suppl. 355, 80,* 63–72.

World Medical Association. (1975). Declaration of Tokyo of the World Medical Association: Guidelines for medical doctors concerning degrading treatment or punishment in relation to detention and imprisonment. *World Medical Journal, 22,* 87–90.

Chapter 10

Concentration Camps

John J. Sigal

Institutional psychiatry only recently formally recognized the potential psychopathological consequences of human exposure to excessive stress as a distinct, definable entity, with the inclusion of Posttraumatic Stress Disorder in the third edition (1980) of the Diagnostic and Statistical Manual (DSM–III) of the American Psychiatric Association (APA, 1980). Yet military experts have known and utilized its consequences at least since biblical times, when armies laid siege to cities until the population's will to resist deteriorated. In World War II, operations researchers documented a rapid decline in the morale of the enemy forces with continued intense bombardment. Much prior to that, the labels "shell shock" and "war neurosis" were widely used to describe the syndrome manifested by soldiers who became psychologically paralyzed as a result of prolonged exposure to combat.

But it was only in studies of survivors of the Nazi concentration camps, and their equivalent in some respects, the Japanese and Korean prisoner-of-war (POW) camps of World War II, that the syndrome became clearly defined and its persistence well-documented over decades.

EARLY SYSTEMATIC STUDIES

The earliest of these studies was conducted 2 years after the war. A team of Danish physicians investigated the physical and psychological effects of all concentration camp survivors living in Copenhagen—some 1300 of them. They found that 44% of the members of the Danish resistance movement who were in concentration camps, had persistent symptoms of a psychological nature that included irritability, depression, impaired memory, disturbed sleep, sexual dis-

orders such as reduced sexual drive and impotence, sleep disturbances, and fatigue (loss of energy, mental fatigue, and difficulty in
concentrating). Half of this group had what they termed severe neuroses (Helweg-Larsen et al., 1952).

Because the symptoms were much more frequent among those who
had lost more than 35% of their weight (resulting from unremitting
forced labor and a starvation diet), the investigators assumed that the
problem would disappear as the survivors became re-integrated into
Danish society and gained weight. They, optimistically, labelled the
syndrome "repatriation neurosis" or "hunger reconvalescence."

By 1954, as a result of an intensive study of 120 survivors, Hermann and Thygesen (1954) observed that the symptoms persisted.
They added nightmares and other manifestations of anxiety, crying
spells, reductions in memory and/or ability to concentrate, and psychotic reactions to the list of typical symptoms, and, recognizing the
enduring nature of the syndrome, changed the label to "the concentration camp syndrome."

A vast number of clinical reports and other studies that utilized
clinic populations or other unrepresentative samples confirmed
these findings among Polish and French non-Jewish, and American
and Israeli Jewish survivors of the Nazi camps as well. Ryn (1990)
reviews the extensive literature on studies of Polish survivors, and
Hoppe (1971), and more recently Berger (1988), review the literature on Jewish survivors. Eitinger and Krell (1985) provide an exhaustive bibliography of all studies in this area.

The tendency to generalize the findings from most of these studies may be questioned because of the potentially unrepresentative
nature of the samples on which they were based. There are, however, some studies that were based on representative samples and
that employed carefully chosen comparison groups. They unequivo-
cally demonstrate the lasting psychopathological effects of this environmental stressor. These studies will be reviewed below.

STUDIES BASED ON UNBIASED SAMPLES
AND USING COMPARISON GROUPS

Military and Para-Military Personnel

Scandinavian studies

Of the approximately 6,000 Norwegians who were in the Nazi concentration camps, some 4,500 survived. About 3,800 were still alive

at the end of 1966 when Eitinger and Strøm (1973) undertook a study of morbidity among a sample of 498 of them (every eighth one) compared to a sample of Norwegians who had not been imprisoned or interned. The samples were matched for the major demographic variables. Health records kept on every Norwegian by the Norwegian Insurance Institute and the Central Register for Psychotics were used as the data base. Those who coded the information did not know to which group the subjects belonged. The survivors were found to have significantly higher rates of neurosis and neurotic reaction, alcoholism, and psychosis. A search of the records of a number of agencies, ranging from the Central Bureau of Statistics to local welfare offices, permitted the investigators to determine that mortality rates as a result of suicide or homicide were significantly higher among survivors than in the general population.

The same investigators later examined the histories of all of the 159 survivors hospitalized for psychoses up to 1976 (Eitinger & Strøm, 1981). Only 15 had received psychiatric treatment prior to their incarceration. In both the 1966 and 1976 studies of this group, the greatest number had what the investigators termed reactive psychoses; that is, psychosis for which there was no discernible organic base. About half of them were well-adjusted prior to the war, went back to work after their liberation, but later became delusional, and finally paranoid. Among the 13 hospitalized exclusively for alcohol-related illnesses (not otherwise specified), 10 had been well-adjusted before the war, had been active in the resistance movement, had experienced severe stress during their incarceration, and had come back as "muselmen" (the last stage of physical and psychological depletion before death in the concentration camps). They turned to alcohol as a way out as they found themselves increasingly less able to cope with the demands of daily living after their repatriation.

American studies

American servicemen imprisoned in the Japanese prisoner-of-war (POW) camps during World War II and in the Korean POW camps experienced malnutrition and stresses greater than their compatriots in the German POW camps. Those in the Japanese camps were also subjected to forced labor and beatings. Thus, there was considerable similarity between their experience and that of those imprisoned in the Nazi concentration camps. Follow-up data from random samples reveal that compared to servicemen from the same military units in the same war theatre, the POWs had significantly higher rates of "mental, psychoneurotic, personality" problems, and injuries resulting from "accident, poisoning or violence" (Beebe, 1975). On the Cornell Medical Index, ex-POWs reported significantly more symptoms of depression, anxiety, sensitivity, anger, and feelings of inadequacy. On the same scale, they also more frequently reported fatigue, palpitations, dyspnea, dizziness, headaches, muscle pains, sleep disturbances, and labile affect.

Common features

The similarity of the findings from the Norwegian and American studies becomes even more striking when one examines the causes of death and a correlate of morbidity in the two studies. The reader will recall that among Norwegian survivors, rates of death as a result of suicide and homicide were higher than among the general population. American Pacific war theatre POWs had significantly higher rates of death by suicide and by accident (motor vehicle and other), but not by homicide (Keehn, 1980). Thus, death by violent means, particularly suicide, appears to be a common denominator. The higher rates of death from cirrhosis of the liver among ex-POWs from the Pacific war theatre in the American studies (Keehn, 1980) parallels the finding of a higher rate of hospitalization for alcohol-related psychoses among the Norwegian survivors.

Finally, parallel to the Norwegian and Danish finding of psychopathology of many sorts being associated with weight loss exceeding 35% (Eitinger & Strøm, 1973; Helweg-Larsen et al., 1952; Thygesen, 1980), in the study of American servicemen, Beebe (1975) found that those with a large number of visual symptoms related to malnutrition were more likely to have a psychiatric diagnosis. He found no relationship between subjects with fewer visual symptoms attributable to malnutrition and psychiatric diagnosis. He also found statistically significant relationships between an index of malnutrition (based on weight loss, edema, visual symptoms, and other symptoms of malnutrition) and the following indices of problems in psychosocial adaptation in both ex-POW groups: difficulty to return to civilian life, current difficulties in civilian life, difficulty making friends, receiving inpatient mental health care, and requiring vocational rehabilitation.

The fact that the rates of postwar morbidity and mortality were higher among American ex-POWs in the Pacific than in the European war theatre offers convincing proof that it was the forced labor

and malnutrition and other excessive stresses, not the imprisonment itself, that were psychopathogenic. (The servicemen interned
in the Nazi POW camps were not subjected to the same harsh conditions as the men in concentration camps or in the Japanese and Korean camps.).

Civilian Survivors

The psychopathological effects of these cruel environments are not
limited to men, despite their greater vulnerability to a variety of
stresses (Holden, 1987). Nor are they limited to military personnel
or members of the resistance. More civilians than military or para-
military personnel were held in the Nazi concentration camps.
(Large numbers were also held in the Japanese camps during World
War II, but there is no comparative documentation on the long-term
effects on these prisoners.) The largest single group were the Jews.
Unlike the military and paramilitary personnel, they continuously
lived under the threat of death. The fact that only 3% of Norwegian
Jews survived deportation by the Nazis compared to 55% to 92% of
other Norwegians, depending on the camps to which they were sent,
attests to this difference.

When the Jews were released, they were not welcomed as return-
ing heroes, given generous rehabilitation services, and integrated
into a supportive family, as were the others. They were often treated
as unwelcome intruders, sometimes even stoned as they attempted
to return to their homes. The majority, wherever they settled, had to
cope with mourning the death of close family members—parents,
spouses, children, and even whole communities. One might, therefore, expect that they would manifest greater psychopathology than
the non-Jewish survivors.

The first reports from self-selected samples confirmed the existence of a very similar pattern of disorders among Jewish survivors.
Krystal and Niederland (1968), reviewing the charts of 149 patients
selected at random from survivors whom they had diagnosed and
treated over 20 years, noted the following signs and symptoms,
which they termed "the survivor syndrome":

sleep disturbances (including anxiety dreams and nightmares)
disturbance of cognition and memory
chronic depressive manifestations
difficulties in relating to people, or social isolation,
transient or long-lasting psychiatric states (they were able to rule

out familial hereditary taint or personal predisposition in 79% of these cases)

psychosomatic disease (including muscle tension, allergy-like symptoms, headaches, palpitation, hyper-ventilation, gastric overacidity, etc.).

It appears that the environmental stressors of the camps nullified the major differences among the pre-camp, camp, and post-camp experiences and in the ethnicity of the POWs and Jewish survivors.

Four controlled community studies based on unbiased samples confirm Krystal and Niederland's findings, one in a specific way, three in more general terms. Their findings are convincing because their data bases were constructed for purposes of general community surveys, not specifically targeted to explore the issue at hand. Concentration camp survivors were subsequently identified by their response(s) to question(s) in a questionnaire that otherwise focused on the matters targeted by the respective studies.

Israeli studies

Three of the studies were conducted in Israel 25 years after the end of World War II. The original purpose of one study was to examine the functioning of menopausal women aged 45 to 54 in a mid-sized Israeli city (Antonovsky, Maoz, Dowty, & Wijsenbeek, 1971). The investigators were able to identify 77 women in their original sample (of 766 whom they contacted) who were concentration camp survivors. They were also able to identify 210 other women of European origin in the sample, whom they used as their comparison group. Compared to the other women, survivors more frequently reported a more negative view of their life situation, a lower sense of self-satisfaction and satisfaction with their capacity to cope with life, a greater feeling of being at loose ends and in a bad mood, and a greater number of worries. These findings were based on composite scores derived from the womens' responses to a number of closed-ended questions.

Among other things, examining physicians were asked to rate the women on a scale of emotional health after they had terminated their examinations; that is, they had not been specifically asked to focus on mental health. They judged almost twice as many women in the comparison group as in the survivor group to be functioning well, and three times as many survivors as in the comparison group as having at least ". . . moderate symptom formation with some interference with life adjustment" (p. 189). It is important to note, however, that raters may not have been blind. That is, they may have known the womens' histories, and that may have biased their ratings. On the other hand, the comparison group might well have included a significant percentage who experienced other forms of prolonged stress, such as being in hiding or in labor camps during World War II. As a result, differences between the groups become more clinically significant.

The data base of the second Israeli study was information obtained during one of a series of periodic general health surveys in a Jerusalem neighborhood as part of a longitudinal study (Levav & Abramson, 1984). Of the 1450 in the sample who were 25 years or older, about 25% (380), equally divided between men and women, were in the Nazi concentration camps. The remainder served as a comparison group. Among them, 71 were born in Eastern Europe and immigrated to Israel in 1941 or later. As a result, a significant proportion of them, too, may have been subjected to Nazi persecution.

Among the questions they were asked was an eight-question, abbreviated version of the Cornell Medical Index (CMI), containing items that referred to feelings of nervousness and unhappiness. It was used as an index of emotional distress. Concentration camp survivors had significantly higher mean scores and rates of emotional distress. The proportion of emotional distress that could be attributed to the camp experience was 16% for men and 22% for women. When adjusted for age and education, a significantly higher percentage of both male and female survivors acknowledged having at least one of the eight symptoms than did their respective comparison groups. Unfortunately, the investigators did not report the frequencies for the individual items.

The third Israeli study was based on the records of some 45,000 people, most of whom had been referred for a periodic or pre-placement health examination at some point between 1977 and 1982; that is, beginning 35 years after the end of World War II (Carmil & Carel, 1986). None were referred for obvious physical or mental health problems, and only a small proportion were retired. The investigators identified a group of men ($N = 755$) and women ($N = 395$) who were in Nazi-occupied Europe at some point during World War II. This group, therefore, was subjected to the Nazi persecution, but was not comprised exclusively of concentration camp survivors. The comparison group was comprised of men ($N = 1366$) and women ($N = 792$) who came to Israel from the same countries but prior to World War II. Among them there were almost certainly a number who had also been subjected to Nazi persecution. The investigators found evidence for greater disturbance among survivors than in the comparison group for females on the following items of a scale derived from the CMI: frequent anxiety, frequently depressed, uncontrolled anger, irrational fears, psychological problems, and psychiatric treatment. Their mean scores were also higher on the sleep disturbance and suicidal thoughts items, but the differences were not statistically significant.

This list resembles closely the list of symptoms reported by clinicians and found in controlled studies of concentration camp survivors. They found no statistically significant differences between the men of the two groups. It is worth noting, however, that men in the survivor group had higher mean scores on all of the preceding items, including the sleep disturbance and suicidal thoughts items. Unfortunately, the investigators did not calculate the combined probability of finding differences in the same direction.

None of the preceding studies provides any information on the reliability of the measures used. Furthermore, in the last two studies, it is difficult to determine the degree of psychiatric impairment that resulted from the subjects' psychological and psychosomatic problems.

Canadian study

In a randomly selected Canadian sample of Jewish household heads in Montreal, investigators were able to identify a similar group of survivors of Nazi persecution (Eaton, Sigal, & Weinfeld, 1982). This study was also conducted more than 3 decades after the end of World War II for purposes other than studying survivors. As in the previous study, a question inserted near the end of the questionnaire permitted the identification of survivors of Nazi persecution and an appropriate comparison group; of the 657 respondents, 135 (99 men, 35 women) answered "yes" to the question, "Excluding service in the Allied Armed Forces, were you in Europe during World War II?" All 133 other respondents, who were Ashkenazic Jews from continental Europe who left Europe before the outbreak of World War II (91 men, 42 women), comprised the comparison group. Within the group of survivors, investigators were able to identify 39 who had spent some time in a concentration camp.

The measure of general mental health used in this study was Langner's 22-item scale. For all its flaws, it has a high reliability and convergent validity (Link & Dohrenwend, 1980). Furthermore, the scale is valid for distinguishing mild levels of psychiatric symptomatology among groups.

Langner (1962) found that 60% of his original sample reported four or more symptoms (sample mean 4.8), compared to 28% in a nonpatient sample (mean score 2.7). Since then, a score above 4 points on his 22-item scale has been widely used as an indicator of psychological distress. In the Montreal study, 29% of the comparison group had four or more symptoms, a percentage about identical to Langner's. Among the concentration camp survivors as a whole, 77% reported four or more symptoms, even more than among Langner's former psychiatric patients. For survivors as a whole, 36% of the male and 64% of the female survivors rated four or more items compared to 22% and 43%, respectively, of the comparison group.

The validity of these findings is suggested by the fact that the percentage of those reporting four or more symptoms decreased with what one might reasonably expect to be decreasingly stressful experiences: 77% among concentration camp survivors, 60% among those in hiding, and 38% among those in resistance groups. A possible anomalous finding was that only 18% of those who were in labor camps reported four or more symptoms.

POSSIBLE CAUSES OF PSYCHOPATHOLOGY IN SURVIVORS

Particularly among military and para-military survivors, an obvious possible cause for psychopathology is brain damage resulting from blows to the head suffered during interrogations. Pneumoencephalograms done on 199 Norwegian concentration camp survivors revealed pathological findings in 84%. Headaches were highly correlated with these findings (Eitinger & Strøm, 1973; Eitinger, 1980). It is important to note, however, that this rate of pathology was based on those referred for neuropsychiatric evaluation and, hence, may be based on an unrepresentative sample. On the other hand, evidence was also found for neuropsychiatric impairment in Canadian Army survivors of the Japanese camps (Klonoff, McDougall, Clark, Kramer, & Horgan, 1976; Kral, Pazder, & Wigdor, 1967).

A second cause is malnutrition combined with forced labor over a prolonged period of time. Caloric intake varied from 500 to 1200 calories a day, depending on the camp and the year (food became less plentiful as the war dragged on, particularly in the last year of the war).

Finally, decline in occupational status and problems in daily living caused by the higher rates of disease in all organ systems (Beebe, 1975; Eitinger & Strøm, 1973, 1981) may be a further physical cause of emotional distress among other survivors and their spouses (Sigal, 1976). The effect of higher mortality and morbidity rates among survivors would be compounded among Jewish survivors. They tended to marry other survivors (Sigal & Weinfeld, 1989). For them, the physical illnesses or psychological distress, or the premature death of their spouses, could add to the psychological burden which they are already carrying.

Family background and pre-existing personality may play a role in the long-term outcome for non-Jewish civilians of the Nazi persecution (for example, political prisoners, criminals, etc.); as a group they were subjected to less stressful conditions. These factors, however, played a negligible role in the long-term functioning of a group of Jewish survivors in whom these variables were explored (Matussek, 1975), albeit in a non-randomly selected sample. For them, the stresses of the camps erased pre-existing individual differences.

By far the most apparent cause of higher morbidity and mortality rates is the demoralization resulting from the unrelenting stresses of cramped quarters, sleep deprivation, unpredictable assaults on person and body, lack of sanitation, continual confrontation with death and disease among one's friends and acquaintances, forced labor, etc. For Jewish survivors there were the additional postwar stresses referred to earlier.

Even these psychosocial stressors may result in lasting biological repercussions in some survivors. Recent studies of Vietnam veterans who were exposed to combat and have been diagnosed as having posttraumatic stress disorder, the signs and symptoms of which are commonly encountered among concentration camp and World War II Pacific war theatre ex-POWs (Davidson, Kudler, Saunders, & Smith, 1990), suggest permanent alterations in their sympathoadrenal function (Kolb, 1987; Kosten, Mason, Giller, Ostroff, & Harkness, 1987; Southwick, Yehudi, Perry, Krystal, & Charney, 1990; Yehudi et al., 1990). On at least some of these measures, the duration of the survivors' incarceration is directly related to the extent of their cerebral dysfunction (Klonoff et al., 1976). The long-term effects of involvement in the Vietnam War and PTSD are discussed at greater length in the preceding chapter on terrorism and torture.

DISCUSSION

The size and nature of the samples in the studies cited above leave no doubt that a significant proportion of the survivors of the Nazi concentration camps and the Japanese POW camps manifest psychological difficulties up to 35 years after their liberation. Women may be more likely to suffer the negative long-term consequences than men. The evidence for gender difference is not clear. Two studies suggest it (Carmil & Carel, 1986; Eaton, Sigal, & Weinfeld, 1982), and one contradicts it (Levav & Abramson, 1984).

One might speculate that this gender difference, if it exists, is because mortality rates are generally higher in men (Holden, 1987). Although the high mortality rates (from disease as well as by suicide, accident, or homicide) in concentration camp and POW camp survivors, most of whom were men, is well-documented (Eitinger & Strøm, 1973, 1981; Keehn, 1980; Nefzger, 1970), there is no comparable data for women, or for civilian survivors. The suggestion that a difference exists between men and women in these symptoms of psychological distress, therefore, remains highly speculative.

The readers should note that those survivors who suffered psychopathological consequences, and even those who experienced subclinical consequences of their wartime experiences, do not form a homogenous group. They can be divided into at least four personality types, namely schizoid, anxious/depressive, paranoid, and normal Type A aggressive (Sigal & Weinfeld, 1989).

Furthermore, not all survivors experience psychosocial dysfunction as a result of their imprisonment. Up to 50% do not. Among those who do, as well as among those who do not, there are outstanding examples of survivors who live active, fulfilled lives, and contribute significantly to the communities in which they have rooted themselves (Giberovitch, 1988; Helmreich, 1988; Ornstein, 1985).

Are the findings reported here, based as they are on events that occurred almost half a century ago, only of historical interest? Unfortunately, they are not. There are still countless countries in which political prisoners, or victims of tribal or other wars, are subjected to torture and forced labor and malnutrition (Amnesty International, 1991). Those who survive, such as survivors of the Cambodian forced labor camps, are likely to suffer the same consequences as the ones we have reported (Carlson & Rosser-Hogan, 1991; Kinzie, Fredrickson, Ben, Fleck, & Karls, 1984).

There is an important caveat to the preceding statement. Without exception, the studies reported in this chapter were based on peoples from the Western, industrialized, or semi-industrialized world. The consequences of similar incarcerations, slave labor, and diet may be different for people of the Third World, primarily agrarian countries. For them, life in the camps may not be as discrepant from their normative expectations. As a result, they may have a higher threshold for tolerance of these adversities. Cultural differences in the presentation and response to symptomatic behavior could also play a role in determining the nature of the long-term consequences (Eisenbruch, 1991).

Only a scattering of clinical reports is available from such contexts. The same repressive regimes that enforce these conditions also prohibit access to the large numbers of people needed for well-designed studies. We are obliged, therefore, perhaps fortunately, to remain in relative ignorance of the full range of the consequences of man's inhumanity to man.

REFERENCES

American Psychiatric Association (1980). Diagnostic and statistical manual of mental disorders, 3rd ed. Washington, DC: Author.

Amnesty International, Report 91 (1991). London, England: Amnesty International Publications.

Antonovsky, A., Maoz, B., Dowty, N., & Wijsenbeek, H. (1971). Twenty-five years later: A limited study of the sequelae of the concentration camp experience. *Social Psychiatry, 6*, 186–193.

Beebe, G. H. (1975). Follow-up studies of World War II and Korean war prisoners: II. Morbidity, disability and maladjustments. *American Journal of Epidemiology, 101*, 400–422.

Berger, L. (1988). The long-term psychological consequences of the Holocaust on the survivors and their offspring. In R. L. Braham (Ed.), *The psychological perspectives of the Holocaust and its aftermath* (pp. 175–221). New York: Columbia University Press.

Carlson, E. B., & Rosser-Hogan, R. (1991). Trauma experiences, posttraumatic stress, dissociation, and depression in Cambodian refugees. *American Journal of Psychiatry, 148*, 1548–1551.

Carmil, D., & Carel, R. S. (1986). Emotional distress and satisfaction in life among Holocaust survivors—a community study of survivors and controls. *Psychological Medicine, 16*, 141–149.

Davidson, J. R. T., Kudler, H., Saunders, W. B., & Smith, R. D. (1990). Symptom and comorbidity patterns in World War II and Vietnam veterans with posttraumatic stress disorder. *Comprehensive Psychiatry, 31*, 162–170.

Eaton, W. W., Sigal, J. J., & Weinfeld, M. (1982). Impairment in Holocaust survivors after 33 years: Data from an unbiased community sample. *American Journal of Psychiatry, 139,* 773–777.

Eisenbruch, M. (1991). From post-traumatic stress disorder to cultural bereavement: Diagnosis of Southeast Asian refugees. *Social Science in Medicine, 33,* 673–680.

Eitinger, L. (1961). *Concentration camp survivors in Norway and Israel.* London: Allen & Unwin.

Eitinger, L. (1980). The concentration camp syndrome and its late sequelae. In J. E. Dimsdale (Ed.), *Survivors, victims and perpetrators* (pp. 127–162). New York: Hemisphere.

Eitinger, L., & Krell, R. (1985). *The psychological and medical effects of concentration camps and related persecutions on survivors of the Holocaust.* Vancouver: University of British Columbia Press.

Eitinger, L., & Strøm, A. (1973). *Mortality and morbidity after excessive stress: A follow-up study of Norwegian concentration camp survivors.* New York: Humanities Press.

Eitinger, L., & Strøm, A. (1981). New investigations on the mortality and morbidity of Norwegian ex-concentration camp prisoners. *Israel Journal of Psychiatry and Related Disciplines, 18,* 173–196.

Giberovitch, M. (1988). *The contribution of Montreal Holocaust survivor organizations to Jewish communal life.* Unpublished master's thesis. McGill University, Montreal.

Helmreich, W. (1988). The impact of Holocaust survivors on American society: A socio-cultural portrait. *Remembering the future: Jews and Christians during and after the Holocaust. Proceedings of the International Scholars Conference* (pp. 363–384). Oxford: Pergamon.

Helweg-Larsen, P., Hoffmeyer, H., Kieler, J., Thaysen, E. H., Thaysen, J. H., Thygesen, P., & Wulff, M. H. (1952). Famine and disease in German concentration camps. Complications and sequels. *Acta Psychiatrica et Neurologica Scandinavica, 34* (Suppl. 83).

Hermann, K., & Thygesen, P. (1985). KZ-syndromet. *Ugeskr-Laeger, 116,* 825–836. Cited in P. Thygesen (1980). The concentration camp syndrome. *Danish Medical Bulletin, 27,* 224–228.

Holden, C. (1987). Why do women live longer than men? *Science, 238,* 158–160.

Hoppe, K. N. (1971). The aftermath of the Nazi persecution reflected in recent psychiatric literature. In H. Krystal & W. G. Niederland (Eds.), *Psychic traumatization: Aftereffects on individuals and communities* (pp. 169–204). Boston: Little, Brown.

Keehn, R. J. (1980). Follow-up studies of World War II and Korean conflict prisoners: III. Mortality to January 1, 1976. *American Journal of Epidemiology, 111,* 194–202.

Kinzie, J. D., Fredrickson, R. H., Ben, R., Fleck, J., & Karls, W. (1984). Post-traumatic stress disorders among survivors of Cambodian concentration camps. *American Journal of Psychiatry, 141,* 645–650.

Klonoff, H., McDougall, G., Clark, C., Kramer, P., & Horgan, J. (1976). The neuropsychological, neuropsychiatric, and physical effects of prolonged and severe stress: 30 years later. *Journal of Nervous and Mental Disease, 163,* 246–252.

Kolb, L. C. (1987). A neuropsychological hypothesis explaining posttraumatic stress disorders. *American Journal of Psychiatry, 144*, 989–995.

Kosten, T. R., Mason, J. W., Giller, E. L., Ostroff, R. B., & Harkness, L. (1987). Sustained urinary norepinepherine and epinepherine elevation in posttraumatic stress disorder. *Psychoneuroendocrinology, 12*, 13–20.

Kral, V. A., Pazder, L. H., & Wigdor, B. T. (1967). Long-term effects of a prolonged stress experience. *Canadian Psychiatric Association Journal, 12*, 175–181.

Krystal, W., & Niederland, W. G. (1968). Clinical observations on the survivor syndrome. In H. Krystal (Ed.), *Massive psychic trauma* (pp. 327–348). New York: International Universities Press.

Langner, T. S. (1962). The twenty-two item index of psychiatric symptoms indicating impairment. *Journal of Health and Human Behavior, 3*, 269–276.

Levav, I., & Abramson, J. H. (1984). Emotional distress among concentration camp survivors—a community study in Jerusalem. *Psychological Medicine, 14*, 215–218.

Link, B., & Dohrenwend, B. P. (1980). Formulation of hypotheses about the true prevalence of demoralization in the United States. In B. P. Dohrenwend, B. S. Dohrenwend, M. S. Gould, B. Link, R. Neugebauer, & R. Wiensch-Hitzig, *Mental Illness in the United States: Epidemiological estimates* (pp. 114–132). New York: Praeger.

Matussek, P. (1975). *Internment in concentration camps and its consequences.* New York: Springer-Verlag.

Nefzger, M. D. (1970). Follow-up studies of World War II and Korean war prisoners. I. Study plan and mortality findings. *American Journal of Epidemiology, 91*, 123–138.

Ornstein, A. (1985). Knowing and not knowing the Holocaust. *Psychoanalytic Inquiry, 5*, 99–130.

Ryn, Z. (1990). The evolution of mental disturbances in the Concentration Camp Syndrome (KZ-Syndrom). *Genetic, Social, and General Psychology Monographs, 116*, 21–36.

Sigal, J. J. (1976). Effects of paternal exposure to prolonged stress on the mental health of the spouse and children: Families of Canadian Army survivors of the Japanese World War II camps. *Canadian Psychiatric Association Journal, 21*, 169–172.

Sigal, J. J., & Weinfeld, M. (1989). *Trauma and rebirth: Intergenerational effects of the Holocaust.* New York: Praeger.

Southwick, S. M., Yehudi, R., Perry, B. D., Krystal, W., & Charney, D. S. (1990). Sympathoadrenal dysfunction in PTSD. Paper presented to the annual meeting of the American Psychiatric Association, New York.

Thygesen, P. (1980). The concentration camp syndrome. *Danish Medical Bulletin, 27*, 224–228.

Yehudi, R., Southwick, S. M. Nussbaum, G., Wahby, B., Giller, R., & Mason, J. W. (1990). Low urinary cortisol excretion in patients with posttraumatic stress disorder. *Journal of Nervous and Mental Disease, 178*, 366–369.

Conclusion

Demonstrating the impact of environment on the mental health of a population is a formidable task. Nevertheless, in the preceding chapters the authors have presented a wealth of knowledge based on the past and current literature, which shows how some disturbing environmental forces can adversely affect the mental and emotional health of individuals. However, our knowledge of the influence of environment on the mind and mood is still very limited and, to some extent, speculative, as compared to the enormous progress and discoveries made in recent years on the role of biological and genetic factors in the manifestation of psychopathology. This book has focussed on shedding new light on an obscure side of our knowledge on the development of psychopathology under the influence of environmental phenomena.

Some environmental and ecological changes occur as a result of human abuse of the environment. These include noise, pollution, nuclear waste, and other toxic exposure and daily fuel combustion resulting in ozone layer depletion, which may result in higher incidence of cancers with subsequent emotional impact and disturbance on the victims and their families. The behavioral consequences of exposure to some of the environmental toxic agents may have far-reaching effects on the life of the generation yet to be born. On the other hand, there are natural and ecological disasters causing either acute physical and mental impact or resulting in posttraumatic stress disorders.

Certain environmental influences, such as the effects of light, nutrition, and substances of abuse on the mood and mind, have been gaining scientific recognition in significant proportion. Environmental changes are not confined to technological disasters. Natural catastrophes such as earthquakes, floods, volcanic eruptions, and large scale drought have caused homelessness, migration, and emotional crises. On the human side, wars and their emotional impact on the current and post-war generations, torture, terrorism, and concentration camp experience are but a few examples of the tragic pain and suffering that mankind has inflicted upon his own species.

Cultural beliefs and attitudes, too, have played an important role in the development of psychopathology. The growing unemployment, homelessness, famine, and refugee camps are other faces of environmental phenomena which have shaken the foundation of human organizations as we approach the end of this century. All of these combined point to the need for a bold and comprehensive evaluation of the effect of our lives on the environment and the impact of environmental disasters, whether natural or man-made, on human mind and behavior. We hope that future researchers will seriously address these questions in the light of broader concepts of biological, psychological, and environmental dimensions of mental health and well-being.

Index

Index

 *Springer Publishing Company*

PROGRESS IN EXPERIMENTAL PERSONALITY AND PSYCHOPATHOLOGY RESEARCH
Volume 15

Elaine F. Walker, PhD, **Robert H. Dworkin**, PhD, and **Barbara A. Cornblatt**, PhD, Editors

Contents: Communication Deviance in Families of Schizophrenic and Other Psychiatric Patients: Current State of the Construct, *D.J. Miklowitz and D. Stackman* • Understanding the Effects of Depressed Mothers on Their Children, *S.H. Goodman* • Childhood Stressors, Parental Expectation, and the Development of Schizophrenia, *A.F. Mirsky et al.* • An Information-Processing Approach to the Study of Cognitive Functioning in Depression, *I.H. Gotlib and S.B. McCabe* • On the Wisconsin, *A.M.J. Wagman and W. Wagman* • Structure-Function Relations in Schizophrenia: Brain Morphology and Neuropsychology, *R.M. Bilder* • Specifying Cognitive Deficiencies in Premorbid Schizophrenics, *R.A. Knight* • Sustained and Selective Attention in Schizophrenia, *M.F. Green et al.*

1992 336pp 0-8261-6090-5 hardcover

PROGRESS IN EXPERIMENTAL PERSONALITY AND PSYCHOPATHOLOGY RESEARCH
Volume 16

Loren J. Chapman, PhD, **Jean P. Chapman**, PhD, and **Don C. Fowles**, PhD, Editors

Contents in the latest volume include schizophrenia, schizotypy, genetic influences on behavior, emotions, and anxiety.

Contents: The Origins of Some of My Conjectures Concerning Schizophrenia, *P.E. Meehl* • A Strategy for Elucidating Genetic Influences on Complex Psychopathological Syndromes, *W.G. Iacono and B.A. Clementz* • Explorations in Schizotypy and the Psychometric High-Risk Paradigm, *M.F. Lenzenweger* • Issues in the Validation of the Personality Disorders, *T.A. Widiger* • Assessment of Normal Personality Traits in a Psychiatric Sample: Dimensions and Categories, *D.L. DiLalla et al.* • Emotion and Psychopathology: A Startle Probe Analysis, *P.J. Lang et al.* • The Genetics of Affective Disorders, *R. Katz and P. McGuffin* • DSM-III-R Dysthymia: Antecedents and Underlying Assumptions, *D.N. Klein et al.* • Anxiety and the Processing of Emotional Information, *A. Mathews*

1992 304pp 0-8261-6091-3 hardcover

536 Broadway, New York, NY 10012-3955 • (212) 431-4370 • Fax (212) 941-7842

⑤ *Springer Publishing Company*

HEALTH ENHANCEMENT, DISEASE PREVENTION, & EARLY INTERVENTION
Biobehavioral Perspectives

Kenneth D. Craig, PhD, and **Stephen M. Weiss**, PhD, Editors

A detailed, current presentation of the relation between behavioral and biological processes for major health risk factors—describing interventions that reduce risks, with emphasis on clinical implications. The key feature of the book is its explicit focus on prevention of life-threatening illness, presented by leading authorities in behavioral medicine.

Partial Contents: How the Brain Affects the Health of the Body, *N.E. Miller* • Brain/Body Linkages in Health Enhancement: Effects of a Lifestyle Change, *J.A. Herd* • Health, Stress, Lifestyle Change, and Health Risk Appraisal, *J.H. Milsum* • Occupational Health Promotion, *G.S. Everly, Jr.* • Program Development for Smoking Prevention and Cessation, *J.A. Best* • Exercise in the Prevention and Early Control of Hypertension: Efficacy and Adherence Issues, *J.E. Martin* • Coronary Prone Behaviors: Intervention Issues, *P.G. Saab et al.* • Prevention of Pain Problems, *P.J. McGrath and I.G. Manion* • Secondary Prevention of Alcohol-Related Problems in Young Adults at Risk, *D.R. Kivlahan et al.* • Female Sexual Dysfunction: Blending Old and New Treatment Modalities, *L.R. Waletzky and S.M. Weiss* • Psychosocial Risk Factors and Cancer Progression: Mediating Pathways Linking Behavior and Disease, *S.M. Levy*

1990   416pp   0-8261-6160-X   hardcover

536 Broadway, New York, NY 10012-3955 • (212) 431-4370 • Fax (212) 941-7842

℗ *Springer Publishing Company*

HANDBOOK OF HEALTH BEHAVIOR CHANGE

Sally A. Shumaker, PhD, Eleanor B. Schron, RN, MS, and Judith K. Ockene, PhD, Editors

"The most prominent authors in the field contribute to this detailed review of the theoretical and empirical literature on the factors that inhibit or promote health-related behavior change.... The extensive collection offers the most thorough examination of factors that influence behavior change, highlighting both the positive and negative influences." —Choice

Partial Contents:
I. Behavior Change and Maintenance: Theory and Measurement, *J.K. Ockene* • Theoretical Models of Adherence and Strategies for Improving Adherence, *M.H. Becker* • Patient–Physician Interactions, *H.S. Friedman and M.R. DiMatteo*
II. Life-Style Interventions and Maintenance of Behavior, *J.M. Wolle* • Life-Style Interventions for HIV-Antibody-Positive Hemophiliacs, *D. Agle* • Dietary Intervention for Coronary Heart Disease Prevention, *B.S. McCann et al.*
III. Obstacles to Life-Style Change and Adherence, *E.B. Schron* • The Social Context and Health Behavior: The Case of Tobacco, *D.G. Altman*
IV. Life-Style Change and Adherence Issues Within Specific Populations, *C.T. Parker* • Patient Adherence in Minority Populations, *D. Lewis et al.* • Life-Style Interventions in the Young, *L.M. Aledort et al.* • Problems with Adherence in the Elderly, *H.P. Roth*
V. Adherence Issues in Clinical Trials, *J.L. Probstfield* • The Interaction of the Recruitment Process With Adherence, *D.B. Hunninghake* • Prerandomization Compliance Screening: A Statistician's View, *C.E. Davis*
VI. Life-Style Change and Adherence: The Broader Context, *S.A. Shumaker* • Adherence and the Placebo Effect, *S.M. Czajkowski and M.A. Chesney* • Personal Responsibility and Public Policy in Health Promotion, *I.M. Rosenstock* • Ethical Issues in Life-Style Change, *R. Faden*

1990   496pp   0-8261-6780-2   hardcover

536 Broadway, New York, NY 10012-3955 • (212) 431-4370 • Fax (212) 941-7842